T0278198

THE COMPLETE GUIDE TO GROWING

FUCHSIAS

THE COMPLETE GUIDE TO GROWING
FUCHSIAS

How to cultivate fuchsias, with practical gardening advice and
an illustrated directory of more than 500 varieties

John Nicholass

Photography by Peter Anderson

LORENZ BOOKS

This edition is published by Lorenz Books
an imprint of Anness Publishing Ltd
info@anness.com
www.lorenzbooks.com
www.annesspublishing.com

© Anness Publishing Ltd 2022

Publisher: Joanna Lorenz
Editorial Director: Helen Sudell
Senior Editor: Felicity Forster
Photographer: Peter Anderson
Illustrator: Liz Pepperell
Maps: Rob Highton
Designer: Lisa Tai
Production Controller: Ben Worley

A CIP catalogue record for this book is available from
the British Library.

All rights reserved. No part of this publication may be reproduced,
stored in a retrieval system, or transmitted in any way or by any means,
electronic, mechanical, photocopying, recording or otherwise, without the prior
written permission of the copyright holder.

PUBLISHER'S NOTE
Although the advice and information in this book are believed to be accurate and true at the time of
going to press, neither the authors nor the publisher can accept any legal responsibility or liability for any
errors or omissions that may have been made nor for any inaccuracies nor for any loss, harm or injury
that comes about from following instructions or advice in this book.

CONTENTS

Introduction

This is a book for anyone who loves fuchsias. It describes how to grow them, which types are best for particular positions in the garden, and how to deal with any problems that might arise in their cultivation. Fuchsias are superb summer-flowering plants. They are fast growing, come in a range of flower colours and sizes and can be used in containers, hanging baskets and as summer bedding in the garden borders. These versatile plants also have a range of growth types – some are upright and bushy, others are trailing or cascading, and some even have a rambling habit, ideal for decorating walls and fences. Fuchsias are very easy to train into different shapes, the standard fuchsia being most familiar.

IN THIS BOOK

Wild fuchsias grow mainly in warm parts of the southern hemisphere, where they enjoy the climate. The first section of this book gives a short history of the fuchsia's distribution, discovery and hybridization.

Next, a section on the fuchsia garden is packed with ideas for growing these rewarding plants, whether as temporary residents in a summer border or as

Top: The large double flower of 'Irene Sinton', with its blush-pink sepals, a full lilac-blue corolla and splashes of pink on the petals. The opening flower bud, sprinkled with raindrops, is about to reveal its inner secrets.

permanent shrubs, or even hedges. There are also tips for growing fuchsias in containers and, for those who really want to extend the growing season of these stunning plants, the book gives instructions for growing fuchsias inside the house, in the greenhouse, in a shadehouse or in a conservatory.

Then comes a section on practical gardening techniques, which explains how to select and buy fuchsia plants, how to train fuchsias into all sorts of shapes, hints on planting containers, taking cuttings, keeping the plants alive over the winter, and dealing with common pests and diseases.

The penultimate section of the book is a directory of over 200 fuchsia cultivars – from standards, trained structures and hanging baskets to hardies, Encliandras and unusual cultivars – with guidance about the ideal varieties for any situation.

At the back of the book, a calendar of care lists the appropriate tasks to be carried out in each season, and a handy chart lists the colour names most commonly applied to fuchsia flowers.

Every gardener will be able to find something in this book to inspire them to experiment with some different fuchsia cultivars and planting techniques.

Left: A mixture of hardy fuchsias growing in a border next to a lawn, with dancing red and purple flowers. A fruiting clematis vine with fluffy seed heads can be seen in the background, scrambling over a fence.

Right: A hardy fuchsia growing strongly against a high stone wall, and partially covering a wrought-iron gate.

Origins and history

The fuchsia belongs to the plant family Onagraceae, a family that also includes the genus *Oenothera* (evening primrose) and the genus *Epilobium*, for example *Chamerion angustifolium* (rosebay willowherb or fireweed). The original discovery of the genus *Fuchsia* was in the southern hemisphere, and the first record of the fuchsia in Western civilization was in the early 18th century. The European explorers and plant collectors of the 18th and 19th centuries brought back many of the species fuchsias from which the range of cultivars we grow today were developed, including hardies, Triphyllas, single and double-flowered fuchsias, and those with upright trailing habits.

GEOGRAPHICAL DISTRIBUTION

There are more than 100 identified fuchsia species found mainly in the southern hemisphere of the world. The majority are originally from South America, with most of the remainder found in Central America, Tahiti and New Zealand.

The genus *Fuchsia* is divided into nine sections, covering the wide range of discovered plant forms. Most are tropical or subtropical shrubs, which vary in height.

F. excorticata from New Zealand is unusual, in that it is a tree growing up to 12–15m (39–49ft) in its native habitat.

The fuchsias from the section known as *Quelusia* originate from the colder southern parts of South America, and these plants allowed fuchsia cultivars to be developed with winter hardiness. Of these, *F. regia*, *F. magellanica* and *F. coccinea* are the most common and the best varieties for areas with cold winters.

Top left: *F. fulgens*, a species fuchsia growing wild in Central America. It has beautiful long red flowers and forms root tubers.

Below left: Many of the known fuchsia species flourish in the wild in South and Central America, where they are mainly found along the chain of the Andes mountains.

Below: Fuchsia species of the section Skinnera originate from New Zealand, where the Maoris used the blue pollen from the flowers of *F. excorticata* for body decoration.

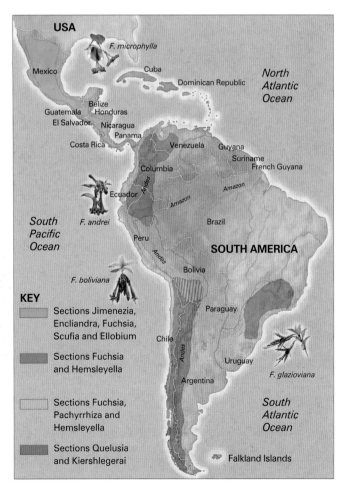

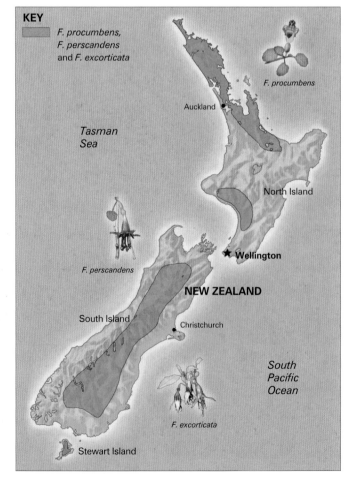

DISCOVERY OF THE FUCHSIA

Father Charles Plumier, a Jesuit priest working as a missionary in San Domingo in the Caribbean, was the first European to record this beautiful plant. He named it *Fuchsia triphylla flore coccinea* in honour of Dr Leonhard Fuchs, a noted 16th-century herbalist and professor of medicine in Germany. The fuchsia was later renamed simply *Fuchsia triphylla* according to the well-known rules developed by the Swedish naturalist Linnaeus.

It should be noted that there are two different pronunciations of the word fuchsia. In Germany, the Netherlands and other parts of Europe the pronunciation is 'fook-sya', while in the UK, USA and Australia the pronunciation is a softer 'fyew-sha'. The first version reflects more closely the fact that the word is based on the German name 'Fuchs'.

ARRIVAL IN EUROPE

It is difficult to establish the exact date when the cultivation of fuchsia species began in Europe. It is likely that Plumier brought some seeds of this exciting plant back to France with him and he would probably have given some of them to other gardeners. There is a reference to the plant *Thiles*, which is the native name of the fuchsia in southern Chile, with an illustration, published in a French botanical journal of 1725.

The first live plant to reach Europe was *F. coccinea*, brought to England by a Captain Firth and presented to Kew Gardens in 1788. James Lee, a horticulturalist and nurseryman in Hammersmith, then a village outside London, obtained a fuchsia plant and propagated it, offering the plants for sale in 1793. After this more plants and seeds quickly arrived and were developed, as we can see in the records at Kew Gardens. First *F. lycioides* arrived in 1796; then *F. arborescens* in 1824; *F. microphylla* in 1827; *F. fulgens* in 1830; *F. corymbiflora* in 1840; and in 1843–44, *F. apetala*, *F. decussata*, *F. dependens* and *F. serratifolia*. Many other species and variants have been discovered.

Above: *F. magellanica*, a profusely flowering species from which many hardy cultivars originate. It is very hardy and grows wild on the mountains of Magellan, one of the coldest parts of South America.

FIRST HYBRIDS

As early as 1825, there were attempts at hybridization between species. The first attempt was to cross *F. arborescens* with *F coccinea* and *F. arborescens* with *F. macrostemma*, but the results were unclear. Over the next 25 years, Europe saw the introduction of many new successful cultivars, several of which were confusingly similar, and also many very different ones under the same popular name, such as 'Queen Victoria'. In 1840 the first cultivar with a white tube and sepals was produced, called 'Venus Victrix'. It is still available commercially, and is reputed to be the parent of many of today's white cultivars, although some experts would dispute this. In 1848, the release of the first double-flowered cultivar, 'Duplex', was credited to William Storey, although this may have had only seven petals.

The early hybridizers

In the last half of the 19th and the first part of the 20th century, several important, prolific hybridizers introduced a tremendous range of new cultivars. Their work is the basis of the range of cultivars now available. Most of this early hybridization took place in Europe, especially in the UK and France, where Félix Porcher's book *Le Fuchsia: Son Histoire et sa Culture* reached its fourth edition by 1874. Although many of these early cultivars are now lost, some – especially the hardy ones – are still grown. However, the naming of new cultivars was then an unorganized process, with many cultivars being given identical names in various counties, while many similar cultivars were given different names.

EDWARD BANKS (ENGLAND)

Born in 1820, Banks ran a fuchsia nursery on the outskirts of Deal, in Kent, and was one of the largest producers of fuchsias in his time. He also hybridized fuchsias and introduced 111 new cultivars, many of which are still grown today, including 'Arabella', 'Blue Beauty', 'Forget-Me-Not', 'Rose of Castile' and 'Rose of Denmark'. He died aged 90, in 1910, when fuchsias were declining in popularity in the UK.

Top: 'Rose of Denmark' was hybridized by Edward Banks and introduced in 1855. It is a hardy cultivar with pink/rose-pink flowers.

Below: 'Phenomenal' is a hardy French cultivar with large double scarlet/indigo-blue flowers. It was hybridized and introduced by Victor Lemoine in 1869.

VICTOR LEMOINE (FRANCE)

One of the most prolific fuchsia hybridizers of his era, Lemoine produced around 450–500 new cultivars, as well as being famous for new varieties of other genera, including lilacs, hydrangeas, pelargoniums and weigela. He was born in Delme in 1823; his family had a long history of being nurserymen and gardeners, and from his early years he had a huge interest in horticulture. He trained with some of the finest nurserymen in Europe and later started his own nursery in Nancy. Among the many fuchsia cultivars he produced that are still widely grown today are 'Abbé Farges', 'Brutus', 'Caledonia', 'Drame', 'Emile de Wildman', 'Enfant Prodigue', 'Flocon de Neige', 'Phenomenal', 'Royal Purple' and 'Voltaire'.

Above: 'Rose of Castile', introduced by Edward Banks in 1855, is a long-established hardy cultivar with white/red-purple flowers.

JAMES LYE (ENGLAND)

One of the best-known English fuchsia hybridizers in the 19th century was James Lye, who produced many cultivars bearing his hallmark of flowers with waxy white tubes and sepals. Born in 1830 in Market Lavington, Worcestershire, he started as a 12-year-old apprentice to the head gardener in the gardens of Clyffe Hall and actually became head gardener when he was 23.

He became interested in fuchsias in the late 1850s, and the first record of one of his fuchsia cultivars was in 1869. He went on to introduce 82 cultivars, most of which had strong, upright growth with the distinctive Lye characteristics. He became famous for growing large specimen pillars

Above: This late 19th-century picture shows James Lye in front of several of his large trained fuchsias in the gardens of Clyffe Hall.

Above: 'Lye's Unique' has single flowers with a long waxy-white tube and sepals, and a beautifully contrasting salmon-orange corolla.

Above: 'Amy Lye' has medium-sized single flowers with a creamy white tube and sepals, and a coral-orange corolla. It is easy to train.

and pyramids, 2.5–3m (8–10ft) high and 1.2–1.5m (4–5ft) in diameter at the base, which had to be transported to exhibitions by horse and cart. Many of the cultivars he produced are still readily available; they include 'Amy Lye', 'Beauty of Trowbridge', 'Charming', 'Harriet Lye', 'Loveliness', 'Lye's Excelsior' and 'Lye's Unique'.

CARL BONSTEDT (GERMANY)

At the end of the 19th century and the beginning of the 20th century, Bonstedt started to produce hybrids from *F. triphylla*, including 'Bornemanns Beste', 'Mary', 'Thalia', 'Coralle', 'Gartenmeister Bonstedt', 'Göttingen' and 'Traudchen Bonstedt'.

These introductions are some of the best Triphylla hybrids available and are still widely grown today.

Born in 1866 in Naumburg, he trained as a gardener at the Pomologischen Institute in Proskau, and later spent some years in Great Britain, notably at Kew Gardens. On returning to Germany, he headed the Botanical Gardens at Rostock from 1892–1900, and then became Technical Director of the Botanical Garden in Göttingen. He was involved in the breeding of other genera, including primroses and lilies. He also wrote and lectured on horticultural subjects, and edited *Parey's Flower Garden*. Bonstedt died in 1953.

OTHER EARLY HYBRIDIZERS

In the later part of the 19th century, Cornelissen hybridized fuchsias in his Belgian nursery, and is best known for 'Madame Cornelissen', a very good hardy cultivar that is still widely available. He also introduced the variegated leaf cultivar 'Meteor', possibly still grown as 'Autumnale'. In Germany, Johan Nepomuk Twrdy produced around 40 cultivars. Among those still available are 'Europa' (1872), 'Papagena' (1870) and 'Schneeball' (1874). Other important hybridizers include Bull, Bass, Henderson, Vietch and Storey in England, and Rozain-Bouchariat and Meillez in France.

Far left: The hot flower colours of 'Gartenmeister Bonstedt', standing out among the surrounding shrubs and palms.

Left: The Triphylla 'Mary', showing its clusters of vivid red flowers and green velvety leaves, is a beautiful sight.

Fuchsia species

Many of the species fuchsias, which mainly originate from South and Central America, are unrecognizable to those who are used to modern fuchsia cultivars. Their form varies from small prostrate spreading plants with upright flowers, to shrubs with glossy leaves and panicle flower spikes, up to small trees. The species fuchsias, unlike their modern hybrid cultivar descendants, will grow true from seed, the main mechanism of their spread and survival in the wild. Categorization of the species is divided into nine separate sections, the largest of which is sub-divided into many different groups. Many of the primary species have several variants that occur naturally in the wild.

SECTION QUELUSIA

The plants in this section come from Argentina, Chile and the south-east coast of Brazil. This section is historically very important to the modern cultivars, since most winter hardiness came from hybridization of this group. It includes *F. alpestris*, *F. coccinea*, *F. glazioviana*, *F. magellanica* and *F. regia*.

   F. magellanica is a hardy shrub originating from the southern mountainous regions of South America. It has small single flowers with a red tube, deep red sepals and a purple corolla, freely produced on an upright bush with small mid- to dark green

Top: The climbing species shrub *F. boliviana* occurs naturally from southern Peru to northern Argentina, and has clusters of striking red tubular flowers.

leaves. This species is very hardy and is an ancestor of many of the fuchsias grown today. It has many natural variants, often grown as hardy garden shrubs.

SECTION FUCHSIA (EUFUCHSIA)

This is the largest section, containing 13 different subgroups of plants found in the tropical Andes, Haiti and the Dominican Republic. The fuchsias in this group are usually tender and have flowers with long tubes and short sepals, and include *F. abrupta*, *F. boliviana*, *F. decussata*, *F. denticulata*, *F. loxensis*, *F. macrophylla*, *F. pallescens*, *F. sessilifolia*, *F. tincta*, *F. triphylla*, *F. venusta* and *F. vulcanica*.

   F. boliviana is a climbing shrub with large hairy mid- to dark green red-veined leaves up to 20 x 10cm (8 x 4in) and

clusters of long red-tubed flowers. It occurs from southern Peru to northern Argentina growing at elevations up to 3,000m (10,000ft), and easily reaching 5m (16ft) in height. It also has a white-tubed variant, *F. boliviana* var. *alba*, which is synonymous with *F. corymbiflora alba*.

   F. denticulata is a very attractive species, easy for the beginner to grow. The flower has a long, light pink to red waxy tube, small pink to light red sepals turning green at the tips and an orange to scarlet corolla. The growth is upright, with large dark green spear-shaped leaves, normally 3–4 per node. It generally flowers best in the spring and autumn, the flowering becoming sparse in the summer. It originates from Peru and Colombia, where it can grow to more than 5m (16ft) in height.

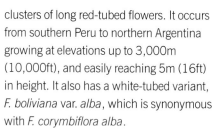

Left: *F. glazioviana* is a species from the cloud forests of southern Brazil, with deep pink and mauve semi-erect flowers.

Right: *F. denticulata* is a species from Peru and Bolivia, and is an easy and rewarding species for the beginner to try. It has striking long flowers with multiple colours.

SECTION KIERSCHLEGERIA
This section, found in central Chile, has only one member, *F. lycioides*.

SECTION SKINNERA
This section is found in New Zealand and Tahiti. The fuchsias have unusual flower colours and blue pollen and include *F. x colensoi*, *F. cyrtandroides*, *F. excorticata* and *F. procumbens*.

F. procumbens is a very unusual species with its prostrate spreading growth, small green fernlike leaves, tiny yellow-green upward-facing flowers with no corolla and blue pollen, and red grapelike fruits. This species is easy to grow, but will benefit from the addition of sharp sand to the growing mix. If you grow it in an elevated position – in a pot on a kitchen stool, for example – it will trail attractively downwards. In time, the long growths can reach 1.5m (5ft).

SECTION HEMSLEYELLA
This section, found in the tropical Andes (Bolivia and Venezuela), contains 14 species, including *F. apetala*, *F. garleppiana*, *F. inflata*, *F. juntasensis*, *F. mezae*, *F. pilaloensis* and *F. salicifolia*.

SECTION SCHUFIA
Plants in this section are shrubs with flowers that are erect on the plant in a corymb-like panicle, and include *F. arborescens*, *F. paniculata* and subspecies.

F. paniculata grows like a shrub, with strong upright growth and large glossy laurel-like leaves. It has tiny pink flowers, held upright in large clusters, and later bears small dark berries. This species is an easy one for the beginner to grow and often known as the lilac fuchsia.

SECTION ENCLIANDRA
This section, which is found growing on the mountainous slopes of Central America and Mexico, has very small flowers and leaves. It includes the species *F. encliandra*, *F. microphylla*, *F. thymifolia* and their subspecies. Many of the fuchsias in this section are quite hardy.

F. encliandra is a rather hardy shrub with tiny rose-orchid to red flowers, small

Above: *F. procumbens* is a hardy prostrate spreading species with upright flowers, and comes from New Zealand.

broad ovate leaves and small black berry fruits, and will grow up to 2.4m (8ft) tall left unchecked in the wild. In cultivation, it grows well in semi-shaded positions.

SECTION JIMENEZIA
This section, found in Panama and Costa Rica, has only one member, *F. jimenezii*.

SECTION ELLOBIUM
This section is found in Central America and Mexico. The fuchsias are unusual in forming root tubers. The section contains *F. decidua*, *F. fulgens* and *F. splendens*.

Above: *F. microphylla* originates from Mexico. It is a fairly hardy shrubby species with tiny but very pretty red flowers which then produce black berries.

Right: *F. paniculata* is a stunning upright shrub originating from southern Mexico and Panama. It has glossy leaves and panicles of tiny purple-pink flowers.

Hybridization trends

Extensive fuchsia hybridization in the last 150 years has resulted in many new cultivars we can still grow today. With this rich heritage in mind, it is fascinating to look at recent hybridization trends around the world. It takes at least five years from sowing the seed that results from the hybridization cross, following a process of selection and testing for genetic stability, until a new cultivar is ready for release to the gardening public. Growing either the seedling or a tip cutting from it without stopping enables growers to assess the growth habit, to see how naturally self-branching it is and most importantly, promotes earlier flowering so that the new fuchsia's flower potential can be judged.

EFFECTS OF CLIMATE CHANGE

All gardeners, not just fuchsia growers, face new challenges from the changing climatic conditions brought on by global warming. Hotter summers, wetter, but milder winters, droughts, and sudden, frequent flooding, together with palpable shifts in seasons are among the increasingly extreme weather events we now experience. This is going to make some aspects of gardening more difficult, but those living in colder latitudes will be able to grow more tender plants as winter temperatures rise, and this could greatly increase the range of viable fuchsias. There are already lists available on the internet giving details of fuchsias that tolerate the heat of the sun, and those that are more resistant to pests and diseases. Most of the fuchsias we grow today have *F. magellanica* blood in them and hybridizers are investigating other species fuchsias to introduce new characteristics.

UNITED STATES

The rapid spread of the fuchsia gall mite since its arrival in California in the early 1980s has caused the fuchsia to drop in popularity in the USA, especially since the big colourful doubles seem to be the most affected by the pest. There are now fewer active hybridizers of fuchsias than in

former years, but those who are still working in the field are focusing on breeding new mite-resistant fuchsias. Nearly all the species are tested for mite resistance, and new cultivars have now been produced; lists of resistant fuchsias are available. You can read articles on the subject via the American Fuchsia Society website, where one author, Dr Peter Baye, has described the results obtained at Annapolis, California and is advocating a wider 'open pollination' programme

from resistant varieties. This pest is now also prevalent in southern England (and spreading north) and in parts of Europe.

Among the hybridizers responsible for large beautiful double cultivars associated with California are Robert Castro, Raymond Hodges, Charles Kennett, Gus Niederholzer, Annabelle Stubbs, Hazard and Hazard, Tiret, Muriel Waltz and Mrs Soo Young.

Below: *F. magellanica* var. *aurea* is a golden-leaf variant of *F. magellanica*, with small red and purple single flowers.

Top: 'Flying Cloud' is a large double, white-flowered, lax spreading cultivar from San Francisco, typical of the flamboyant Californian cultivars. It was hybridized by Victor Reiter from San Francisco and released in 1949.

Above: 'Apricot Ice' is a recent single-flowered cultivar. The flowers are crisp apricot-cream and a lovely rich apricot.

AUSTRALIA

Ronald Lockerbie was the first prolific hybridizer of fuchsias in Australia, followed by Richardson, Richardson/Yandina and Southall. The preference in Australia, as in the USA, seems to be for double cultivars, and especially those that are suitable for baskets. Some of the best of these have become available in other countries, for instance 'Australia Day', 'Happy Wedding Day' and 'Marlene Gilbee'. There was a stir when a new variety named after Ronald Lockerbie was reputed to be the first yellow fuchsia, but sadly it turned out to be more of a cream colour, at least in northern European light conditions.

NEW ZEALAND

There are very different growing conditions from the southern tip of the South Island to the northern point of the North Island. The cultivars hybridized in New Zealand are a mixture of single, semi-double and double cultivars, both upright and trailing. Some well-known hybridizers are Sharpe and Proffit, who intorduced the cultivar 'Apricot Slice', and Butcher, who has introduced a number of cultivars with the prefix 'Omar', many grown outside New Zealand.

EUROPE

In Europe there has been a revival of fuchsia hybridization, with prolific hybridizers such as Carel Roes and Herman de Graaff in the Netherlands, Marcel Michiels in Belgium, Karl Strümper in Germany, René Massé in France, and Edwin Goulding and Mick Allsop in the UK. There have been some interesting new flower colours, such as the aubergine fuchsias started by de Graaff, as well as large doubles with very long tubes, and some unusual cultivars obtained by crossing back or between the species – all produced by the efforts of these dedicated enthusiasts.

Right: 'Hazel' is a large double-flowered, lax-growing fuchsia hybridized by Richardson of Australia and released in 1985.

Above: 'Gerharda's Aubergine' is a beautiful fuchsia that has a vigorous trailing habit and looks wonderful in a hanging pot.

LOOKING FORWARD

One challenge that remains is to produce a true yellow fuchsia, which will doubtless happen at some point in the future. Hybridizers are also trying hard to develop gall mite-resistant and heat-resistant fuchsias with a bigger range of flower sizes and colours for fuchsia lovers to grow.

THE FUCHSIA GARDEN

Fuchsias flower profusely in the summer, often blooming from late spring right through to the first autumn frosts. A greenhouse can extend that flowering period even further, with plants either kept under cover all year round, or brought outside for the warmer months. This chapter will give you many ideas for using fuchsias in a garden scheme. Large hardy fuchsia cultivars look splendid alongside other evergreen and deciduous shrubs to provide some areas of the garden with colour interest all the year round. Many hardy fuchsias will make a beautiful flowering hedge as a division within a garden. Non-hardy fuchsias make excellent summer bedding plants. Grown on their own as specimen plants, cultivars such as 'Border Queen' and 'Celia Smedley' can be really striking. Triphylla hybrids such as 'Thalia' or 'Coralle', mixed with other traditional summer bedding plants, make an attractive natural border. Smaller, more compact fuchsias can be excellent edging plants for flowerbeds or for the rockery.

Left: This splendid example of the hardy cultivar 'Margaret Brown', with its pretty single flowers, is more than 1.8m (6ft) tall, and looks beautiful growing among other shrubs such as weigela and camellia.

Top left: 'Brenda White' is an attractive single-flowered cultivar which is perfect for a border edging plant or small standard. It has lightish foliage and a truly classic bell-shaped flower.

Top middle: 'Tennessee Waltz' is a beautiful hardy with large red and lilac-lavender semi-double flowers. It is excellent as a permanent planting or for use in a summer border.

Top right: 'Celia Smedley' has medium to large neyron-rose/currant-red single flowers and is excellent for a bedding plant used in the centre of a border.

Single specimen fuchsias

Large fuchsia plants can make striking, eye-catching centrepieces when grown as specimen plants. When grown in large pots using a large single plant or multi-planting placed in the centre of a terrace or patio, they will clamour for your attention. Alternatively, for a display requiring less maintenance, plant them in the ground in the main garden borders, or dominating a small border in a paved area. They can make a striking focal point when grown against the right background. For example, you can choose a flower colour that contrasts well with a ground cover of chippings or slate, or the backdrop colour when grown in front of a fence or hedge.

SELECTION AND PLACEMENT

With such a range of flower colours and sizes, and a long summer-flowering period, using fuchsias as specimen feature plants gives very satisfying results. If you are lucky enough to live in an area with mild winters, where the stems of hardy fuchsias survive, you can make them part of a permanent planting scheme. Otherwise, specimen plants need winter protection to survive. This will allow them to start into growth again in the late winter and early spring, and will ensure they look good each year. Large specimen plants can be formed from single plants trained as shrubs or bushes, or one of the trained shapes. Alternatively, to obtain a large specimen in a short time, the multi-plant technique works well.

Use these specimen plants to create a focal point on terraces or patios, in the middle of lawns, on the edges of wide steps, beside gates or doorways or on large areas of gravel or stone chippings. They also look very striking in low stone or brick walls, which have a planting area built into them, or in a square stone pot placed on top of a wide wall – as long as it is stable and cannot be knocked over or blown off by the wind. Pick the right fuchsia for the height of the wall – for a low wall, an upright-growing variety will look best, and for a medium or high wall, a more lax variety will create a flowing effect, cascading downward.

Top left: 'Thalia', a Triphylla hybrid, has racemes of long brilliant red flowers contrasting perfectly with its dark olive-green leaves, and flourishes in full sun.

SUNNY AND HOT AREAS

Triphylla hybrids are a natural choice for sunny and hot areas, where they will reward you with continuous flowering through the summer. Grow them in the ground or in large porous clay pots to help keep the roots cool. This is one of the most important factors to ensure fuchsias do well when exposed to full sun.

Above: This striking shrub of 'Hawkshead', planted permanently in the ground, is covered with small white flowers contrasted against the small dark green leaves.

DAPPLED SHADE AREAS

Areas with dappled shade are ideal for growing most fuchsias, as they recreate the conditions where the species grows naturally in the wild. Good examples

SINGLE SPECIMENS

Plants that form a good natural shape with distinctive flowers that stand out from the foliage are superb to use as specimen plants.

Full sun: 'City of Leicester', 'Coralle', 'Falling Stars', 'Gartenmeister Bonstedt', 'Genii', 'Joan Pacey', 'Nancy Lou', 'Other Fellow', 'Tennessee Waltz', 'Thalia'
Dappled shade: 'Border Queen', 'Lady Kathleen Spence', 'Lilian', 'Misty Blue', 'Rolla'
Shady: 'Alaska', 'Constellation', 'Evensong', 'Flirtation Waltz', 'Florence Mary Abbot', 'Iceberg', 'Lady Kathleen Spence', 'Ting a Ling'
Shady against white background: 'Gruss aus dem Bodenthal', 'Haute Cuisine', 'Marin Glow', 'Ortenburger Festival', 'Roesse Blacky', 'Royal Velvet', 'Symphony'

Above: 'Richard John Carrington' is a bush cultivar and has medium-sized single flowers with bright cerise sepals and a blue-violet corolla. This compact hardy plant has light green foliage that ages to dark green.

are on the edges of the shade cast by open tree canopies, in the shade created by artificial structures, or near east- or west-facing walls.

While you can use almost any of the fuchsia cultivars in these areas, the pastel-coloured varieties look at their best in dappled shade, as their flower colours intensify.

SHADY AREAS

Fuchsias will grow well in light shade, although this can reduce the amount of growth they will make in a season. An ideal situation would be a wall that gets the early morning and the late evening sun, painted white or a light colour, so that it will reflect any available light back on to the plant. Many of the white or light pastel-coloured fuchsias will do well here, as the whites stay really white in the shade, rather than taking on pink hues, as sometimes happens when they are in bright sunlight.

Right: 'Genii' is a superb hardy cultivar whose foliage becomes a vivid yellow-green in a sunny position, contrasting beautifully with the delicate red and purple single flowers. Here, it is growing by a path together with other shrubs.

Alternatively, you can use fuchsias with very dark flower colours, as many of them have a tendency to bleach in the sun. In shadier conditions, they will maintain their deep colours without fading. The flowers will not show up as well as light-coloured ones, though, unless you give them a light background, such as a painted wall or perhaps a golden-leaved hedge.

Right: 'Other Fellow' drips continuously with waxy white and coral-pink single flowers on a vigorous plant with mid-green foliage. It is a really eye-catching fuchsia when grown as a single specimen.

Specimen plants as features

When they are given sufficient root room and encouragement, many of the more vigorous fuchsias can grow into large plants quite quickly. Placed at key locations in the garden or on the garden boundaries, they make excellent eye-catchers. The large feature fuchsias can be divided into the non-hardy and hardy kinds. In temperate climates, non-hardy ones need to be grown in large pots and moved into a greenhouse or conservatory every winter, so that they can keep growing from year to year. Hardy varieties can be left in the ground all year. In very cold areas, however, where winter temperatures may kill the wood structure back to the ground, then they should be treated like non-hardy types.

FAST-GROWING HALF-HARDY FUCHSIAS

These are best grown in large pots, either using a single plant grown over a few years, allowing it to reach a suitable size, or the multi-plant technique described later in this book. Growing fuchsias to a large size in pots requires quite a lot of watering and feeding, but the rewards are high. The plants make good eye-catchers when in flower, especially some of the Triphylla cultivars, and the pots are easy to remove and replace with a flowering or winter-berrying substitute when they stop

Top: A large specimen of the hardy fuchsia 'Riccartonii', permanently planted in the west of England. This plant is around 4m (13ft) high and is covered in flowers.

performing. Good vigorous contenders include the following:
• 'Barbara', an upright cultivar with medium-sized bell-shaped single pink flowers. As it is not very self-branching, it needs some early pinching to encourage it to form a bushy plant.
• 'Celia Smedley', with large white blushed pink and red single flowers. It makes a lot of heavy wood quickly, is a strong upright and responds well to intense feeding.
• 'Checkerboard', a strong upright with long arching branches covered with unusual, attractive single flowers with a red tube, white sepals and a deep red corolla.
• 'Kolding Perle', another strong upright producing long branches covered with medium-large white and red single flowers.

• 'Lady Isobel Barnett', a strong-growing and upright cultivar that is one of the most floriferous. It has rosy-red and rose purple flared single flowers and will be eye-catching for long periods.
• 'Phenomenal', an old, fast-growing strong upright with bushy growth. Because of the weight and size of its large double red and deep indigo blue flowers, the main branches need cane supports in the early years, to prevent them from snapping.

FAST-GROWING HARDY FUCHSIAS

Many of the hardy varieties make a significant amount of growth in a single season, and several grow 1.5m (5ft) a year. When grown in areas with milder winters, typically zone 9 and above, temperatures will not be low enough to kill the old wood down to the ground, and these fuchsias can therefore be pruned down to the main framework. Over a few years, they will make large plants, and one of the best examples concerns a 'Riccartonii'. One was planted on the island of Valentia off the south-west coast of Ireland in 1854. By 1870 it had reached a circumference of 36m (120ft) and, by 1905, it was 76m (250ft) and had reached the cliff edge. The island's climate is windswept, mild and wet. As the branches bend over in the wind and touch the ground, they root readily, making new plants and eventually forming a large thicket covered with flowers.

Left: A large hardy fuchsia is growing over an old brick wall, dripping its flowers on to the pavement outside.

Above: *F. magellanica* var. *molinae* is a fantastic hardy fuchsia with vigorous growth, whose alternative US name of 'Maiden's Blush' comes from the small white and pale pinkish-lilac flowers.

Above: The classic red and purple flowers of *F. magellanica* var. *gracilis* are delicately hanging on its beautiful arching branches. It is a wonderful fuchsia, and is seen in many gardens.

That is very unlikely to happen in your garden but, with suitable annual pruning and shaping, it is possible to obtain a substantial shrub using a hardy fuchsia. Those worth trying include:

• 'Hawkshead', with upright growth of 1.3m (4ft) a year, small white flowers and dark green foliage. The flowers remain white even in direct sun.

• *F. magellanica* var. *gracilis* or *F. m.* var. *gracilis* 'Variegata', both with spreading, arching growth of 1–1.2m (3–4ft) a year and dainty red and purple flowers, and the latter with silvery variegated leaves. It looks very good on a hill or elevated position.

• *F. magellanica* var. *molinae*, with upright growth of 1.5m (5ft) a year and small white and pale lilac flowers.

• 'Mrs Popple', a strong-growing hardy cultivar which strong upright branches and plentiful medium-sized scarlet and violet-purple single flowers. This cultivar will easily grow 1–1.2m (3–4ft) in a season.

• 'Riccartonii', which has upright growth of 1.5m (5ft) a year and small single red and purple flowers.

Right: These hardy fuchsias, growing under the shade of a large horse chestnut tree, are overhanging a narrow roadway and making it almost impassable.

Groups of specimen plants

Large fuchsias grouped together in pots or planted permanently in the ground look spectacular when in flower from early summer onwards. If you choose plants with contrasting flower colours and possibly different foliage colours, the impact can be even greater; on the other hand, if you use several plants of the same variety, you can create the effect of a single, much larger specimen. In milder climates, typically Zone 9 and above, groups of hardy fuchsias can be trained into large shrubs to form a large, easy centrepiece needing minimal attention. Groups of pot-grown fuchsias can also be effective, especially when arranged in tiers, one above the other, making them easily visible from a distance.

GROUPS OF HARDY FUCHSIAS
Here are some suggestions for groups of three hardy fuchsias to place close together – either planted out permanently or in pots – with a choice of different sizes, depending on how much space is available.

For a group of large plants, place 'Riccartonii' at the back, which has upright growth of 1.5m (5ft) a year, with small single red and purple flowers, and *F. magellanica* var. *molinae* beside it; it will reach the same height and give small white and pale lilac flowers. In front of these two,

Top: 'Beacon Rosa' is a lovely hardy fuchsia with self pink flared single flowers that contrast well against the dark green leaves, which have a serrated edge.

the lower-growing *F. magellanica* var. *gracilis* 'Variegata' looks very attractive, with spreading arching growth of 1–1.2m (3–4ft) a year and dainty red and purple flowers and silvery variegated leaves.

A group of medium-sized hardy fuchsias could include 'Hawkshead' at the back; it has upright growth of 1.2m (4ft) a year and small white flowers with dark green foliage. Grow it beside the upright 'Margaret', which puts on 90cm (3ft) a year, and has small single rose-pink and light rose-coloured flowers and light green foliage. 'Genii' goes in front, making an attractive domed bush to a height of 70cm (28in), with golden-green foliage and delicate cerise and violet flowers.

If you only have space for small plants, 'Beacon' is a good choice for the back, with its upright growth of 60cm (2ft) a year, darkish green serrated foliage and deep pink and mauve-pink single flowers. 'Santa Cruz' grows to the same height and has bronze-green foliage and red and reddish-purple semi-double flowers. Use 'Lady

Below left: This pair of 'Mrs Popple' hardy fuchsias, covered with a mass of red and purple flowers, has been planted either side of a flight of steps, guarding the ascent to the rear garden above.

Below: 'Riccartonii' growing in front of the *Canna* 'Tchad'. This is a hardy fuchsia; it is strong growing and often found naturalized in hedgerows.

Thumb' to the front, with its natural mound-forming, bushy compact growth of 40cm (16in) a year, small dark green foliage and red and white semi-double flowers.

GROUPS OF FAST-GROWING NON-HARDY FUCHSIAS

When creating groups of pots, using three again works very well, with two at the back and a third at the front or vice-versa. For a bigger feature, with more height, try a large, raised pot with one or more cascading or upright plants, surrounded by several pots on the ground. You could also use a half or full standard, or a trained shape such as a pillar, in the middle of a group.

For the first possible trio, try 'Celia Smedley' at the back with its large pinkish-white and red flowers and mid-green leaves, contrasting well with 'Phenomenal', an old fast-growing cultivar with large double red and deep indigo-blue flowers. 'Happy Wedding Day' to the front has good strong arching growth and large flared double white flowers.

Another effective group could use the upright 'Royal Velvet' at the back with light to mid-green foliage, crimson red and deep purple double flowers, joined by 'Nancy Lou' with full pink and white double flowers and dark green foliage. 'Annabel',

in front, has lax upright growth, pale green foliage and medium to large white double flowers.

A final suggestion, with all upright, bushy and erect-flowered single cultivars, involves 'WALZ Jubelteen' with light green foliage, pink and pinkish-orange single flowers alongside 'Pink Fantasia' with its dark green foliage and red and violet single flowers. In front, 'Dawn Fantasia' has cream and green variegated foliage and single pale pink and pink flowers.

Above left: A tremendous and highly colourful group of hardy cultivars, including 'Joan Smith', 'Rufus', 'Rose of Castile', 'Genii' and 'Rose of Denmark', planted on a sloping border.

Above: These established plants of the hardy cultivar 'Tom Thumb', forming a compact mound, are covered in flower at the front of a herbaceous border.

Below: This superb mixture of hardy fuchsias planted in a long bed surrounding a sculpted grass area with another island bed in the centre is just coming into flower.

Red and white fuchsias

The dancing flowers of red and white fuchsias stand out waving in the breeze, especially in the dawn or evening. A wide choice of red and white fuchsias is available, with single, semi-double or double flowers, in upright or trailing growth habits. Most have red sepals and a white corolla, though there are some with the colours reversed. The colours show up well, since red complements green,

and the white makes a good contrast. Cultivars with red sepals and a white corolla were among the first hybridized cultivars. Some that are still cultivated today include 'Madame Cornelissen', introduced in 1860, and 'Snowcap', introduced in 1888. Fuchsias with white sepals and a red corolla include *F. boliviana* var. *alba*, a species with these characteristics, plus 'Waternymph' from 1859, 'Beauty

△ **'Brookwood Belle'** A sturdy, upright, short-jointed cultivar with medium-sized double flowers with cerise sepals and a pink corolla flushed white with red veining on the petals. It makes a good pot plant. This fuchsia was hybridized by Gilbert in the UK in 1988.

△ **'Toby Foreman'** A new cultivar introduced in 2007, hybridized by Peter Waving. It is a small single-flowered fuchsia with deep rose sepals and a white corolla. It has vigorous, short-jointed and bushy growth and is likely to prove a popular cultivar.

△ **'Frosted Flame'** A lovely lax fuchsia with single flowers with white sepals and a barrel-shaped flame-red corolla with white patches at the petal base. It is excellent grown in a half basket and may also be trained as a weeping standard.

△ **'Sir Matt Busby'** This is a trailing fuchsia with small to medium double flowers with red sepals and a flared white corolla with red veins, rather like a smaller version of 'Swingtime'. It grows very well in mixed baskets and containers.

△ **'Snowcap'** This fuchsia is an old hardy cultivar which has proved very adaptable over the years. It has medium-sized semi-double flowers with red sepals and a white corolla with red veins. It can be trained into most shapes, or left to grow as a shrub.

of Trowbridge' from 1879 and 'Lye's Elegance' from 1884. Some fuchsias with white sepals, such as 'Celia Smedley', acquire a pink blush with more direct sunlight. There are some superb showy red and white fuchsias. 'Swingtime', the big American trailing double, is very popular and well worth growing, and other trailing cultivars include 'Princessita', 'Frosted Flame', 'Land van Beveren' and 'Sylvia Barker'. Introductions such as 'Nellie Nuttall', 'Ernie' and 'John Bartlett' are very floriferous singles. Growing red and white-flowered cultivars as large structures works well because of the way the flowers stand out, showing up well from quite a distance. A fan shape of 'Swingtime' or a pyramid of 'Snowcap' will look stunning in the garden with their flowers moving in the wind.

△ **'Lancashire Lad'** This is an upright double-flowered cultivar with red sepals and a red-veined white corolla, with a pretty frill at the edges of the petals. The flowers stand out against the dark green foliage and it grows well in containers or borders.

△ **'Swingtime'** This is perhaps the most popular of all the red and white trailing fuchsias. It has large, full, fluffy double flowers and medium-sized mid- to dark green foliage. It looks superb in a basket or as a weeping full or half standard.

▷ **'Sylvia Barker'** This is a floriferous single-flowered cultivar with small to medium flowers with a long waxy white tube and white sepals, and a smoky red short corolla. The growth is lax but quite vigorous, so this fuchsia is very good for baskets, half baskets and hanging containers or pots.

△ **'Nellie Nuttall'** A compact self-branching plant, quite slow-growing, with beautiful semi-erect single flowers with red sepals and a white corolla. This fuchsia is superb grown as a small standard, as a compact bedding plant or in small containers.

Fuchsias as summer bedding

Many gardeners use a variety of plant types and sizes within summer bedding schemes and fuchsias can be very useful as part of these schemes. The best fuchsias for summer bedding are those that tolerate being in full sun and display their flowers well. There is quite a choice of available colours, both in flower and in foliage. The summer garden border is the ideal spot for fuchsias of different growth sizes, leaf colour, and flower sizes and shapes. They will suit all sorts of bedding schemes, from mass planting to more informal arrangements. A useful tool in planning summer bedding schemes is the colour wheel, which gives a guide to complementary colours.

MASS PLANTING SCHEMES

Formal schemes for large areas require compact and uniform plants so that the edges in the design remain clearly defined, and several fuchsia cultivars fit these requirements. The raisings by Tabraham, including the Seven Dwarfs series and the Thumbs, are ideal as they are very small and compact. Use them as edging plants in their own right, or interplant them with other

Top: 'Pink Fantasia' is a floriferous single with masses of upward-facing pinkish-red and violet mauve flowers. It is an excellent choice for bedding.

suitable bedding subjects for edging. Alternatively you could plant them in blocks in a background of edging or ground-cover plants, which will contrast well against the fuchsia's foliage and flowers. The effect can look quite spectacular with the small fuchsia flowers moving in the breeze and sparkling in the sun, or lighter colours and whites standing out in the dusk. Avoid over-feeding these small cultivars to keep their dwarf and compact growth.

Fuchsias with variegated foliage are also worth using as formal summer bedding plants, since the leaf colours intensify in the bright light of the sun, and the growth becomes sturdier. Some cultivars worth trying are 'Autumnale', 'Sunray' and 'Tom West' (which is almost hardy). These have some of the best foliage colours, but they are not quite as compact, so are not suitable for edging. A newer one that is more compact is 'Baby Thumb'.

PLANTS FOR MIXED BEDDING

Use fuchsias that grow to larger sizes in mixed bedding schemes, either as single plants or in groups. The best cultivars are those that have upright and self-branching growth, display their flowers well and are happy in a sunny position. Some of the darker-coloured blooms bleach and fade with strong sunlight and many whites change to shades of pink, so bear this in

Left: 'Tom Thumb' is a compact hardy cultivar from France, introduced in 1850. It is seen here flourishing at the front of a border, contrasting beautifully with the perennial *Kalimeris incisa* 'Charlotte'.

Above: Planted with a mixture of fuchsias, this pale foliage cultivar cleverly delineates the edge of the border.

mind when choosing cultivars. The leaf colours of many fuchsias are mid-green, but some cultivars have quite pale or dark green leaves, so consider this too while planning combinations of colour.

There are plenty of beautiful fuchsias to try in mixed schemes. 'Mickey Goult' is a good small pink single, vigorous and upright, covered in small semi-erect pink single flowers over a long period. 'Bow Bells' is a strong-growing single cultivar with white sepals and a magenta corolla that is an excellent summer bedder. 'Lye's Unique' has waxy white sepals and a salmon-orange corolla; 'Other Fellow' is

VARIETIES FOR SUMMER BEDDING

The following are suggestions for fuchsias that are suitable for single-season use as a summer bedding plant for mass or single planting.

Edging or mass planting: 'Alwin', 'Bambini', 'Baroness van Dedem', 'Bashful', 'Ben Jammin', 'Doc', 'Dopey', 'Geoffrey Smith', 'Grumpy', 'Happy', 'Lady Thumb', 'Mischief', 'Sleepy', 'Sneezy', 'Son of Thumb', 'Tom Thumb', 'Tsjiep', 'Vobeglo'
Group or single planting: 'Bon Accord', 'Border Queen', 'Coralle', 'Dawn Fantasia', 'Jack Siverns', 'Nellie Nuttall', 'Nice 'n' Easy', 'Olive Smith', 'Pink Fantasia', 'Rose Fantasia', 'Rose Quartet', 'Snowcap', 'Thalia', 'Thamar', 'Tom West', 'Upward Look', 'Variegated Pink Fantasia', 'WALZ Jubelteen'
Single planting: 'Alan Titchmarsh', 'Celia Smedley', *F. boliviana* and *F. boliviana* var. *alba*, 'Mrs Lovell Swisher', 'Other Fellow', 'Sharpitor'

Above: A fuchsia border, including 'Genii', 'Thalia' and 'Checkerboard', giving an impressive, flower-filled overall effect.

a lovely pink and white single; 'Jack Siverns' is a new vigorous bush with aubergine flowers that should make a very nice bedding plant; and 'Snowcap' is a semi-double with red sepals and white corolla. The Triphyllas are excellent for summer bedding, and some suggestions are: 'Thalia', with dark foliage and orange flowers; 'Coralle', with sage-green foliage and orange flowers; 'Andenken an Heinrich Henkel', with dark green to purplish-red foliage and pinkish-orange flowers; or how about trying 'Firecracker', the variegated-leaf sport from 'Thalia'.

PLANTS FOR SINGLE PLANTING

Some fuchsia plants grow quickly into large spreading shrubs, and therefore they are excellent for planting as single specimens in the border or any other space that needs filling with summer colour. Some examples are 'Celia Smedley', 'Checkerboard', most of the larger *F. magellanica* variants and the larger Triphylla hybrids.

Far left: 'Autumnale' has beautiful yellow and green foliage when young, which matures to red and salmon with yellow. The single flowers are red and purple.

Left: 'WALZ Jubelteen' is a vigorous upright with masses of pale pink and pinkish-orange upward-facing single flowers. It is excellent for bedding.

Triphyllas as summer bedding

The long tubular flame-red and orange flower clusters of the Triphyllas standing out against the backdrop of their large dark velvety leaves are a superb sight in a summer border. Their tolerance of sun and continuous flowering with vivid colours are the reasons that many professional gardeners use Triphylla cultivars in parks and public gardens, planting them in summer borders. These fuchsias blend happily with many other hot-coloured bedding plants such as red zonal pelargoniums, vivid red salvias or yellow and orange marigolds, complemented by the cooler blues and whites of edging plants such as ageratum, alyssum and lobelia.

USING TRIPHYLLAS

Once they start to flower, the terminal clusters of flowers last a long time and, when they finish, side shoots from below the main clusters carry on the show. This means that once they start flowering they do not let up until the first frosts, or until their removal to make way for planting the spring bedding schemes.

When used in summer bedding they can be treated as annuals and either left in the ground until they are killed by the frost or removed and discarded. If you want to save them for next year, they need to be lifted before the first frost. Pot them up into fairly dry compost (soil mix), prune them once and keep them at a minimum of 4–5°C (39–41°F). In spring, water them and spray lightly to bring them back into growth.

RANGE OF COLOURS

While the majority of the terminal-flowering Triphyllas are different shades of red, pink and orange, other colours are available if you include the Triphylla types that have Triphylla-shaped flowers which are also axial-flowering. For notably different

Top: The Triphylla cultivar 'Mary' is a beautiful slightly lax-growing plant with long green velvety leaves and large clusters of vivid red flowers.

Right: This Triphylla cultivar 'Thalia' has been used as a bedding plant in front of shrubs and climbers, and is just starting to come into flower.

colours try 'Roger de Cooker' with a white tube and sepals and a rose corolla, 'Jaspers Triphywhite' with a rose-white flower, 'Pabbe's Torreldöve' with a magenta-purple flower and 'Our Ted' with a white flower. In addition, there are cultivars with different flower sizes. Smaller-flowered cultivars include 'Adinda' with small pink flowers, 'Anja Robbens' in magenta-rose, 'Bessie Kimberly' (red), 'Boy Marc' (orange-red), 'Eruption' (magenta-pink), 'Pan' (purple-red-rose) and 'Sparky' (red-purple). Medium-sized cultivars include 'Billy Green' (salmon pink), 'Coralle' (orange-red), 'Gartenmeister

Left: This 'Gartenmeister Bonstedt' is growing with *Corynocarpus laevigatus* 'Picturatus', *Metrosideros mexicana*, *Iresine lindenii* (bloodleaf) and *Justicia brandegeana* (shrimp plant).

white or pastel blue petunias or white zonal pelargoniums. For a cool border choose the white or pink-flowered Triphyllas or Triphylla types, again mixing them with white and blue bedding plants. Useful Triphyllas include 'Adinda', 'Billy Green', 'Roger de Cooker', 'Fulpila', 'Phaidra' and 'Orient Express'.

Finally, try spot planting using large Triphylla fuchsias in a summer bedding scheme creating focal points to catch the eye, with the quick-growing, free-flowering 'Thalia' and 'Coralle' being high on the list. In a sunny border, they will thrive for the whole summer in a riot of colour. Also, quarter standards grown from Triphylla cultivars are excellent for creating differences in height along a summer bedding scheme and, again, will flower continuously from midsummer on, but remember that they will need heated winter protection if you wish to keep them for next year.

Below: The Triphylla cultivar 'Thalia' is excellent for summer bedding. The long red flowers contrast well with the olive-green leaves. *Helichrysum petiolare* 'Limelight' would make a good companion plant.

Bonstedt' (orange), 'Insulinde' (red-orange), 'Mary' (brilliant red) and 'Thalia' (orange-red). 'Orient Express' is an unusual Triphylla type that has very long flowers with pinkish-white sepals and a rose corolla.

VIVID BORDERS

An excellent way of using these Triphylla fuchsias is in groups or blocks with other similarly hot-coloured bedding plants. For example, the brilliant yellows and oranges of French or African marigolds go perfectly with the flame oranges and reds of the Triphylla fuchsias to create a vivid border.

Red-hot salvias can also be used in this way, and why not try orange-flowered Triphyllas such as 'Gartenmeister Bonstedt' or 'Coralle' with blocks of yellow rudbeckia or tagetes? Zonal pelargoniums, including the bi- and tri-colour leaf types, with intense red flowers will also happily sit in blocks alongside the Triphylla fuchsias.

COOL AND MIXED BORDERS

Alternatively create a border with alternate patches of hot and cold, mixing blocks of red and orange Triphyllas with cooler plants such as blue ageratums, white impatiens,

Upward-looking fuchsias

Traditional fuchsias hang delicately down from the leaf axils, hence the origin of their common nickname, 'ladies' eardrop'. In recent years, hybridizers have produced many more fuchsias with semi-erect and erect flowers ('upward-looking'). Semi-erect means the plants hold flowers horizontally, and erect means they hold flowers upwards so that you look down from above into the corolla. This gives the plants a surprisingly different character, even though the flower forms are the same as the hanging varieties. They are excellent used as half-hardy bedding plants in groups or individually, mixed with bedding plants that are more traditional.

FIRST UPWARD-LOOKING FUCHSIAS

The first recorded cultivar of this type, 'Bon Accord', was hybridized and introduced in 1861 in France by the grower Crousse, and is still widely cultivated. It is not naturally self-branching and needs frequent pinching in the early stages of growth. Sent from France to the USA, it then later reappeared in England as a new introduction under the name 'Erecta Novelty'. This name still appears in hybridization parent lists today. It was not until 1968, over 100 years after the first upward-looking fuchsia was created, that the next significant introduction appeared – 'Upward Look',

with carmine and rose-purple flowers, hybridized by Cliff Gadsby using 'Bon Accord' as one of the parents.

CURRENT RANGE OF CULTIVARS

Nowadays, one can choose from an extensive range, including small to medium single or semi-double-flowered cultivars. Quite recently, the first semi-erect small double-flowered cultivars have appeared, but no fully erect ones yet, although it can only be a matter of time. It will have to be a

Top left: 'Minirose' is a small free-flowering cultivar with semi-erect single flowers of very pale pink and cyclamen-purple. It flowers continuously for long periods.

Left: 'Bon Accord' is the first recorded cultivar with truly erect flowers. Its small single flowers, with their white tube, white sepals flushed pink and pale purple corolla, look really stunning in a low border.

Above: 'Alison Patricia' has small semi-erect single or semi-double flowers with dark pink sepals and a violet corolla. It is an upright, compact and very floriferous fuchsia.

small double, or the weight of the flowers will pull the flower head downward.

'Pink Fantasia' was first introduced in 1989, and has been used extensively both as an exhibition plant and for summer bedding. It has thrown a number of sports, including 'Rose Fantasia', which fits its parent's name more aptly, and variegated forms such as 'Variegated Pink Fantasia', 'Colne Fantasy' and 'Dawn Fantasia'. Plant them together in blocks to form part of your bedding schemes, using different varieties for colour contrast.

The erect-flowering cultivars are all upright growers that are not especially self-branching and will grow to 60–72cm

Left: 'John Bartlett' is a floriferous upright fuchsia with semi-erect red and white single flowers, often producing three flowers from each leaf axil.

(24–30in) from a 15cm (6in) tall plant bedded out in the late spring. Try mixing them with traditional bedding plants, choosing ones that grow to similar heights and give good colour contrasts. Consider petunia, impatiens, salvia (but be careful with the colours), nicotiana, antirrhinum, godetia, verbena or dianthus as a starting point, but let your creativity put your own personal mark on the border.

You can also use them as spot plants in bedding schemes to make focal points in the border, and the large range of colours means you are sure to find one that complements the rest of the planting scheme. 'Vobeglo', a Dutch dwarf erect-flowering cultivar, works well as an edging plant or a spot plant in the rockery. Many of the dwarf varieties also make excellent small standards, which are good for planting in bedding schemes.

Semi-erect types can also be used to great effect. They are not upward-looking, but they do hold their flowers out well from the foliage, which makes them excellent for planters and bedding out in the garden. You will also find a more varied choice of colours and flower sizes in this group.

The list in the panel gives suggestions for both erect-flowering and semi-erect fuchsias that have a range of colours and sizes, which you might consider for use in your own bedding schemes.

Below: 'WALZ Jubelteen' is a bushy cultivar with small erect pink to pinkish-orange single flowers that seem to sparkle in the sun.

UPWARD-LOOKING CULTIVARS

The range of erect-flowering cultivars is increasing year on year. The lists below contain some of the current fuchsias of this group that grow well.

ERECT-FLOWERING TYPES

'Bon Accord'
'Estelle Marie'
'Ivana van Amsterdam'
'Joan Goy'
'Pink Fantasia'
'Rose Fantasia'
'Thamar'
'Upward Look'
'Variegated Pink Fantasia'
'Vobeglo'
'WALZ Jubelteen'

SEMI-ERECT-FLOWERING TYPES

'Alison Patricia'
'Bob Pacey'
'Brookwood Lady'
'Harvey's Reward'
'John Bartlett'
'Mickey Goult'
'Minirose'
'Nellie Nuttall'
'Nicis Findling'
'Pabbe's Kirrevaalk'
'Sparky'
'Superstar'
'Susan Skeen'

'Pink Fantasia'

Triphylla fuchsias

The fuchsia cultivars that make up the Triphylla Group should be in everybody's collection because of their graceful foliage and striking racemes of flowers. They make very good summer bedding plants, as they will happily tolerate full sun, and while not being the quickest fuchsia to flower in early summer, once they start they will continue blooming right up to the first frosts. This group of fuchsias also does very well planted in pots or large containers. The plants have large, long and narrow leaves which are often velvety in texture and range in colour from a bronzy green to a rich purple-green colour. The flowers have long tubes and grow in terminal racemes or clusters. Although each cluster of flowers lasts quite a long time, that stem cannot grow any further, since this is a terminal

△ **'Thalia'** This is probably the Triphylla cultivar that most people will recognize. The long racemes of orange-red flowers contrast beautifully with its dark olive-green foliage. This fuchsia is really superb as a summer bedder and will also make a good standard.

△ **'Whiteknights Cheeky'** This plant is a Triphylla-type fuchsia, with flowers in the leaf axils and not just in terminal racemes. The flowers are long, Tyrian purple in colour and carried erect. It is an unusual plant with an interesting flower colour.

△ **'Coralle'** Also known as 'Koralle', this is a striking fuchsia with racemes of long orange flowers that contrast beautifully with the large sage-green leaves. This cultivar is slightly more tolerant of cold temperatures in the winter than other Triphyllas.

△ **'Billy Green'** This is a lovely Triphylla-type fuchsia with long salmon-pink flowers and velvety light olive-green leaves. It is so vigorous in growth that it quickly makes a large specimen plant. It is easy to grow and highly recommended.

△ **'Insulinde'** A newer Dutch Triphylla hybrid by Herman de Graaff, introduced in 1991. It is a very striking fuchsia, with vivid orange racemes of flowers and very dark bronze-green foliage. It grows vigorously in full sun, making it very good for bedding schemes.

point. Fortunately, side shoots produced a little further down the stem quickly form new flower clusters, often taking over before the first flush is finished, giving almost continuous blooms throughout the summer and into late autumn. The flower colours are mainly self-colours of reds, oranges and pinks, but a few new colours like whites and aubergines and even multiple colours, for example 'Orient Express', with a pink corolla and pinkish-white and red sepals, have been commercially produced. They need careful feeding and watering and seem to respond very well to a high-nitrogen feed, which helps to prevent the yellowing of lower leaves. This class of fuchsias is frost tender – most varieties need a minimum winter temperature of 5°C (41°F).

△ **'Sparky'** An unusual fuchsia with smallish semi-erect Triphylla-type flowers of deep red, with small bronzy-green, red-veined foliage. It is very useful for small mixed planters, being slightly smaller and more compact in growth than the traditional Triphyllas.

△ **'Our Ted'** This is the first truly white Triphylla cultivar, hybridized by Edwin Goulding. It has racemes of creamy white flowers and rather dark green glossy foliage. This is not an easy cultivar to grow and it hates being overwatered, so it is one for the experts.

◁ **'Gartenmeister Bonstedt'** One of the beautiful Triphylla hybrids introduced by Carl Bonstedt in 1905. It is very similar to 'Thalia', the main difference being a pronounced bulge in the orange-red tube. It is excellent as a summer bedder.

△ **'Mary'** This is a superb Triphylla raised by Carl Bonstedt as far back as 1897. It has racemes of vivid bright crimson flowers and velvety sage-green foliage. It is not the easiest plant to grow, but can make a very nice standard or a spectacular specimen.

Fuchsias in the shrub border

If you are fortunate enough to have a large garden, you are likely to have a shrub border, or at least some area of the garden planted with shrubs. These can be extremely interesting areas, with so many shapes and sizes of shrubs, different leaf textures and colours, evergreen and deciduous plants, and some kinds of flowers at most times of the year. Hardy fuchsias grown as part of a permanent planting scheme behave like deciduous shrubs or herbaceous perennials, depending on the winter temperatures. They are useful grown among spring-flowering and autumn-flowering shrubs to give some blooms and colour in the summer months. They also show up well against dark evergreen shrubs such as camellias.

FUCHSIAS AND SHRUBS

The height and spread of shrubs can vary tremendously, even within the same genus of plants, and it is quite an art to arrange them so that they complement each other and are all clearly visible. When established, they have the advantage of being quite low-maintenance, needing only annual pruning and mulching, and the ground beneath them remains reasonably weed-free because of the amount of shade, with perhaps species like ground ivy being the major problems. Large fuchsias as shrubs can add an extra dimension, providing extra pockets of colour, especially with winter- and spring-flowering shrubs.

Top: This fuchsia species *F. arborescens* is growing happily in a border, showing off its large, glossy green leaves. The flower heads are in various stages of development, from panicles of pink flowers to ripe berries.

CHOOSING THE RIGHT FUCHSIAS

In areas of the shrub border with plant heights of up to 2m (6ft), grow fuchsias to add vibrant pockets of summer colour and interest, especially among spring-, autumn- and winter-flowering shrubs.

Above: Fuchsias 'Katie Susan', 'Brenda White' and 'Love's Reward' used as edging plants for a shrub border, contrasting with a purple-foliaged berberis.

In parts of the world where the frost will not kill fuchsias down to the ground in the winter, you can use vigorous-growing hardy fuchsias such as *F. magellanica* var. *molinae* or 'Riccartonii' in taller parts of the border, where they can reach heights of 3–4m (10–13ft). This may work in fairly cold areas too, since shielding from the evergreen shrubs will give some extra frost protection, allowing more growth than in the open.

While the larger hardy fuchsias are the easiest to grow, since they become a permanent part of the shrubbery, it can also be interesting to grow some of the large

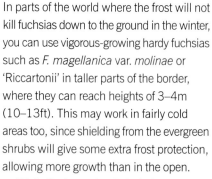

Left: The hardy cultivar 'Garden News', with its rose-pink and magenta-rose double flowers, is seen here growing among other flowering plants and shrubs in a border.

tender species as temporary residents, such as *F. boliviana* or *F. boliviana* var. *alba,* both of which grow as a climbing shrub. Alternatively, *F. arborescens* or *F. paniculata*, with their upright racemes of tiny pink-purple flowers, large glossy leaves and clusters of berries later in the season, merge beautifully into the shrub border, adding extra interest for many months.

FUCHSIAS AS EDGING

Another way to use fuchsias in the shrub border is to grow them as dot plants along the edges, between the shrubs and a lawn or a paved or gravelled area. This can give nice spots of colour against the background of the leaves and structure of the shrubs. Use the larger-growing varieties in gaps in the border toward the front, and more compact-growing ones right along the edges. When growing them in this situation, it is better to treat them as bedding plants.

TEMPORARY RESIDENTS

Plant out fuchsias, especially those trained as standards or pillars, as temporary residents in the summer in the shrub border. This works especially well in a spring-flowering shrub border with plants such as rhododendrons, camellias, azaleas and other similar evergreen shrubs. Usually pruning of these takes place in the late spring or early summer, and in the created spaces fuchsia standards of an appropriate

height can give excellent patches of summer and autumn flower in an otherwise green border. Full or half standards of red and white flowered cultivars such as 'Snowcap' and 'Celia Smedley', or red flowered such as 'Rufus' or 'Olive Smith', are very effective. Pillars of cultivars such as 'Phyllis' or 'Kolding Perle' can also be effective. With pillars, a space where the plant is visible almost down to the ground will give the best results.

Below: This striking hardy species variant *F. magellanica* var. *gracilis* 'Tricolor' is displaying its variegated foliage to perfection here, planted among a selection of other flowering plants and shrubs.

Above: An unusual use of the species fuchsia *F. denticulata* as a tall edging plant, with its pretty pink, red, green and orange-red long tubed flowers along the edge of border.

HARDY FUCHSIAS AND COMPANION SHRUBS

The following tall-growing hardy fuchsias and companion shrubs can be used together to create some interesting shrub border designs.

LARGE HARDY FUCHSIAS

F. magellanica var. *molinae*, *F. magellanica* var. *versicolor*, 'Hawkshead', 'Margaret', 'Margaret Brown', 'Mrs Popple', 'Mrs W.P. Wood', 'Riccartonii', 'Sharpitor', 'Waldfee'

COMPANION SHRUBS

Deciduous, spring-flowering:
Cornus, Forsythia, Genista, Lonicera, Ribes, Sambucus, Spiraea, Syringa, Viburnum, Weigela
Evergreen, spring-flowering:
Brachyglottis, Camellia, Ceanothus, Choisya, Daphne, Garrya, Ilex, Magnolia, Mahonia, Osmanthus, Pieris, Pittosporum, Prunus, Rhododendron, Skimmia, Tamarix, Viburnum

Fuchsias in the rockery

Many of the smaller hardy or half-hardy fuchsias can be used to great effect in the rockery. A number of cultivars will only grow to 45cm (18in) in a season if you cut them back hard at the start of the season. This type usually has quite small flowers, which are in proportion and keeping with other rockery plants. A rockery may include many of the low-growing and smaller-flowered plants commonly available, with alpines such as *Armeria juniperifolia*, *Aurinia saxatilis*, *Dianthus alpinus*, *Draba aizoides*, *Gentiana acaulis* and *G. septemfida*, *Primula marginata*, *Saxifraga*, small conifers, miniature shrubs and heathers or other small plants or your choice.

ROCKERY PLANTING

The smaller fuchsias can do very well in these situations, enjoying the good drainage conditions in most rockeries and contrasting well with the green foliage of the heathers or small conifers. Use the hardy varieties as a permanent planting, and the less hardy ones as a spot planting, but be careful not to plant hardy varieties in a soil-filled depression in a rock, which will fill with water when it rains. The resulting waterlogging will certainly kill them over the winter.

Top: 'La Campanella', with its stiff trailing growth and smallish leaves, is excellent for growing over low rocks. It has round buds and semi-double flowers, with white sepals flushed pink and an imperial purple corolla.

SMALL-FLOWERED HARDY FUCHSIAS

The prostrate-growing New Zealand species *F. procumbens* is an interesting choice, as its fern-like foliage will creep and spread over rocks. It is medium hardy and you can use it as a permanent planting. The flowers are very small, upright with a yellow-green tube, green sepals but no corolla, and blue pollen on the anthers. It forms grape-like fruits, which turn pink-red when ripe.

The Thumb varieties – 'Tom Thumb', 'Lady Thumb', and the variegated 'Baby Thumb' and 'Son of Thumb' – are good rockery plants, along with the series hybridized by Tabraham, named after the seven dwarfs: 'Bashful', 'Doc', 'Dopey', 'Grumpy', 'Happy', 'Sleepy' and 'Sneezy', which all have annual

Above: 'Sharonelle' is a compact bush cultivar with semi-erect single flowers. It is ideal for use in the rockery.

growth of only 22–45cm (9–18in). The Seven Dwarfs fuchsias are often planted alongside the cultivar 'Snow White', but this is a larger double white trailer, not suitable for the rockery.

Two very hardy varieties, *F. magellanica* var. *pumila* and 'David', are excellent choices, with small foliage and flowers, and these also only grow to 45cm (18in). 'Papoose' is a low-growing, spreading, hardy cultivar, which can also be encouraged to trail over rocks.

Others worth considering are 'Alice Hoffman', 'Bouquet', 'Elf', 'Forget-Me-Not', 'Liebriez', 'Red Imp', 'Thornley's Hardy', which has a trailing habit, and 'Tinker Bell' (note that this is the cultivar raised by Tabraham, not the one with the same name raised by Hodges).

Left: This selection of small-flowered fuchsias is growing with a variety of companion plants in a multi-levelled rockery. Note how the foliage of the variegated cultivar 'Tom West' stands out in the sun.

Above: Ferns, small conifers, miniature campanulas and other rockery plants accompany fuchsias in this steep rockery.

DWARF HARDY FUCHSIAS

The following are some recommendations for compact, hardy and half-hardy small-flowered varieties that are excellent for use in a rockery.

Hardy: 'Alice Hoffman', 'Bashful', 'David', 'Doc', 'Dopey', 'Geoffrey Smith', 'Grumpy', 'Happy', 'Lady Thumb', *F. magellanica* var. *pumila*, 'Papoose', *F. procumbens*, 'Sleepy', 'Sneezy', 'Son of Thumb', 'Tom Thumb', 'Thornley's Hardy'
Half hardy: 'Andrew Hadfield', 'Auntie Jinks', 'Ben Jammin', 'Harry Grey', 'La Campanella', 'My Little Cracker', 'Nellie Nuttall', 'Pink Rain', 'Postiljon', 'Sophie Louise', 'Sharonelle', 'Superstar', 'Tom West', 'Twinny', 'Westminster Chimes', 'Vobeglo'

SMALL-FLOWERED HALF-HARDY FUCHSIAS

Use these as spot plantings in the rockery over the summer. If you are in a very mild area they may survive the winter, but cut them back hard in the late winter or early spring to keep them small. The best plants for this situation are the low-growing types with small flowers, especially the ones that throw their flowers outward. The types used for showing at exhibitions grown in 9cm (3½in) pots are a very good choice for spot planting in a rockery.

Some cultivars to consider are 'Andrew Hadfield', 'My Little Cracker', 'Nellie Nuttall', 'Sophie Louise', 'Sharon Leslie', 'Sharonelle', 'Superstar' and 'Twinny'. Try also some of the smaller growing Encliandra types, but beware, some of them are strong growers. Try *F. hemsleyana*, variegated 'Lottie Hobby', 'Miniature Jewels', *F. microphylla* and its subspecies. You can also consider growing the smaller cascading types, to trail over the rocks. Some suitable cultivars are 'Auntie Jinks', 'Harry Grey', 'Pink Rain' and 'Westminster Chimes'.

Left: This bright collection of fuchsia cultivars is thriving on a warm rockery slope, giving an interesting combination of textures and shapes.

Above: *F. procumbens* is a hardy prostrate-growing species from New Zealand. It is excellent for a rockery because it scrambles energetically over the rocks.

Pink and white fuchsias

There are many fuchsias with pink and white flowers, and those with darker foliage show up the pale flowers especially well. The pink shade softens the hardness of the white and gives a warmer feeling. These fuchsias can be a great way to create a transition between cool and hot colours in the garden. There are many varieties in this colour range to choose from, bearing both white

sepals with a pink corolla and pink sepals with a white corolla, but one point to remember is that the shades of both pink and white may change in the sun. Many white varieties keep their pure white only in the shade, turning to pink in full sun, and pink shades may become deeper in the sun. Some examples of cultivars which do this are 'Shelford', 'Katrina Thompsen' and 'Trudi Davro'. If you

△ **'Shelford'** This is a superb single-flowered cultivar that is very adaptable and possible to grow in most forms. Although white in the shade, the medium-sized single flowers become pink in the sun.

△ **'Margarite Dawson'** This is a borderline hardy cultivar with strong upright growth and quite large mid-green leaves. The medium double flowers have rose-pink sepals and a pink-veined white corolla.

△ **'Miss California'** This is a spreading semi-lax, semi-double-flowered cultivar with pink sepals and a white corolla. Grown as a bush it will need some support, and in a basket, weights to pull down the branches.

△ **'Camcon'** This is a single-flowered cultivar, making an upright, bushy and very floriferous plant, with attractive sparkling flowers. The flowers have white sepals flushed with pink and a deep pink corolla. It makes a good small pot plant or a smaller standard.

△ **'Harlow Carr'** This is a very pretty cultivar with lovely single flowers having pink sepals and a flared white corolla. It is excellent to grow as a standard and as a trained shape. The dark green foliage enhances the flower display, allowing them to stand out.

want to grow a pink and white in a shady area, make sure it is a variety that has natural pink colours that will not fade. One of the best double-flowered bush fuchsias with pink sepals and a white corolla is 'Nancy Lou', hybridized by Annabelle Stubbs and almost discarded because it did not have the trailing habit she believed was commercially necessary. 'Miss California' and 'Harlow Carr'

also have pink sepals and a white corolla, while 'Margarite Dawson' is a double with similar colours. 'Other Fellow' is a cultivar with lovely white sepals and a pink corolla, and 'Flirtation Waltz' is a superb double with similar colours. 'Puts Folly' is a trailing single cultivar with white sepals and a deep pink corolla, while 'Impala' is a double with the same characteristics.

▷ **'Other Fellow'** This is a very floriferous single-flowered cultivar with a longish waxy white tube, waxy white sepals and a coral-pink corolla. It thrives in direct sun and makes an excellent bedding plant.

▽ **'Trudi Davro'** This is a trailing cultivar, excellent for hanging baskets or pots. It has small to medium double flowers with pale pink sepals and a fluffy white corolla. The flower is almost white in the shade, but the sepals gradually gain pink shades with exposure to the sun. The flowers stand out against the dark green leaves.

△ **'Countess of Aberdeen'** This is an old cultivar first introduced in 1888. It has a beautiful small single flower with a longish ivory-white tube, white sepals and a corolla which is almost white in the shade, but gradually becomes pink with exposure to the sun. It dislikes overwatering.

△ **'Sophisticated Lady'** This is a lax-growing large-flowered double American cultivar with a pale pink tube and sepals, and a white corolla. It is an excellent cultivar for use in baskets and containers.

Permanent fuchsia beds

Hardy fuchsias can form the basis of fantastic low-maintenance beds, giving colour in the garden for much of the year. They flower continuously from early summer to the first autumn frosts – much longer than most shrubs and perennials. In some temperate areas, especially on the west and south-west coasts of Europe touched by the Gulf Stream, it is possible to grow half-hardy varieties as permanent plantings right through the milder winters. In warmer areas that have entire frost-free growing seasons, it is even possible to grow almost all fuchsia types permanently, although they might need some shading during the hotter months, and pruning in the cooler months.

CHOOSING SUITABLE HARDIES

This section focuses on fuchsias that are recognized hardy types when grown in a climate with hard winters, typically around USA Zone 7, which will remove all the leaves and kill the growth down to ground level. It is always a good idea to look at local public gardens to see which hardy fuchsias grow well in your area.

You can choose hardy fuchsias in a wonderful range of heights, flower sizes, types and colours, varying from small, dwarf singles, through medium-sized doubles and semi-doubles, up to the large,

rapid-growing *magellanica* hybrids, thanks to the efforts of many different hybridizers since the early 19th century. The growth made from ground level during the season ranges from a modest 13cm (5in) in the case of the spreading *F. procumbens*, up to 1.2m (4ft) for *F. magellanica* var. *molinae* and 'Margaret'.

PERMANENT BED DESIGNS

When planning a hardy fuchsia bed, do as much research as possible and get advice from your local fuchsia specialist nursery, as well as from neighbours or

your local gardening society. You also need to check the different flower colours and typical annual growth of the plants before deciding how to lay out your border. Although most hardy fuchsias have mid or dark green foliage, there are some cultivars with pale green, golden or variegated leaves. Use these as eye-catching individuals or groups to create extra interest.

The easiest plans are for borders backing on to a high wall, fence or hedge, where the aim is to create an increase in height from the front to the back of the border, with some differences or undulations in height

Top: A single flower of *F. magellanica*, with its red sepals and purple corolla. This hardy shrub is commonly found in gardens, where it thrives with little attention. It also makes a good hedging plant.

Right: A group of hardy fuchsias growing and flowering together as permanent plantings, carefully protected by a windbreak of small trees and shrubs.

Above: *F. magellanica* var. *variegata* is a single-flowered hardy fuchsia that makes an attractive low bush. The crimson-red sepals and purple corolla contrast well with the pale green foliage, which is edged with cream.

Right: 'Empress of Prussia' is an old and very floriferous hardy cultivar with scarlet and magenta flowers. It was almost lost from cultivation, but luckily found again.

Above: 'Purple Splendour' is a strong, upright, hardy cultivar growing to 60cm (2ft), and was introduced by Sunningdale Nurseries in 1975. The lovely single flowers have crimson sepals and a blue-purple corolla.

along the length of the scheme. These borders can be different shapes – rectangular, square, semi-circular or with an uneven scalloped edge – with the colour of the backdrop chosen to enhance the fuchsia display.

A more elaborate design involves surrounding a bed by a path on all sides, or placing the bed in the middle of a lawn. Such designs are more common in public or botanical gardens, where there is space to create large beds that are best viewed from all sides. Make sure that the larger plants are in the middle, with the smaller ones at the edges and a gradation in size between the extremes. Surrounding the border with low hedges, grown from a dense, evergreen plant such as box, helps to shelter the fuchsias from the worst of the cold winter winds.

The choice of hardy fuchsias is very subjective, but if you select carefully you will have a beautiful show of colour right through summer and autumn.

RELIABLE HARDY FUCHSIAS
This list contains some high-quality fuchsias recommended for permanent fuchsia beds, arranged by the height of their seasonal growth.

Small: 'Abbé Farges', 'Alice Hoffman', 'Baby Thumb', 'Beacon Rosa', 'Beranger', 'Bouquet', 'Carmen', 'Constance', 'David', 'Dollar Prinzessin', 'Elfin Glade', 'Happy', 'Heidi Ann', 'Lady Thumb', 'Liebriez', *F. magellanica* var. *pumila*, 'Papoose', 'Son of Thumb', 'Thornley's Hardy', 'Tom Thumb'
Medium: 'Achievement', 'Ariel', 'Beacon', 'Blue Gown', 'Brutus', 'C.J. Howlett', 'Chillerton Beauty', 'Garden News', 'Glow', 'Herald', 'Howlett's Hardy', 'Lady Bacon', 'Mauve Lace', 'Phyrne', 'Prosperity', 'Red Ace', 'Rose of Castile', 'Rufus', 'Snowcap', 'Tennessee Waltz', 'W.P. Wood', 'White Pixie'
Large: 'Abundance', 'Army Nurse', 'Charming', 'Diana Wright', 'Empress of Prussia', 'Enfante Prodigue', 'Exmoor Gold', 'Graf Witte', 'Greatham Mill', 'Hawkshead', *F. magellanica* var. *molinae*, 'Madame Cornelissen', 'Margaret', 'Margaret Brown', 'Mrs Popple', 'Waldfee', 'Whiteknights Amethyst'

Fuchsia beds with bulbs

Growing winter- and spring-flowering bulbs and corms among fuchsias is a superb way of extending the period of interest in a hardy fuchsia bed. They add a wide range of vibrant hues. Although fuchsias have a very long flowering period, in colder areas – where the winter is cold enough to make them shed their leaves and kill growth down to the ground – the fuchsia beds will be bare from late autumn or early winter to spring, when the fuchsias start to regrow. Even in mild winters, when the woody structure and the leaves may remain, the fuchsias will not be in flower. This is the perfect opportunity to create a colourful display of winter- and spring-flowering bulbs.

BULB PLACEMENT

The arrangement of the bulbs will partly depend on how formal the garden is, and whether you want a random mixture of different flowers or neat blocks of one type, but a good general guideline is to put plants of similar sizes together, with the tallest at the back of the border – or in the middle of a bed that is viewed from all sides – and the smallest at the front edge where they are easy to see.

THE FRONT TO THE MIDDLE

Excellent choices for the front of the hardy fuchsia border include hyacinths, dwarf irises, *Hyacinthoides non-scripta* (English bluebells), *Anemone blanda*, scillas and even the spring-flowering cyclamen

Top: A hardy fuchsia bed with underplanted flowering narcissi and hyacinths. The fuchsias, cut down to the ground in the early spring, are just starting to shoot again.

and smaller fritillaries, such as *F. meleagris* (snake's-head fritillary) and *F. pyrenaica*. However, avoid the quick-spreading *Muscari* (grape hyacinth) because it spreads very

quickly unless you contain it by planting in a bottomless bucket sunk in the ground. Grow the medium-high bulbs and corms from the front to the middle of the bed, allowing them to emerge through the bare fuchsia stems. This group includes tulips – the single early kind, double early kind, Kaufmanniana and some species – and different types of daffodils, ranging from the miniatures to the medium high. Avoid the double types if you have strong winds.

Above: The tall spectacular flowers of *Fritillaria imperialis* (crown imperial) are a good choice for use at the back of the border, while small cupped narcissi suit the middle.

Left: A continuous bed of hardy fuchsias surrounding a scalloped lawn underplanted with hundreds of flowering narcissi. In places it is just possible to see the brown stems of the fuchsias.

Above: The lovely flowers of *Leucojum aestivum* (summer snowflake) grow on delicate long stems that resemble those of the humble snowdrop.

THE MIDDLE TO THE BACK/CENTRE

In the middle of the bed, you can plant *Fritillaria pontica* or *F. pallidiflora*, *Iris tuberosa* and some early summer-flowering bulbs, such as alliums. You should avoid *Hyacinthoides hispanica* (Spanish bluebell) because it spreads almost uncontrollably, and more importantly, causes problems by hybridizing with the threatened wild English bluebell. Possible plants for the middle to the back of the border depend largely on the backdrop, but *Fritillaria raddena*, *F. verticillata* or *F. imperialis* (crown imperial), *Leucojum aestivum* (summer snowflake) and some of the late spring or early summer-flowering lilies, such as 'Connecticut King', *Lilium mackliniae* or *L. nanum*, are very effective.

LOOKING AFTER THE BULBS

Before planting the bulbs, check the requirements of each type, and make sure the conditions are suitable. You should also remember that you must be able to reach the fuchsias to prune them in late winter or early spring. When the bulbs have finished flowering, allow the foliage to die down naturally to ensure that the bulbs build up their strength for next year's display.

SOME RECOMMENDED DAFFODILS

	FRONT	MIDDLE	BACK
'Trumpet'	'Little Beauty' 'Little Gem'	'Foresight' 'Silent Valley' 'W.P. Milner'	'Arctic Gold' 'Bravoure' 'Mount Hood'
Large-cupped	'Bantam'	'Decoy' 'Sempre Avanti'	'Ice Follies' 'Pineapple Prince'
Small-cupped		'Sinopel'	'Barrett Browning'
Double	'Manly'	'Irene Copeland'	'Acropolis' 'Golden Ducat'
Jonquil	'Pipit' 'Sugar Bush'	'Hillstar'	
Tazetta	'Minnow'	'Canary Bird' 'Winston Churchill'	
Cyclaminieus	'Jack Snipe' 'Jetfire'	'Peeping Tom'	
Species	*N. triandrus*	*N. cyclamineus* *N. jonquilla*	

'Barrett Browning'   'Pipit'   'Peeping Tom'   *Narcissus triandrus*

SOME RECOMMENDED TULIPS

	FRONT	MIDDLE	BACK
Single early	'Calgary'	'Apricot Beauty' 'Keizerskroon'	
Early double	'Monte Carlo' 'Viking'	'Foxtrot'	'Mondial'
Kaufmanniana	'Johann Strauss' 'Zampa'	'Corsage' 'Oriental Splendour'	
Single late		'Andre-Rieu' 'Broadway'	'Maureen' 'Wisley'
Darwin hybrid		'Ad Rem'	'Burning Heart' 'Oxford'

'Apricot Beauty'   'Keizerskroon'   'Monte Carlo'   'Johann Strauss'

Fuchsia beds with spring flowers

The use of winter- and spring-flowering shrubs and a wide range of other perennials in the hardy fuchsia bed is another excellent way of generating extra shapes and colours and extending the flowering season. Choosing the right shrubs and carefully looking after them with appropriate pruning ensures that the bed stays the way you visualized it. The size of the shrubs is important to make sure that you arrive at a fuchsia bed inter-planted with shrubs and not a spring-flowering shrubbery inter-planted with fuchsias. Utilizing small dwarf evergreen shrubs that are amenable to pruning will ensure there is some background of green foliage in the border for the whole of the year.

SELECTING SHRUBS

It is important, when choosing shrubs, to select those with a similar build – both in terms of height and width – to the fuchsias. If you use larger shrubs, or those that you cannot prune to keep them at the right size, they will quickly dominate the bed, and the fuchsias will look like an after-thought. You must also check that the design allows both the shrubs and fuchsias sufficient room to grow, so that the space is well filled but no plant gets crowded out.

Top: A pale pink single fuchsia growing among prettily coloured blooms in a late spring-flowering basket brightens the mood and welcomes the summer.

Remember also that fuchsias are not scented, but many winter- and spring-flowering shrubs are, so you should try to think of fragrance as well as colour when making your choice.

EVERGREEN SHRUBS

These are an excellent choice because, in addition to their colourful flowers, the leaves give attractive blocks of colour throughout winter. Try to choose compact plants growing to a maximum of 1.5m (5ft) high, because larger plants will need vigorous annual pruning to prevent them becoming too big, and in some cases, this may inhibit the flowering. Of course, some

of the bigger ones will not be amenable to pruning. The best evergreens include smallish azaleas or rhododendrons, daphnes, early-flowering hebes (such as *Hebe macrantha* or *H. ochracea*), pieris, spiraea, skimmia and viburnum. For the front of the bed, winter- and spring-flowering heathers are ideal, but again they require heavy clipping after flowering to keep them at a reasonable size. There are some suggestions of suitable shrubs at the top of the page opposite.

DECIDUOUS SHRUBS

Alternatively, you can use deciduous, late winter- or spring-flowering shrubs to add colour in spring. Again, opt for shrubs with similar dimensions to your fuchsias, but it is also possible to use larger shrubs such as forsythia or weigela, as long as you prune them hard after flowering each year. There is a list of suggested small deciduous shrubs opposite.

Another approach involves using winter- and spring-flowering perennial plants or sub-shrubs to create interest among the dormant fuchsias. *Helleborus orientalis* and *H. niger* are excellent choices because they will have plenty of room to flower in winter, and the fuchsias will help to provide the shade they love in summer. Aquilegias are equally effective, but note that you ought to remove the seed-heads to prevent them from spreading too much. If the front of the fuchsia bed is free-draining, large alpines or rock plants – for example *Iberis sempervirens*, *Cassiope* and *Andromeda polifolia* 'Compacta' – can also be grown.

Above: This gorgeous azalea in full flower in the late spring is an ideal shrub to inter-plant among hardy fuchsias. It is amenable to a light pruning after flowering to keep it to size. It is accompanied by the clump-forming perennial *Aurinia saxatilis* (golden alyssum) and a deep pink alyssum.

EVERGREEN AND SEMI-EVERGREEN SHRUBS

	HEIGHT X SPREAD	LEAVES	FLOWERS	HARDINESS
Daphne odora 'Aureomarginata'	1.5 x 1.5m (5 x 5ft)	Dark green, glossy, edged with yellow	Fragrant, purple-pink, mid-winter to early spring	Hardy
Daphne retusa	75 x 75cm (30 x 30in)	Leathery, glossy	Fragrant, pink and white, late spring to early summer	Very hardy
Erica carnea 'King George'	20 x 30cm (8 x 12in)	Dark green	Deep rose-pink, mid-winter to early spring	Hardy
Hebe brachysiphon 'White Gem'	75cm x 1m (30in x 3ft)	Small, glossy, green	Racemes of small white flowers, early summer	Very hardy
Ledum groenlandicum (Labrador tea)	75 x 75cm (30 x 30in)	Dark green	White, mid-spring to early summer	Very hardy
Mahonia aquifolium (Oregon grape)	1 x 2m (3 x 6ft)	Glossy, spikes, green	Fragrant, small, yellow, spring	Very hardy
Prunus laurocerasus 'Otto Luyken'	1 x 1.5m (3 x 5ft)	Narrow, glossy, dark green	White spikes, late spring	Very hardy

Daphne retusa

Erica carnea

Mahonia aquifolium

Prunus laurocerasus

DECIDUOUS SHRUBS

	HEIGHT X SPREAD	LEAVES	FLOWERS	HARDINESS
Chaenomeles x *superba* 'Rowallane'	75cm x 2m (30in x 6ft)	Dark green	Large, red, spring	Very hardy
Forsythia x *intermedia* 'Minigold'	2 x 2m (6 x 6ft)	Mid-green	Small, yellow, mid-spring	Very hardy
Spiraea thunbergii	1.5 x 1.5m (5 x 5ft)	Narrow, pale green	White, spring	Very hardy
Viburnum x *juddii*	1.5 x 1.5m (5x5ft)	Dark green	Fragrant, pink-white, mid- to late spring	Very hardy
Weigela florida 'Foliis Purpureis'	75cm x 1m (30in x 3ft)	Dull purple or purplish-green	Pink, funnel-shaped, late spring to early summer	Very hardy

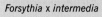
Forsythia x *intermedia*

Spiraea thunbergii

Viburnum x *juddii*

Weigela florida

Fuchsia beds with hedging

Beds of fuchsias defined and protected by low hedges are a very attractive addition to a formal garden, with the colours of the fuchsia flowers contrasting with the greens of the hedging. There are two main advantages to using hedging around a fuchsia bed. The first is practical: closely growing dense evergreen hedging will give protection on exposed, windswept sites from the added wind chill in the coldest months, enabling you to grow fuchsias where it might not otherwise be possible. The second is aesthetic: you can create a striking feature by dividing a bed into different areas, with each section containing either a group or a single specimen fuchsia, or just have one small bed surrounded by a hedge.

HEDGING PLANS

Taking a hedging plan to its limit by including coloured gravel pathways to divide the fuchsia beds and intricate designs of hedges and edging, a hedged fuchsia garden could approach a knot garden or even a parterre. Although this extreme needs a large, flat space with a suitable vantage point so that it can be viewed from above, it is possible to apply the techniques and principles to smaller areas. For example, a garden could include a central paved area with several paths radiating outwards and a circular path around the outside. Each segment of the circle could be defined by dwarf box hedges enclosing a single variety of fuchsia. This would be

an excellent way to display individual fuchsias without the plants intermingling, as they often will in hardy beds with continuing growth later in the season.

The plants can be set out in single or double rows, depending on the width of the desired hedge. It will take a few years before it reaches its final size and density, after which it needs maintaining at that size and shape. For larger boundary hedges, especially those where you require a strong windbreak, yew (*Taxus baccata*) is perfect. Clip it to below its final height at first, to encourage dense growth all the way from the ground up. Different varieties are available with colours ranging from golden-yellow to the traditional dark green.

When planning a hedge, large or small, always make sure that you have easy access for clipping a few times each year.

Also note that taller hedges can be used to make an attractive backdrop for the fuchsias. When the background is dark opt for bright flower colours, and when it is pale yellow or green choose darker flowers, to make sure that they really stand out.

Top left: 'String of Pearls' is an upright fuchsia with long growths covered in pretty single or semi-double flowers coloured China-rose and rose purple.

Below: An arrangement of fuchsias in a bed divided into compartments with low hedging. Other large fuchsias are visible in the background, along with agaves in large pots.

Above left: This bed of mixed hardy fuchsias is flowering happily in the summer, and will be well protected during the winter months with a low evergreen hedge on two sides.

Above: This tall hardy fuchsia covered in flowers is starting to envelop the fountain statue of a cherub on a dolphin. The fuchsia is large because of the hedge protection.

SUITABLE FUCHSIAS TO USE AGAINST HEDGING

White, pink or red fuchsias display well against green hedging.

White: 'Alaska', 'Annabel' (hardy), 'Flying Cloud', 'Happy Wedding Day', 'Hawkshead', 'Sleigh Bells', 'White Joy'
White and pink: 'Baby Love', 'Countess of Aberdeen', 'Grandma Sinton', 'Hidcote Beauty', 'Micky Goult', 'Other Fellow'
White and lavender: 'Alberttina', 'British Stirling', 'Doreen Redfern', 'Eden Lady', 'Lady Kathleen Spence', 'Lilian', 'Violet Bassett-Burr'
White and red: 'Beauty of Trowbridge', 'Celia Smedley', 'Checkerboard', 'Hiawatha', 'Nellie Nuttall', 'Snowcap' (hardy)
White and purple: 'Bon Accord', 'City of Leicester', 'David Lockyer', 'Estelle Marie', 'Kegworth Carnival', 'Lena' (hardy), 'Marin Glow', 'Preston Guild', 'Quasar', 'Rose of Castile Improved' (hardy), 'Stanley Cash'
Pink: 'Barbara', 'Beacon Rosa' (hardy), 'Cotton Candy', 'Elfriede Ott', 'Leonora', 'Margaret Brown' (hardy), 'Pink Bon Accord', 'Regal' (hardy), 'Rose of Denmark' (hardy), 'String of Pearls'
Red: 'Achievement', 'Caledonia' (hardy), 'Kwintet', 'Mephisto', 'Nettala', 'Phyllis' (hardy), 'Rufus'

TYPES OF HEDGING

There are a number of plants that will make good hedges, but for the low formal kind different varieties of box (*Buxus*) are the most suitable. The following list includes those for different hedge sizes. The best range is available from specialist nurseries.

	TYPE	HEIGHT	LEAF
Buxus microphylla	Low	82cm (32in)	Small, dark green
Buxus microphylla 'Faulkner'	Medium	1.5m (5ft)	Green; red/bronze in winter
Buxus sempervirens 'Blauer Heinz'	Dwarf	30cm (12in)	Small, bluish-green
Buxus sempervirens 'Elegantissima'	Medium	1.5m (5ft)	Green and cream variegation
Buxus sempervirens 'Green Gem'	Low	82cm (32in)	Bright green
Buxus sempervirens 'Suffruticosa'	Low	82cm (32in)	Bright green

Buxus microphylla

Buxus microphylla 'Faulkner'

Buxus sempervirens 'Elegantissima'

Buxus sempervirens 'Suffruticosa'

Fuchsias in cottage gardens

The words 'cottage garden' summon up a vision of a chocolate-box picture: a thatched cottage with white walls and a wonderful garden with all kinds of annual and perennial flowering plants growing by a weaving path in informal beds and borders. Stone walls around the boundaries will have cascading and rambling plants all over them, covered in flowers. Hardy fuchsias are one of the components of this image and a cottage garden would be incomplete without them. The cottage garden is particularly associated with old dwellings in the countryside in England, but it is perfectly possible to create a cottage-style garden in a town or city.

PLANTS FOR COTTAGE GARDENS

Cottage gardens always have many different plants crammed into a small space, yet they are quite low-maintenance, with many perennial and self-seeding annual plants. A vegetable and herb garden would also be part of the traditional theme. The pathways are an integral part of these gardens, usually made of flagstones or cobbles, with a main path leading to the front door, and other paths snaking off to encourage exploration of other parts of the garden. All these paths help to break the garden up into separate areas, leading you from one to another.

Typical examples of cottage garden plants are achillea, alliums, buddleia, Canterbury bells, carnations, columbines, cornflowers, delphiniums, echinacea, euphorbia, foxgloves, gladioli, hollyhocks, lilies, hardy pelargoinums, phlox, poppies, rudbeckia, snapdragons, stocks, sweet Williams, and of course the spring-flowering bulbs such as crocuses, daffodils and tulips. The list would not be complete without roses, especially the old-fashioned scented varieties and climbing or rambling roses. Other climbing plants often found in this setting are clematis and honeysuckle. All the climbing plants grow up walls, pergolas and trees, or just scramble where they will, through the other plants.

SUITABLE COTTAGE FUCHSIAS

In the 19th century, fuchsias were not part of a cottage garden, as people considered them to be tender plants. Once it was realized that many were hardy, gardeners enthusiastically adopted them as another

Top left: A hardy fuchsia growing among a clump of hosta plants. The small red and purple flowers stand out beautifully against the pale green of the hosta leaves.

Left: A large double-flowered fuchsia growing in a pot by a pond, surrounded by other plants. It looks beautiful set against the contrasting background of a white wall covered with wisteria and pyracantha.

Above: A cottage garden hardy fuchsia growing among flowering shrubs, with a white-flowering *Choisya* (Mexican orange blossom) shrub in the background.

hardy perennial in their planting schemes. Since the 20th century, extensive use has been made of many of the *F. magellanica* varieties, along with many of the early hardy single-flowered cultivars. *F. magellanica* var. *molinae* is an excellent choice, with its white and pale lilac flowers on long stems, which will reach 1.5m (5ft) or more in a single year. In a sunny spot, the ideal fuchsias would be *F. magellanica* var. *aurea*, with its elegant growth and golden yellow foliage, *F. magellanica* var. *riccartonii*, or *F. magellanica* var. *gracilis* 'Tricolor' (or 'Variegata') with its variegated foliage.

There is a lovely story that illustrates how these cottage gardens can be repositories for older plants. The fuchsia cultivar 'Empress of Prussia' was introduced by Hoppe in 1868, but the plant became lost from commercial cultivation for many years. In 1957, a London fuchsia enthusiast was on holiday in Devon and noticed a large fuchsia growing in a cottage garden. The owners did not know the name of the cultivar, but they were sure that the plant had been growing there for at least 50 years. Subsequent identification proved it was the long-lost 'Empress of Prussia', and it was reintroduced by the grower Bernard Rawlins. 'Empress of Prussia' is a good hardy plant with a medium to large single flower, with a vivid scarlet tube and sepals and a reddish-magenta corolla. It is very floriferous, having as many as eight blooms on each pair of leaf axils, and will grow to 90cm (36in) in one season.

COTTAGE-STYLE CONTAINERS

Another important feature in cottage gardens is the use of unusual containers. Different shapes and sizes can work well,

Below: Two large hardy fuchsias, both in full flower, growing either side of shallow steps in front of a cottage wall, surrounded by other cottage garden plants.

as long as they look old, and preferably might have been part of the original cottage inventory. Remember that they should have enough drainage holes, and beware of using metal containers, which can become very hot in the sun. There are many possibilities, such as weathered terracotta (clay) pots, chimney pots, terracotta drainpipes placed vertically with the top full of plants, stone sinks, buckets or watering cans. Filling these with fuchsias, especially the older single cultivars, creates a splendid display. Suitable cultivars include 'Blue Beauty', 'Corallina', 'Countess

Above: The hardy fuchsia 'Army Nurse' growing among *Sorbus* 'Sunshine', hibiscus and *Potentilla fruticosa* 'Elizabeth'. 'Army Nurse' is a strong cultivar, with semi-double flowers with red sepals and a mauve-blue corolla.

of Aberdeen', 'Drame', 'Mauve Lace', 'Rose of Castile', 'Snowcap' and 'Tom Thumb'. Light-coloured or variegated-leaf cultivars such as 'Old Somerset', 'Sunray' or 'Tom West' are also valuable, as they will stand out well in darker corners or against dark green foliage.

Aubergine fuchsias

Fuchsias with different shades of purple in the corolla have been in commerce for many years. As a further refinement of this colour, hybridizers started to release fuchsias in aubergine shades in the mid-1980s. The Dutch hybridizers, especially Herman de Graaff, introduced some beautiful and vivid aubergine cultivars, including 'Aubergine', 'Gerharda's Aubergine' and 'Haute Cuisine'. There is quite a choice of aubergine fuchsias with flowers of different sizes from small singles to large doubles, and habits of growth from trailing to strongly upright. New aubergine-coloured cultivars are still being released every year. The photographs on these pages give an idea of some of the cultivars that are available. An excellent way to grow them is as standards or in hanging baskets, so you can see

△ **'Debron's Black Cherry '** This is a single-flowered cultivar with a dark reddish-purple tube and sepals, held slightly down with reflexed tips. The corolla is quarter flared and dark purple. It was hybridized by Monnier in the USA and is listed as hardy. It was released in 2012.

△ **'Gerharda's Aubergine'** This trailing fuchsia has small to medium single flowers with a deep red/aubergine tube and sepals and an aubergine corolla. It has mid- to dark green leaves and is excellent for baskets. It was hybridized by Herman de Graaff of the Netherlands and released in 1989.

△ **'President George Bartlett'** A semi-double cultivar with a burgundy-red tube and sepals and a deep aubergine corolla. It is excellent when trained as a standard, with its slightly lax growth habit. It was hybridized by Bielby/Oxtoby and named after a former British Fuchsia Society president.

△ **'Ben Jammin'** A small, compact plant, borderline hardy, superb for growing as a mini standard or a small pot plant. It has small to medium single flowers with pale pink sepals flushed aubergine and a dark aubergine corolla, and mid- to dark green foliage.

△ **'Jessica Reynolds'** A floriferous medium-sized single-flowered cultivar with beautiful white sepals flushed with aubergine and an aubergine corolla. It has neat, compact self-branching growth, excellent for growing standards, with mid-green leaves.

the beauty of the flowers at eye level. They will also contrast well with pastel and white-flowered cultivars in mixed baskets, containers or planting arrangements. There are two aubergine fuchsias which are listed as hardy: 'Ben Jammin', a small compact-growing single, and 'Dorothy Handley', a vigorously upright semi-double that will grow 75cm (30in) in one season. A fuchsia that is good for summer bedding is 'President George Bartlett'. Lax types for baskets include 'Art Deco', 'Haute Cuisine' and 'Ratatouille'. An attractive Triphylla type named 'Pabbe's Torreldöve' has aubergine-blue flowers. 'Whiteknights Amethyst' is an unusual hardy fuchsia with blue pollen, hybridized from *F. excorticata*, and is in the parentage of many aubergine fuchsias.

△ **'Tarra Valley'** This fuchsia resulted from an interspecies hybridization cross and has very unusual single flowers with a long light greenish-yellow tube, short greenish-white sepals and an unusually coloured dark red/aubergine/purple corolla.

△ **'Haute Cuisine'** A superb double-flowered cultivar with dark red sepals and a deep aubergine corolla, contrasting beautifully with its light to mid-green leaves. It has a vigorous but stiff trailing habit, and is excellent for baskets and patio containers.

▷ **'Jack Siverns'** This cultivar has a vigorous and bushy growth habit, and is excellent grown as a specimen plant or a standard. The flowers are single and medium in size, with aubergine sepals blushed with pink and an aubergine corolla.

Standard fuchsias

One of the best ways to display fuchsias is by growing them as standards of different heights, making vibrant focal points around the garden. They look like small trees covered in flowers and, from a distance, attract the eye to different parts of the garden, standing out against fences and hedges. There are many places in most gardens that are ideal for standard fuchsias, where they will greatly enhance the view. Excellent places include either side of an entrance gate, next to a doorway, by a fence, against a non-flowering evergreen background, such as a conifer hedge, and in the hardy fuchsia border, where they give extra height and colour. Also try growing them in groups of identical standards in a more formal border.

SMALL STANDARDS

The smaller standards look wonderful on the edges of steps, around a patio or pond, and you can even use miniature standards in rockeries. Where it is impossible to set any of these plants in the ground, they will need some kind of support to keep the pot and standard upright, especially in windy conditions. Quarter standards, often referred to as table standards, will make an attractive display on a garden table.

Top: 'Royal Velvet' is a strong double cultivar with red and violet flowers. It makes a superb half standard, but tie the head in well as the weight of the flowers can break branches.

GATEWAYS, WALLS AND CORNERS

Large standards grown to either side of a gateway are very striking, especially when the gate is in a low boundary wall or fence about 1–1.5m (3–5ft) high. In addition, the wall or fence gives a good anchoring point and supports the standards while also giving them some protection. Standards can be equally effective to either side of a front door, creating a beautiful entrance and a good topic of conversation.

Below: Two attractive wrought iron planters either side of an archway planted with standards of the double flowered fuchsia 'Annabel', finished with bedding plants.

Above: A standard of the hardy cultivar 'Lady Thumb' growing among ferns by a doorway, carefully placed to stand out against a white wall. The small flowers and compact growth habit are excellent for a smaller standard.

Full and half standards are very impressive against taller walls, when combined with half baskets and wall pots to brighten up the background. Choose plants with flower colours that will complement the brickwork. If the wall is a dark colour, pastel shades or lighter coloured flowers are best, while a rendered wall painted with a light colour needs darker flowers. In both cases avoid using the hottest, sunniest brick walls because in the middle of summer it

Left: 'This quarter standard of 'WALZ Jubelteen' is growing by a path with its pot set into the soil. Covered with prolific pale-pink and pinkish-orange single flowers, it is a wonderful sight.

CREATING EXTRA HEIGHT

Standard fuchsias are excellent for raising the height and increasing the impact of other displays. For instance, in a group of pots of different sizes and heights, adding one or more standards at the back can create a much more impressive effect. Similarly, you can place a standard at the back of a border, against a hedge or fence, when extra height is required and there is a need for a focal point to draw the eye upward. Standards with white or lighter pastel-coloured flowers look splendid against dark fences and hedges, and deeper-coloured cultivars are best against light walls or golden-yellow hedges. Red and white flowers stand out well against mid-green hedges, while standards grown from variegated cultivars make excellent eye-catchers anywhere, with the best foliage colours developing in bright conditions. Use the same technique in the hardy fuchsia border, adding variations in height with standards and even some spectacular early colour if the standards are already in flower, forced into growth, early in the year, in the protective warmth of a greenhouse.

Below: The cultivar 'Miss California' grown as a quarter standard. It has a wiry and slightly lax habit of growth, giving a weeping effect with pink and white flowers.

will probably be too hot for the fuchsias. If you do use a standard in a hot spot, ensure it is a sun-tolerant type, and in any case protect the pot (and the plant's roots) with shading or sink it into the ground.

Weeping standards are ideal for an internal corner, with the profusion of flowers filling up what might otherwise be an awkward space. Periodically turn the standard 45 degrees so that you get a fully rounded shape, otherwise it will produce all its growth towards the light.

Left: 'Cambridge Louie' is a strong-growing single-flowered cultivar, which makes a very good quarter or half standard. When grown in plenty of sun, its growth is stronger and harder.

STEPS, PATHS AND BORDERS

Putting half or quarter standards at the edge of garden steps creates a terrific effect. The standards help define the edges and simultaneously soften the transition between the steps and garden. Similarly, position them along the edge of a path – provided it is wide enough – and they will help delineate the outline. Quarter standards are also excellent in summer bedding borders, especially when surrounded by many low-growing plants. This technique is commonly, and very effectively, used in parks, botanical gardens and other public displays.

Standard fuchsias again make excellent specimen plants, and placing a full standard in a small, circular bed in the centre of a lawn creates a brilliant focal point. Plant the remainder of the circular bed with other bedding plants to complement the standard's height and colour. A weeping standard grown in such a scheme will often be a spectacular sight with its masses of flowers raining down on its cascading branches.

Below: A half standard with pink and white flowers, growing in an attractive pot. Standing on paving close to a gate, it makes a really eye-catching feature.

TERRACES AND PATIOS

Another exciting way of using standard fuchsias is along the edge of a terrace or patio. If you are constructing a new terrace or patio, sink some large pots into the ground around the edges for placing the standards in over the summer. This technique will help keep the plants' roots cool and the stems upright. You can use these same pots for bulbs and spring-flowering plants, until the time comes to bring out the standards in summer.

Fuchsias grown in this way help define the edge of a patio, and create lovely bursts of colour. In the case of patios surrounded

Top: Four standards planted in the ground above a mass of bedding plants, including alyssum, lobelia, marigolds and pelargoniums at the back of a semi-circular border.

Left: A full standard of the hardy 'Margaret' growing against an evergreen background, close to a bench seat and surrounded by colourful containers of ageratum, begonias and pelargoniums.

by a low border wall, create some planting areas within the wall, hollowing out the centre along the top, and plant the standards here. Half or full standards placed close to bench seats against light-coloured walls can also look very pleasing and make the seat a little more of a private place.

PONDS

Just as paths can be defined and dramatically brightened by standard fuchsias, so too can ponds. Use larger standards to create spot features, placing them in the line of sight, while smaller standards are ideal for highlighting the outline. The fuchsias thrive on the humidity of the air and soil near the pond, but do not place them so close to the edge that the falling flowers drop into the water, spoiling the effect.

PERGOLAS

When using the standards to soften hard landscaping, try placing them around the outside of pergolas, arches and other similar structures to help hide the sharp edges of the vertical posts. The posts, in turn, provide additional support for the standard, preventing them from being blown over. If you have extra standards, position some inside large pergolas to complement the other plants, hanging baskets and containers, to create extra focal points.

CHOOSING STANDARDS

The following cultivars are suggestions for growing different types of standard. The measurements show the length of clear stem between the surface of the soil and the lowest branch of the head. The measurements are for classification guidance only, and the actual dimensions and size very much depend on you. It is possible to grow standards with even longer stems, perhaps up to 1.8m (6ft), although handling and overwintering them will be very difficult.

Miniature standard 13–25cm (5–10in): 'Baby Bright', 'Marilyn Olsen', 'Nellie Nuttall', 'Sophie Louise', 'Tom Thumb'
Quarter or table standard 25–46cm (10–18in): 'Chang, 'Estelle Marie', 'Genii', 'Katrina Thompsen', 'Paula Jane', 'Rose Fantasia'
Half standard 46–76cm (18–30in): 'Annabel', 'Border Queen', 'Checkerboard', 'Garden News', 'Olive Smith', 'WALZ Jubelteen'
Full standard 76–107cm (30–42in): 'Achievement', 'Amy Lye', 'Barbara', 'Celia Smedley', 'Mrs Lovell Swisher', 'Snowcap'
Weeping standard 46–107cm (18–42in): 'Brutus', 'Ernie Bromley', 'Eva Boerg', 'Falling Stars', 'Jack Shahan', 'Swingtime'

Left: A miniature standard of 'Midwinter' covered in white single flowers. This size of this standard makes it suitable for a table decoration, or you can use it in the rockery.

Above: Full standards of 'Snowcap' and 'Celia Smedley' with their pots sunk into the ground either side of an entrance gate. They are wired to the wall and ground for support.

Trained fuchsias

A well-grown fuchsia trained into a shape like a pyramid or a fan can be a stunning sight and can make a real focal point in a garden. A pyramid or pillar can make a striking freestanding display in the middle of a lawn, while a trained fan or an espalier can cover a large area of a wall or fence. Before embarking on growing large trained fuchsias for display as specimens in the garden, it is important to consider how they will be stored for the winter, as they are best kept ticking over in green leaf. It is easier if you live in an area without frosts, where leaving them outside all year without winter protection is possible, but most growers will need heated protection big enough to overwinter these structures.

PYRAMIDS

Large pyramid shapes will grow more than 3m (10ft) over a few years with the right care and growing conditions, but smaller specimens of 1m (3ft) or more in height may be grown in a single season and still make a very impressive show. As the plants

Top: A young pyramid in its first full year of growth, in flower against a background of Japanese anemones and *Fatsia japonica*.

age, the wood becomes harder and stronger, and they are better able to stand the ravages of strong winds and heavy rains, but during the first year when green growth is maturing to wood, some extra protection and support is needed. It is therefore important to make sure the centre stake or cane is in good condition and strong enough, especially the part that stands in the compost (soil mix), which is more prone to rotting. The best time to

change the cane is when you cut back the plant in the autumn. Use ties such as PVC tape, and check the tightness as the stem thickens. Tying the top of the cane to an overhead support helps to stabilize the structure and will reduce the chances of it blowing over in strong winds.

PILLARS

This form of training develops an attractive column of flowers, with the diameter of growth being very similar at the top and bottom of the structure. When a pillar is in full flower, it makes a very attractive and eye-catching sight, which is sure to raise many comments. This type of structure is ideal to place either side of a doorway or gateway, as the girth at the base does not restrict placement.

CONICALS

The conical form of training is intermediate between the pyramid and the pillar. It is trained in a similar way to a pyramid, but has a narrower base, forming a slimmer, tapered shape compared to a pyramid. The end result resembles an elegant tree. Conicals are easy to use in similar ways to both pyramids and pillars, but during winter storage they do not take up quite as much floor area as pyramids.

Far left and left: A trained shape of 'Brutus', dripping with red and purple flowers and growing with the top of the cane tied up to a pear tree. In the earlier picture (far left), the plant training was toward a pyramid. In the later picture (near left), pruning the base of the plant produced a narrower conical shape.

Above: A small-scale trained pyramid of the cultivar 'Midwinter', flowering for the first time with its white single flowers.

Above: A small pillar of the cultivar 'London 2000', trained up to the desired height. Next, the side growth will be filled out.

You may use all of the forms above in a similar way to large standards, but they look especially impressive when placed either side of a doorway, or at the edges of a patio or yard where they will help to highlight the corners and edges. They will also stand out beautifully as a feature in the centre of a lawn or as a centrepiece in an arrangement of pots.

Right: A young conical of the cultivar 'Little Beauty', grown to a height of 2m (6ft), flowering for the first time. As the plant gets older, the growth will thicken up.

FANS AND ESPALIERS

The usual way to grow fans and espaliers is against a wall, where they can benefit from the shelter and warmth (especially if it is a house wall) and an easy means of supporting them. Choose a wall that receives a reasonable amount of sun, but ideally not full sun all day.

If you don't have a suitable wall, you can also train fuchsias against a wire fence where you can see them from both sides, provided the fence is strong enough. In both cases, be aware that these shapes,

especially the fan shape, will have a large frontal surface area. A specimen measuring 2m (6ft) high and wide can present a surface area of $1–1.5m^2$ ($1.2–1.8$sq yd) to the wind, resulting in a huge pressure on the structure . Therefore, it is important to secure it well against the wall or fence, ideally by ties between the wall or fence and the top of the frame, to prevent the wind from damaging it. If there is a border along the wall or fence, try to sink the pot partially or completely in the ground to help keep the roots cool. You may also plant the specimen in the soil but it will be tricky removing it at the end of the season.

When in full flower, such plants can be breathtaking, making superb focal points. A double cultivar, such as 'Annabel', 'Lillian Annetts' or 'Swingtime', will look truly spectacular when grown as a fan, and it will be well worth moving it to a warm place every winter, enabling it to grow to an impressive size.

Top left: A magnificent fuchsia fan grown from the cultivar 'Lillian Annetts'. This structure measures more than 2m (6ft) high and wide, and was grown by Chris Woolston.

Top right: This small fan of 'Waveney Gem' has been grown in a 13cm (5in) pot. Placed on a lawn against a stone wall, it is displaying its flowers forward.

Left: A young espalier of the red and white double-flowered cultivar 'Swingtime', being grown on a framework of green canes.

OTHER TRAINED SHAPES

Topiary shapes can be very successful if you position them where they will catch the eye, for example on low walls, perched on top of entrance pillars or even on purpose-built stands. Ensure that you fix the pots securely so they cannot blow off, and they will be sure to create a lot of interest. There are so many different wire-framed shapes now available that you could even create a tableau of different animal images along the top of a wall. You can also create individual letters and numbers, and even

Above: A topiary cat shape grown from a vigorous Encliandra cultivar inside a wire mesh former. Note how the ears have filled but the feet and tail need more growth.

a living message along the top of a wall. If you use the Encliandra types, let them flower, just clipping off any long growths to keep them tidy and maintain the shape of the basic framework. Use miniaturized versions of rings, fans, pyramids and other trained shapes to enhance walls, pillars, porchways and steps.

CLIMBING FUCHSIAS

Some fuchsias have such vigorous, rampant growth that they are very difficult to train in a conventional way. While they might not be true climbers, since they do not twist around supports like a vine, and they do not have tendrils or leaves that curl around and attach the plant to supports, such as a clematis, some do make

excellent clambering plants. You can grow them permanently in a greenhouse or against a fence, a pergola or a simple post by using large plants started into vigorous growth in the greenhouse.

Good candidates include the species *F. boliviana*, *F. regia* and the cultivars 'Giant Cascade', 'Lady Boothby', 'Pride of the West', 'Royal Purple' and 'Wisteria'. In recent years, some large companies have promoted 'Lady Boothby' especially for this purpose. When left to grow unstopped, this cultivar makes long, extended upright growths with minimal side shoots until it starts to flower, with attractive cerise and dark purple small single flowers near the growing tips. Removing the growing tips will promote branching.

Fuchsias grown in this way need tying to supports, just as you would secure a climbing rose, to prevent the supple growth from being broken off. Both *F. regia* and 'Lady Boothby' are hardy and therefore may be planted permanently, and will shoot from the base again if killed down to the ground in winter. The other mentioned cultivars need winter protection or should be grown outside only in milder, frost-free climates.

Below left: This climbing fuchsia cultivar of 'Lady Boothby' has been planted against the wall of a house, trained and supported on a wire mesh secured to the wall.

Below: This vigorous and well-established hardy fuchsia looks quite at ease climbing naturally up a fence, covered in wild columbine and other creeping and trailing plants.

Blue fuchsias

Blue shades in fuchsia flowers vary from a lilac or lavender blue through deeper blues to violets in the corolla. White, pink or red sepals usually accompany them, and those with white sepals are ideal for shady corners of the garden. Many fuchsias have names starting with 'blue' but some of these have no blues at all in the flower, so do look carefully at the description in a catalogue.

There is still no real royal blue fuchsia, but plenty of pale blue fuchsias of a similar shade to wisteria, and many darker blues that tend more toward violet. All fuchsias change colour through the life of the flower, usually starting with the most intense colour and fading as they age. Mix fuchsias with white sepals and a blue corolla with plain white fuchsias and other pale-coloured plants to

△ **'Irene Sinton'** A double-flowered trailing cultivar, with blush-pink sepals and a full lilac-blue corolla with pink splashes on the petals. This fuchsia is excellent in a hanging pot or basket, although it can be prone to botrytis early in the year.

△ **'Holly's Beauty'** This superb American cultivar is part of the California Dreamers collection. The large double flowers have pink-blushed white sepals and a pale lilac-blue corolla. With its trailing habit, it is excellent for hanging baskets.

△ **'Lilac Lustre'** This is an upright bush cultivar with medium-sized double flowers with broad rose-red sepals and a powder-blue full corolla. The flower buds are very fat, almost like little red bulbs waiting to burst, adding to its beauty.

△ **'Delta's Sara'** This is an upright vigorous cultivar with beautiful semi-double flowers with white sepals and a mid- to deep blue corolla with white splashes at the petal base. Listed as hardy in some catalogues, try it as a garden bedder.

△ **'Lilian'** This is a lovely single-flowered cultivar with pink sepals blushed white and a pastel pink-lilac corolla. The flower colours contrast beautifully with the anthers, which are a deep red before they break with pollen. It is well worth growing as a quarter standard.

make a cool collection in a shady corner. Some suitable fuchsias for this setting are 'Andrea', 'Azure Sky', 'Blue Veil', 'Carmel Blue', 'Claire Evans', 'Crystal Blue', 'Lady in Blue', 'Lilian' and 'Whickam Blue'. Many fuchsias have either deep pink or red sepals with various shades of blue in the corolla, and these give a much warmer impression. These look their best in groups or in mixed plantings in containers with other plants with red, white, blue and even yellow flowers, to give an exciting contrast of hot and cold colours. Some good cultivars here are 'Angela Rippon', 'Blue Gown', 'Blue Lace', 'Carina Harrer', 'Fort Bragg', 'Happy', 'Jomam', 'Kobold', 'Lady Beth', 'Lilac Lustre', 'Little Beauty', 'Party Frock', 'WALZ Blauwkous' and 'Winston Churchill'.

▷ **'Winston Churchill'** This is a superb cultivar, with medium-sized double flowers with deep pink, green-tipped sepals and a lavender-blue corolla that matures to pale purple. It has upright, bushy and self-branching growth with wiry stems and narrow dark green leaves.

▽ **'Sophie Louise'** This is a compact and bushy cultivar with small single flowers with pink-blushed white sepals and a tight purple-blue corolla. It is extremely floriferous and makes a superb smaller standard and pot plant.

△ **'Carmel Blue'** This is a vigorous shrub cultivar that will grow to a large plant quite quickly. It has attractive single flowers, with pink sepals blushed white, and blue petals with a white splash at the base. The flowers lose their shape as they age and become rather open.

△ **'Love's Reward'** This is an aptly named cultivar with white and violet-blue single flowers, held semi-erect. The upright bushy growth and bright mid-green leaves make it ideal for growing as a small pot plant or a beautiful quarter standard.

THE CONTAINER GARDEN

Fuchsias are an ideal choice for growing in containers, both on their own and as companion plants in mixed plantings. There is a tremendous range of colours to blend with every colour scheme, from the traditional red and purple through whites, pinks, blues, aubergines, indigos and violets. Stately standard fuchsias stand to attention, demanding respect and displaying their flowers proudly, while fans or pyramids make striking architectural features. Large double-flowered trailing fuchsias, such as 'Swingtime' or 'Haute Cuisine', display their flowers at the ideal eye level in hanging baskets, demanding a closer look. Variegated-leaf cultivars such as 'Golden Marinka' in hanging containers, or 'Firecracker', 'Tom West' and 'Sunray' in freestanding containers, can add some variation of leaf colour. This chapter contains examples of different types of containers to use, tips on caring for the plants, and ideas for placing and grouping them into eye-catching displays, even co-ordinating the colours to create different moods within the garden.

Left: This trailing fuchsia has been planted in an old wooden wheelbarrow, along with different coloured lobelias, catmint and other bedding plants.

Top left: 'Cambridge Louie' is a vigorous and bushy single-flowered cultivar that thrives in containers placed in sunny positions around the garden.

Top middle: 'Cloth of Gold' has beautifully coloured foliage that looks wonderful in hanging containers, where the colours can be appreciated at eye level.

Top right: The beautiful double-flowered cultivar 'Walsingham' works beautifully when used in either planters or hanging containers.

Large pots

Grown alone as specimen plants or mixed with other plants, fuchsias make an excellent show in large pots around the garden. They make pleasing focal points on terraces, steps and patios. By using different varieties, you should find one to suit every part of the garden – most fuchsias do best in partial shade, where a lot of other flowering shrubs would be less happy, but in sunny positions the Triphylla hybrids are ideal. For a specimen, it is best to start with a large single plant, or multiple plants (at least three) of the same variety. For a mixed pot, try different fuchsias with contrasting flower colours, or mix fuchsias with begonias, busy Lizzies, pelargoniums and foliage plants.

TYPES OF POT

There are many different shapes, sizes and finishes of pot, including colour-glazed and unglazed types, manufactured from many materials such as stone, cast concrete, plastic and fired clay. The unglazed terracotta (clay) type is the best choice for fuchsias, as the pots breathe and help to cool the root ball by evaporation. The glazed type can also work well and is a good choice if you want a particular colour scheme. Try to avoid pots with very narrow necks, as it is often difficult to remove large plants at the end of the season. An alternative is to grow the plant in a separate smaller pot, which then sits in the neck of a

large pot. Do not choose a container with a narrow base in a position exposed to wind, as it could blow over – wide-based pots are more stable. You can stand pots on clay pot feet to improve drainage.

SINGLE-SPECIMEN FUCHSIAS

In pots up to 30cm (12in), you can achieve a good effect by using a large fuchsia plant brought into growth early in the year, or three or more smaller plants of the same variety. Preferably, plant it up in the early spring, so the plant can establish itself in the pot. Pinch out the growing tips until early to mid-spring and then let it grow on and it will be in flower in early summer. Double-flowered and Triphylla hybrids need a little longer to come into flower, so stop the pinching out a few weeks earlier. Grouping some of these large specimen plants together in a large garden can also be very effective. Try using a large Triphylla fuchsia with hot red-orange flowers such as 'Thalia' or 'Gartenmeister Bonstedt' at the back of a display, and in front, place two pots with slightly more lax white-flowered cultivars such as 'Annabel' or 'Shelford'.

Top left: Multiple plants of the cultivar 'John Bartlett' grown in a glazed black pot placed in the middle of a lawn.

Above right: This large blue pot has been multi-planted with the cultivar 'Shelford', and placed on the edge of a flight of steps.

Left: The hardy cultivar 'Tom Thumb' has small red and purple flowers. This example, grown in an aged terracotta pot standing on a terrace, is just coming into flower.

RECOMMENDED TRIPHYLLA CULTIVARS

Many of the cultivars hybridized by Carl Bonstedt, including 'Bornemann's Beste', 'Coralle', 'Gartenmeister Bonstedt' and 'Thalia', are strong growers that will quickly form a large plant. 'Traudchen Bonstedt' is trickier to grow but has beautiful salmon-pink flowers and dark foliage, while 'Mary' will always make a spectacular, eye-catching plant with its vivid red flowers and attractive green leaves and slightly more lax growth, which creates a large, arching shape. Grow it in a dark glazed pot to contrast strongly with the vivid flowers. Other older cultivars worth trying are 'Obergartner Koch', hybridized by Sauer in 1912, with bright orange flowers and dark foliage, and 'Leverkusen', hybridized by Rehnelt in

Left: 'Chantry Park' is one of the more lax-growing Triphylla types, with long scarlet flowers. It is excellent for planting around the edge of a large pot.

Right: This large multi-planted pot of the Triphylla 'Coralle' is in full flower, fringed with conifers and standing on smooth granite rock in full sun in a front garden in Sweden.

FUCHSIAS FOR LARGE POTS

Many of the wide range of beautiful fuchsias will look superb in large pots. Below is a list to consider.

Triphyllas: 'Billy Green', 'Coralle', 'Gartenmeister Bonstedt', 'Georg Bornemann', 'Mary', 'Thalia'
Single-flowered: 'Cambridge Louie', 'Celia Smedley', 'Joy Patmore', 'Lady Isobel Barnett', 'Lenora', 'Other Fellow', 'Shelford'
Semi-double-flowered: 'Delta's Sara', 'Miss California', 'President George Bartlett'
Double-flowered: 'Annabel', 'Blue Waves', 'Garden News', 'Royal Velvet'
Foliage: 'Autumnal', 'Cloth of Gold', 'Golden Marinka', 'Popsie Girl', 'Sunray', 'Tom West'

'Joy Patmore'

Right: This Triphylla fuchsia in a large terracotta pot basking in the sunshine is covered from top to bottom with racemes of long-tubed orange-red flowers.

1928, with rose-cerise flowers produced very freely. Of the more recent cultivars, 'Firecracker' (the variegated leaf sport from 'Thalia') is well worth growing, but do not overwater it. 'Brian Kimberley' has very long, pale orange flowers and light sage-green foliage, 'Insulinde' has bright orange flowers and very dark, slightly shiny leaves,

'Len Beilby' has scarlet-red flowers and very vigorous growth, and the free-flowering 'Roos Breytenbach' has a pinkish-red tube and sepals, and an orange-red corolla with vigorous growth. One newer, unusual cultivar is 'Pabbe's Torreldöve' with purple-magenta flowers, hybridized by Tielko Koerts in 1996.

You can also mix in different companion plants such as begonias or pelargoniums. The Pendula begonias and ivy-leaf pelargoniums look particularly good around the edges of a pot. Zonal pelargoniums are excellent in the centre, especially the bi- and tricolour leaf types such as 'Frank Headley' and 'Mrs Pollock'. Try using a striking foliage plant like a canna with a white or pale pink-flowered fuchsia. Other foliage plants such as *Helichrysum petiolare* 'Limelight' or 'Variegatum' are useful as fillers. Make use of some of the variegated leaf fuchsias such as 'Tom West', 'Sunray' or 'Golden Marinka', as these have both beautiful foliage colours and flowers. These mixed pots will look lovely with a few edging plants such as lobelia, the small blue trailing campanula or *Bacopa* 'Snowflake' around the sides. Fuchsias combine well with many different plant species, so it is worth experimenting with some of your own favourites.

With a minimal amount of care, adequate watering and feeding through the summer, these pots will give months of colour and pleasure.

Above: A large white stone pot filled with *F. arborescens* and trailing plants *Lotus berthelotii* and *Iresine lindenii*.

Right: An attractive blue-glazed pot planted with a standard of 'Tom West' and some trailing ivy, set against an aged blue fence.

Below: A terracotta bell pot, standing on the edge of steps, filled with fuchsias, including 'Thalia', 'Cotton Candy' and 'Auntie Jinks', as well as zonal pelargoniums and other companion plants.

Above: A large terracotta flowerpot, planted with multiple plants of 'Thalia', placed at the top of steps by a lawn. The plant is just coming into flower in midsummer.

There are also Triphylla-type cultivars that are worth considering because of their vigour or unusual flower colours. These cultivars have Triphylla-shaped flowers, and tend to be more axial- than terminal-flowering. Look out for the vigorous and free-flowering 'Billy Green' with pink self flowers and 'Efried Ott' with plenty of salmon-pink flowers, 'Orient Express' (one of a series of cultivars named after famous trains by Goulding), with a pretty pink and white flower, and 'Roger de Cooker', with white and rose flowers.

MIXED CONTAINERS

It is a good idea to use different fuchsias with contrasting flower colours, but similar growth habits. An example of a good mix of double-flowered types is 'Royal Velvet' with 'Alaska', or 'Annabel' with 'Haute Cuisine'. Try planting upright types in the centre and more lax or trailing types on the outside.

COMPANION PLANTS FOR LARGE POTS

The following are ideal companions for fuchsias in mixed pots.

Larger flowering plants: *Begonia*, *Calibrachoa* (million bells), *Dahlia* (dwarf varieties), *Dianthus*, *Gazania*, *Impatiens*, *Matthiola* (stock), *Nicotiana*, *Osteospermum*, *Pelargonium* (angel, ivy-leaf, scented-leaf and zonal), *Penstemon*, *Petunia*, *Salvia*, *Verbena*
Larger foliage plants: *Canna*, *Coleus*, *Helichrysum*, *Nemesia*
Compact edging plants: *Ageratum*, *Alyssum*, *Bacopa*, *Campanula*, *Diascia*, *Hedera* (compact ivies), *Lobelia*

Dianthus

Helichrysum

Lobelia

Urns

Fuchsias, especially those with a lax shape, make a very attractive picture when grown in an elegant urn on a patio or flight of steps. Usually an urn is in the shape of a large vase, and sits on a pedestal or feet. Such containers are available in many different shapes, finishes and colours, and are made from materials including cast iron, plastic, terracotta (clay), GRP (glass-reinforced plastic) and carved or reconstituted stone. Shapes vary from the tall, slim and elegant, such as the Venetian urn, to the Versailles type and the larger bowl-shaped urns (the Regency type), which are usually placed on a pedestal and base. Often they have surface decoration with elegant relief patterns that add to the attraction.

URN PLANTING IDEAS

The smaller, narrower type of container is best suited to growing a single fuchsia cultivar, either a group or a single plant. The best varieties have lax or semi-trailing compact growth so that they trail over the edge of the container but do not completely cascade or they will hide its beauty. Alternatively, plant it with a fuchsia that grows in the shape of a compact dome, leaving the urn completely visible. Hardy cultivars often exhibit these characteristics and good examples include 'Dollar Prinzessin', 'Genii' and 'Lady Thumb'.

The large pot or bowl-shaped containers are better suited to mixed fuchsia cultivars or a mixed planting. Use smaller trailing fuchsias around the edge and an upright bushier plant in the middle for a really striking effect. Alternatively, use a large-flowered cultivar with arching growth that will easily fill a large container. Good varieties include 'Annabel', 'Celia Smedley', 'Checkerboard' and 'Royal Velvet'. Always choose cultivars whose flower and leaf colours will complement or contrast with the container. An urn made from light coloured stone, such as the creamy pale yellow Bath stone, is best with a darker flowered cultivar.

Top: This small blue urn, planted with the cultivar 'Martin's Umbrella', is standing on a patio in front of larger pots containing cannas and hostas.

Right: This embellished lead urn looks impressive and dramatic, planted with 'Marinka', a red single-flowered trailing fuchsia, around the edges, and the Triphylla cultivar 'Thalia' in the centre.

Conversely, a dark cast-iron container, or a clay container glazed with a dark colour, may look better with a cultivar with a white or pale-coloured flower.

Using a mixture of plant types, with fuchsias as just one component of the whole display, is also an inspiring way of using these containers, especially the bowl-shaped kind. There are many suitable companion plants but zonal pelargoniums, especially the single-flowered types that tolerate the rain or those with variegated

Left: This attractive embossed terracotta urn is standing on a brick paved patio, and is planted with the hardy fuchsia 'Tom Thumb'. Other fuchsias and plants provide a background of contrasting textures and colours.

foliage, such as the bi-color leaved 'Frank Headly' or the tricolor leaved 'Mrs Pollack', are excellent choices. Ivy-leaf pelargoniums are also effective, offering a tremendous choice of colours and trailing-cascading growth. Good single varieties include 'Crocodile', 'Surcouf', 'Sugar Baby' and the red or pink 'Mini Cascade'. Variegated leaf varieties include 'Hederinum Variegated',

Below: A terracotta strawberry pot planted with many different fuchsia cultivars, including 'Roesse Blacky', 'Waveney Gem', 'Emma Louise' and 'Land van Beveren'.

'Jips Twink', 'L'Elégante' and 'Pac Ekva'. If planting the urn with mainly upright plants, then compact lobelia, campanula or alyssum can be used to trail around the edge of the container.

An attractive way of positioning urns planted with fuchsias is by placing a matching pair either side of a doorway with a wide set of steps leading up to them. They are also excellent as a single feature on a patio or terrace, or in multiple groups around the edges or in corners where a wall gives a lovely backdrop.

Finally, try planting fuchsias in urn-shaped containers with planting pockets on the side designed for growing herbs or strawberries. Use the smaller trailing varieties such as 'Auntie Jinks', 'Harry Grey', 'La Campanella' or 'Gordon Thorley' around the edges and a more vigorous cultivar in the top, and it will reward you with a mound of colour throughout summer.

Below: A large blue urn planted with a Triphylla and other fuchsias and trailing plants, standing on paving in front of a white-painted brick wall.

Troughs and boxes

Fuchsias grown in troughs and boxes are marvellous for brightening many areas of the garden, such as low walls, roof patios and paved areas. They are also probably the best way to grow fuchsias if you have no garden – they can sit on a broad windowsill, or on the ground next to the house wall. There are many different types of trough made of various materials, including terracotta (clay), wood, plastic, stone, concrete and metal. It is best to avoid metal ones, as the roots can become very hot in the sun. Some have feet to stand on; some have a tray to stand in; yet others are made to hang on a wall. Troughs standing on windowsills, walls or roofs must be fixed down securely.

WALL TROUGHS

These containers, usually made from metal strips in a framework, are hung on a wall. They need lining with moss, plastic or a suitable bespoke liner before planting. Several different shapes are available, such as wall-mounted hay feeders. Ensure the wall fixings are strong enough to support the weight, as these containers can often be very heavy when fully planted. Try planting these with trailing fuchsias along the front edge and more compact upright varieties behind, or mixed with other companion plants such as begonias and pelargoniums.

Top: An attractive square black pot made of glass-reinforced plastic, with a mixed planting of fuchsias, lobelia, nepeta and petunias, standing on paving in front of a raised bed.

Below: A small terracotta trough planted with compact fuchsias, upright at the back and trailing at the front, including 'Love's Reward', 'Emma Louise' and 'La Campanella'.

Left: An elegant trough made of plastic, planted with the fuchsia 'Dollar Prinzessin' and companion plants.

TROUGHS FOR LOW WALLS

When placing troughs on top of low walls, make sure that the wall is sufficiently thick for the container to stand firmly on it, again fixing it down well. The best walls for fuchsia troughs are typically up to 1.5m (5ft) so that it is easy to access them for watering and maintenance. Trailing fuchsias, especially really prolific varieties such as 'Cascade', 'Put's Folly' and 'President Margaret Slater',
look wonderful cascading down the wall. If the trough is wide enough, plant some compact upright cultivars along the centre as well. Try using small standards as another way of lifting the centre of the trough and creating some extra interest.

FREE-STANDING TROUGHS

Troughs of various sizes can be used around the garden as stand-alone features or as part of larger container displays. Placing them around the edges of terraces, decks or patios to help define the edges can be very useful, both as a decoration and as a safety aid. Larger containers of stone, such as old drinking troughs, are often very impressive, especially if they have an aged look with lichen and moss growing on the stone and in the crevices.

Plant these types of containers with fuchsias, or fuchsias mixed with other plants, and they will make a colourful display for the whole summer. Use standards or other trained shapes such as pyramids, pillars or conicals in bigger troughs, ensuring the size of the plants fits the scale of the trough.

Right: A plastic square pot planted with a standard bay tree. The companion plants in the pot are *Fuchsia* 'Pink Fantasia', an erect-flowered fuchsia with red and mauve flowers, and *Cineraria maritima* 'Silverdust'.

WINDOW BOXES

Where the windowsills on a house are big enough, window boxes can look very attractive planted with fuchsias and companion plants. The best type are those with a flat base which will sit firmly on the windowsill; they must also be fixed or clamped in some way to prevent them falling off. Plant them in a similar way to the wall troughs described earlier, with trailing fuchsias at the front edge for those viewing from outside, and compact upright cultivars for viewing from both inside and outside, but make sure that the whole display does not obstruct the view out of the window.

PLANTING BOXES

Square boxes for planting made of plastic or hardwood can be very attractive, and are excellent homes for a tall centre plant with smaller edging or cascading plants surrounding them. They will look splendid with a standard fuchsia in the middle and trailing fuchsias around the edges. Alternatively, you can grow another tall plant such as a conifer or a standard bay, and add trailing fuchsias in the base.

Below: A cast concrete trough planted with red and white single fuchsias and white flowered bacopa as an edging plant, standing on the edge of decking.

FUCHSIAS FOR TROUGHS AND BOXES

There are a great many fuchsias that will work well in troughs and boxes. Listed below are some of the most suitable lax and upright cultivars.

Lax and cascading types: 'Auntie Jinks', 'Cascade', 'Devonshire Dumpling', 'Emma Louise', 'Eva Boerg', 'Golden Marinka', 'Harry Grey', 'Haute Cuisine', 'Land van Beveren', 'President Margaret Slater', 'Seventh Heaven', 'Susan Green', 'Swingtime', 'Waveney Gem'
Upright types: 'Alison Patricia', 'Annabel', 'Border Queen', 'Dollar Prinzessin', 'Maria Landy', 'Mickey Goult', 'Millennium', 'Minirose', 'Miss California', 'Paula Jane', 'Pink Fantasia', 'Thamar', 'Twinny'

Hanging baskets

Hanging baskets are an excellent way of showing off the beauty of fuchsia flowers because you have to look up into them. There are many different trailing fuchsia cultivars, ideal for baskets. You can fill a basket with several plants of one particular cultivar, a mixture of different kinds, or fuchsias with companion plants – all look very impressive. Good growth habits for hanging baskets vary from the lax or spreading upright growers, to the stiff trailers and those that cascade over the sides of a basket. Some of the large double cultivars used in baskets do not trail very much until the flowers start to open, when the weight of the flowers drags the branches downward.

THE BEST SITES

You can use fuchsia-based hanging baskets in many places around the house and garden. They are commonly found suspended from strong brackets on the side or corners of the house, and beside doorways. You could try hanging them from tree branches, especially spreading trees with strong boughs such as Bramley Seedling apple trees. You can also hang them from the eaves of the roof if they have sufficient overhang, or even within the arch of a pergola if it is high enough. You can also use baskets to enliven

Top: The lovely lax cultivar 'Wendy's Beauty' has a double flower with white tube and sepals and an unusual pale violet-purple corolla, and works well in hanging baskets.

garages, sheds and other outbuildings, or any corners that look dull and need brightening in summer.

A further option involves using tiered baskets, which perch on top of each other using special support stands, or using those built around a single support pole. Ensure that the base of these is wide enough or weighted down to prevent it from blowing over in the wind. Baskets

Above: This basket planted with fuchsias, impatiens and begonias is in full flower, and stands out beautifully against a white wall.

Left: A plastic container hanging from a tree branch, planted with 'Susan Green'. This vigorous fuchsia cultivar has beautiful, classically shaped single flowers with green-tipped, pale pink sepals and a coral-pink corolla.

can even be placed on pedestals, chimney pots or special metal basket stands to create a lovely display.

Where fuchsias outscore many other plants is in creating a showy and long-lasting display in a shady position, where it might be too dull for many traditional colourful bedding plants, such as pelargoniums and verbena, to perform well. Choose cultivars with white or light-coloured flowers, or at least those with pale sepals, because they will stand out better in shady conditions.

SINGLE-CULTIVAR BASKETS

Baskets planted with a single cultivar produce a mass of flowers of the same colour, and invariably make a strong impact. Another effective tactic is using two baskets – with similar-shaped flowers but in contrasting colours – say, to either side of a door. For example, you could use 'Janice Ann' in one basket and 'Harry Grey' in the other. Use at least four plants, each in a 9cm (3½in) pot, in a 30cm (12in) basket, or at least seven in a 40cm (16in) basket. When making the final pinching out, stop all the growing tips at the same time so that all the plants flower simultaneously.

Above: A lovely hanging basket planted with the fuchsias 'Cascade', 'Marinka', 'Seventh Heaven', 'Sir Matt Busby' and 'Veenlust', together with pretty lobelia, ivy-leaf pelargoniums and begonias.

In a dark corner, where a white or pastel-coloured cultivar is the best choice, use fuchsias such as 'Devonshire Dumpling', 'Harry Grey', 'Natasha Sinton' or 'Walsingham'. In a brighter area, a more strongly coloured cultivar will stand out even better, with a double-flowered red and white, such as 'Swingtime', or a pink and red, such as 'Seventh Heaven', being excellent choices. Strongly coloured single-flowered fuchsias (such as 'Caradella', 'Marinka' or 'Postiljon') also work very well. Cultivars with vigorous, cascading growth, such as 'Cascade', 'President Margaret Slater' or 'Put's Folly', are less suitable for single-cultivar baskets because they flower at the end of long branches, and you will end up with no flowers in the middle. It is better to use these cultivars in mixed baskets.

Above: 'Rocket Fire' growing in a wicker hanging basket. The double flowers of this fuchsia have an unusual frilled corolla with pink outer petals and purple inner petals.

Different foliage colours can also make quite an impact, and cultivars with variegated foliage, such as 'Alton Water', 'Arcadia Gold', 'Barbara Norton', 'Golden Lena', 'Golden Marinka', 'Rosemarie Higham' and ''t Voske' (a variegated sport from 'Auntie Jinks'), are ideal. Alternatively, use fuchsias with a distinctive leaf colour adding to the display. Suitable examples include 'Autumnale' (young leaves start green and yellow but mature to red and salmon with splashes of yellow), 'Ernie Bromley' (bright yellow-green), 'Golden Anniversary' (large double, light green new foliage) and 'Tropic Sunset' (double, red-bronze foliage).

MIXED FUCHSIA BASKETS

Baskets planted with a mixture of different kinds of fuchsia can be extremely effective. Use either several plants of just a few different cultivars to a predetermined colour plan or a random mix of several different cultivars. Try to use a short-jointed, slightly lax cultivar in the centre of the basket with the more trailing, cascading types around the outside and this will ensure a superb, all-over coverage of flowers. Intermixing doubles and singles will ensure plenty of flowers over the whole basket. The large double flowers are impressive, but not always as freely produced as the single flowers. Using alternate cascading and lax cultivars around the edges gives an interesting variety of the depth of trailing growth and flowers.

When deciding how to arrange multiple plants of just a few cultivars, there are several different approaches. One is to mix plants with similar growth habits but contrasting flower colours. So, use 'Auntie Jinks' and 'Harry Grey' alternately around the edges with a slightly lax cultivar, such as the white single-flowered 'Shelford' or the double 'Ruth King', in the centre.

Above: Tiered baskets with stands are an excellent way to display fuchsias. This twin basket has been planted with many cultivars in front of Japanese anemones.

COMPANION PLANTS FOR MIXED BASKETS

Creating mixed summer baskets using fuchsias opens a whole world of different combinations. There are masses of possible companion plants. Some gardeners like to insert plants through the sides of the basket to obtain the full cascading effect quite quickly, but this is probably unnecessary with a mixed fuchsia basket. Instead, use cultivars that are fairly stiff and semi-upright, such as 'Annabel' or 'Ruth King', in the centre of the scheme surrounded by a ring of lax types, such as 'Seventh Heaven' or 'Millennium', and trailing or cascading cultivars around the edges, such as 'Cascade' or 'Auntie Jinks'. Contrasts of foliage and flower colour help to create a basket that is attractive from every side.

Inter-planting with ivy-leaf pelargoniums, such as 'Balkonvit' (white), 'Mauve Beauty' (freely produced deep mauve flowers), 'Sugar Baby' (miniature ivy-leaf and pink flowers) and 'Pak Ekva' (small, variegated leaves and pink flowers), generates extra interest. Pendula begonias, which grow from corms or seed, come in a range of colours including red, orange, yellow and pink, and create a wonderful cascade of colour. Their foliage comes in different colours, varying from light green to dark reddish-green. They grow big and bushy, with large leaves, so take care that they do not crowd out the other plants – use no more than one or two in a large basket.

Left: A hanging basket planted with fuchsias, attached to a wall bracket by a door. Other plants in the basket include zonal and ivy-leaf pelargoniums, ivy, *Glechoma hederacea* 'Variegata' (catmint), trailing lobelia and *Calibrachoa*. Beneath the basket are some colourful upright begonias.

Above: A mixed hanging basket planted with the fuchsias 'Deep Purple', 'Herman de Graaff', 'Ruby Wedding' and 'Auntie Jinks' with begonias and pelargoniums.

Smaller flowering plants can be used to fill gaps between the larger plants, and improve the stunning effect. Good possibilities include cascading lobelia, bacopa, small trailing campanula, diascia, busy Lizzie, surfinia, trailing viola and verbena, all of which mix really well with fuchsias in a basket. Trailing foliage plants, such as *Glechoma hederacea* 'Variegata' (catmint) and variegated ivies, add long, dangling stems and beautiful, variegated leaves, giving extra depth to the display.

Above: A hanging basket planted with bright pink fuchsias and yellow Pendula begonias decorating a building. Note the convenient watering system.

FUCHSIAS FOR HANGING BASKETS

There are far too many suitable fuchsias to list, but these are some of the best. They include a wide range of colours, with different growth habits and flower sizes. Note that while the largest doubles look spectacular, others produce more flowers.

STIFF CULTIVARS

'Haute Cuisine'	Double
'Janice Ann'	Single
'La Campanella'	Semi-double
'Rigoletto'	Double
'Swingtime'	Double
'Waveney Gem'	Single

LAX CULTIVARS

'Annabelle Stubbs'	Double
'Cecile'	Double
'Chantry Park'	Triphylla type
'Deep Purple'	Double
'Golden Anniversary'	Double
'Postiljon'	Single
'Purple Rain'	Single
'Seventh Heaven'	Double
'Trudi Davro'	Double
'Walsingham'	Double
'WALZ Citer'	Single
'Wendy's Beauty'	Double

TRAILING CULTIVARS

'Ashley and Isobel'	Single
'Auntie Jinks'	Single
'Emma Louise'	Double
'Eva Boerg'	Semi-double
'Golden Marinka'	Single
'Harry Grey'	Double
'Hermiena'	Single
'Kon Tiki'	Double
'Land van Beveren'	Single
'Marinka'	Single
'Pinch Me'	Double
'Red Spider'	Single
'University of Liverpool'	Single
'Vanessa Jackson'	Single

CASCADING CULTIVARS

'Cascade'	Single
'Pink Rain'	Single
'President Margaret Slater'	Single
'Trailing King'	Single
'Trailing Queen'	Single

'Cascade'

'Cecile'

'Haute Cuisine'

'Marinka'

Hanging pots

Fuchsias grown in hanging pots are a tremendously flexible way to brighten many a dull corner. Hang them from tree branches, pergolas, under storm porches or any other places that need a floral lift. The cascading and long-lasting flowering habit of trailing fuchsias planted in hanging pots will bring a lot of pleasure throughout the entire summer. A hanging pot is usually made of plastic, with plastic detachable hangers and a detachable watering tray measuring up to 26cm (10in) in diameter in colours of black, green or terracotta. When buying this type of pot, pay particular attention to the quality of the plastic hangers as this is the part most likely to fail.

PLANTING HANGING POTS

Plant up small pots (up to 20cm [8in]) with a trailing fuchsia cultivar, using up to five plants depending on the pot size. Plant larger pots with a mixture of fuchsia cultivars or mixed plantings, according to your preference. After the short time needed to establish themselves, these will grow rapidly and start to flower, and from then on they will need regular watering and feeding. On very hot, windy days, water them until the lower tray fills and the compost is saturated. The plants will soon use up the water in the lower tray, which acts as an extra reservoir.

PLACING HANGING POTS

Hanging pots are ideal to brighten up all sorts of odd places and neglected corners in the garden. They have the advantage of being lighter than hanging baskets, and do not need such strong supports. Suspending them in the lower branches of trees works very well, since they add extra colour and the tree provides them with dappled shade from the sun in the hottest parts of the day. Hang them directly on smaller branches, using the plastic hook

Above: A hanging pot planted with the fuchsia cultivar 'Trudi Davro', with its double white flowers. The sepals are white in the shade but become pink when placed in the sun.

that came with the pot, or make some heavy wire hooks to fit over thicker branches, but remember to put some protection over the branch to prevent the wire cutting into the bark of the tree.

Another excellent way to display these pots is hanging from a large post, which has crosspieces placed horizontally and at right angles to each other at intervals up the post. Other good places for hanging are from pergolas, from overhanging roof eaves, or on small brackets attached to walls, sheds or fence posts. Even in a small garden, using a bit of thought will reveal a number of places where hanging pots will add interesting colour.

Top left: 'Golden Marinka' is a beautiful variegated leaf sport from 'Marinka'. It has yellow-cream, green variegated leaves with bright red flowers, and looks lovely when grown in a hanging pot.

Left: A hanging pot of 'Waveney Gem' in full flower hung from a maple tree looks beautiful against the foliage.

VARIETIES FOR HANGING POTS

Most trailing or cascading fuchsia cultivars will work very well in hanging pots, but the best ones are those with compact and self-branching growth, especially for the smaller pot sizes, as they will make a more dense mass of flowers and foliage. In hanging pots with mixed plantings, the compact growth of the fuchsia is less important, as the other plants will fill the spaces. Double-flowered fuchsias work very well – the smaller double types such as 'Emma Louise', 'Kon Tiki' or 'Ratatouille' are ideal. In larger pots the bigger American doubles such as 'Holly's Beauty' also work well.

Above: This aged 'Bramley' apple tree is giving superb dappled shade to several hanging pots and baskets of fuchsias.

Below: 'Princessita' is an excellent cultivar for hanging pots or baskets, with its long-lasting white and red single flowers.

FUCHSIAS FOR HANGING POTS

Cascading or trailing fuchsia cultivars look superb in hanging pots. The list below suggests some suitable fuchsia cultivars for different-sized pots.

SMALLER POTS
'Ashley and Isobel'
'Auntie Jinks'
'Caradella'
'Chantry Park'
'Emma Louise'
'Golden Marinka'
'Harry Grey'
'Hermiena'
'La Campanella'
'Princessita'
'Susan Green'
'Trudi Davro'

'Harry Grey'

LARGER POTS
'Annabelle Stubbs'
'Cecile'
'Golden Anniversary'
'Holly's Beauty'
'Irene Sinton'
'Pink Marshmallow'
'Seventh Heaven'
'Wendy's Beauty'

'Irene Sinton'

Half baskets and wall troughs

Fuchsias planted in half baskets or wall troughs attached to walls or fences are superb ways of creating splashes of colour around the garden. A half basket, as the name suggests, is a container of a demi-hemispherical shape usually constructed of PVC-covered or galvanized heavy wire mesh. The flat side sits against the wall with the hanging points at the back of the basket suspended on screws or hooks. A variation of this is a three-quarter hemispherical shape, designed to sit neatly on an outside corner wall, looking rather unusual and eye-catching. A wall trough is typically made of flat metal strips with a flat back, curved base and rounded ends, and can be much longer than a half basket.

ADVANTAGES

Hanging from screws or hooks fixed into a wall or a strong fence, all these containers are less prone to wind damage than hanging baskets that swing when blown around. The plants also benefit from the warmth of the wall, especially if it is a house wall, as protection from frost at the beginning and end of the season. The planting scheme is very much a personal choice, but here are some suggestions.

Top: A colourful half basket, planted with fuchsias, Pendula begonias, impatiens and a small-leaved trailing ivy.

Below: This half basket, lined with sphagnum moss and planted with double fuchsias, is mounted on a white brick wall.

PLANTING WITH THE SAME CULTIVAR

This is best for the half basket and, normally, five to six plants will be sufficient to make a stunning display. Consider the site and choose a cultivar that will tolerate these conditions. If you are using an open sunny wall, make sure that a heat-tolerant cultivar is used, for example one of the lax Triphylla types such as 'Chantry Park' or 'Mantilla'. Also consider the background colour of the wall or fence. A dark surface, such as brick, is better suited to the lighter coloured cultivars such as 'Shelford' and 'Harry Grey' and some of the red and whites like 'Swingtime', 'Sir Matt Busby' and 'Wilson's Pearls' because the flowers will stand out. Conversely, lighter surfaces need darker coloured flowers such as 'Haute Cuisine', 'Millennium', 'Ruby Wedding' or 'Janice Ann'.

PLANTING WITH MIXED FUCHSIAS

Both half baskets and wall troughs suit mixed cultivars and can give a superb show. For the former, try fuchsias with colours that complement each other and, if possible, have similar flower sizes, although this is less important for large troughs. Also use cultivars with a cascading habit at the front of the container and those with stiffer, more upright growth at the

Below: This half basket of 'Shelford' is of exhibition quality, grown by Steve Andrews. He grows these baskets outdoors on a fence in the west of England.

Above: This trough, suspended from balcony railings in a wire cage, has been planted with the Triphylla cultivar 'Professor Henkel' and a variegated ivy, *Hedera helix* 'Golden Cecile'.

Above: Bright yellow, black-eyed pansies, planted together with the fuchsia cultivars 'Swingtime' and 'Nancy Lou', show up well against this plain white-painted brick wall.

back. Good cascading cultivars include 'Auntie Jinks', 'Cascade', 'Kon Tiki', 'Marinka, 'President Margaret Slater' and 'Susan Green'. Those with more of a stiff lax habit include 'Annabel', 'Cecile', 'Haute Cuisine', 'Land van Beveren', 'Ruby Wedding' and 'University of Liverpool'. One of the advantages of using mixed cultivars is that some will be flowering while others are forming their second flush of buds, so there will always be some colour and interest.

MIXED PLANTING

Wall troughs are big enough to combine trailing fuchsias with other trailing and cascading plants, with ivy-leaf pelargoniums and Pendula begonias being two of the most reliable. Both flower over a long period, with many flower colours. Other possibilities include bacopa, diascia, helichrysum, impatiens, lobelia, nepeta, petunia or surfinia, verbena and viola. Remember, however, that most of these need more sun than fuchsias – for partial shade, choose begonias, impatiens, lobelia or some violas.

Also choose trailing fuchsias with complementary flower colours, both small single and large double-flowered types.

Right: A perfectly co-ordinated stone trough on a stone wall, planted with the white double-flowered cultivar 'Annabel'.

Fuchsias with different coloured or variegated foliage give added interest, with 'Ernie Bromley', 'Golden Marinka', 'Tom West' and 'Popsie Girl' being good choices. Companion plants can also be chosen for similar characteristics, with two lively possibilities being 'Pac Ekva',

a small variegated leaf ivy-leaf pelargonium with single red flowers, and *Bacopa* 'Golden Leaves' with its small golden leaves and lilac-blue flowers. For variegated foliage only, try *Glechoma hederacea* 'Variegata' or some of the excellent variegated ivies.

Wall pots

Fuchsias give a stunning display of colour for several months in wall pots. They are ideal for an individual 'spot' of colour or for arranging in groups on a wall, fence or other strong structures. There is a tremendous range of shapes and materials, varying from what might be called a half pot with a flat back but rounded front, to a wall planter that is something between a half hanging pot and half basket, to ornate wall pots with a decorative back plate. For hot, sunny walls the unglazed terracotta kind is best, because of the cooling effect from water evaporating through the porous surface. However, they will dry out very quickly, so use larger pots for these situations and be prepared for frequent waterings.

WALL POT TYPES

Available shapes include the deep-tapered kind that comes down almost to a point, half-tapered pots that are shallower with a flat base, pots with a scalloped rim, traditional wall pots with a larger body and wall urns with a completely circular rim. Another has the body of an urn sliced through at 45 degrees giving the result of a flat back on the cut side. This gives an inclined complete circular rim so the plants are leaning outwards, helping them to trail down the wall.

PLANTING WALL POTS

As wall pots are usually smaller than other containers, they tend to work best with a few plants of just one type of fuchsia, or perhaps two in a larger wall pot. Two or three small plants in 8cm (3in) pots or a single plant in a 12cm (4in) pot should be sufficient for the smaller pots, while larger ones may require more plants, depending on their size. Typically, five small plants or two to three larger plants will suffice.

SUITABLE CULTIVARS

For pale coloured singles and semi-doubles try 'Bertha Gadsby', 'Jean Dawes', 'Ostfriesland', 'Pink Rain', 'Postiljon' and 'WALZ Citer'. Paler coloured doubles include 'Claudia', 'Frank Unsworth', 'Harry Grey' and 'Powder Puff'. Darker coloured singles and semi-doubles include 'Auntie Jinks', 'Cascade', 'Derby Imp', 'Fiona Jane',

Top: A small wall pot, tapered almost to a point, planted with a flared single-flowered fuchsia hanging on a red brick wall.

'Forest King', 'Hermiena', 'La Campanella', 'Marinka', 'President Margaret Slater', 'Thornley's Hardy' and 'Trailing Queen'.

Darker coloured doubles include 'Emma Louise' and 'Kon Tiki'. Triphylla types include 'Chantry Park', 'Daisy Bell' and 'Mantilla'. Variegated foliage types include 'Autumnale' and 'Golden Marinka'. An unusual choice to try is *F. procumbens*, which makes a good trailing plant for a wall

pot. Although the flowers are rather small, they hold themselves off the fern-like foliage, showing their blue pollen; after flowering later in the season, grape-like fruits are produced.

Below: This ornate terracotta wall pot, hung on a brick wall in a gap created in the climbing vine, has been planted with the fuchsia 'Daisy Bell', which carries small orange and vermilion single flowers.

Above: The Triphylla-type 'Chantry Park' is an excellent fuchsia for wall pots because of its long-tubed red flowers and its ability to tolerate direct sunlight.

Above right: This double-flowered cultivar 'Bella Rosella', grown in a standard terracotta pot, is sitting in a heavy metal holder fixed to a white wall.

DISPLAYING WALL POTS

Use flower colours to contrast with the colour of the wall, for example growing the dark flowers of 'Janice Ann' against a white wall or the white flowers of 'Harry Grey' against red brick.

Consider how the colour of the pot and the finish will work with the flower and wall colours. Arrange groups of hanging pots to fill up a large wall space. Arranging three pots in a triangle with one pot at the highest position or a stretched triangle with the bottom two pots at different levels can be very attractive, as can diamond arrangements of four pots or star displays of five pots. Finally, note that hanging pots tend to dry out quickly and that you should use water-retaining gels to tackle the problem, and slow-release fertilizers to keep the plants growing well.

Right: This old wall-mounted basin has been adapted for garden use, planted with fuchsias and hung on a white brick wall.

Chimney pots

Chimney pots salvaged from house demolitions and rebuilding work make excellent containers for growing fuchsias, or as stands for fuchsia pots and baskets. Many are quite tall and will lift the fuchsia flowers up closer to eye level or when used in groups of pots and containers will raise part of the overall exhibit. Planted with a trailing fuchsia, they can look spectacular with a cascade of flowers tumbling down the body of the pot. Groups of planted chimney pots of different heights and styles can also be used to great effect. They are tremendous containers for planting fuchsias or fuchsias mixed with other plants, and come in a wide range of sizes, colours and styles.

TYPES OF CHIMNEY POT

There is a tremendous range of chimney pots in different shapes and sizes, to use for planting, or grouped together to form displays. The tall type is excellent as a stand-alone feature or placed at the back of a display or group of plants to raise the height. Other shorter chimney pots can be grouped together with more traditional pots to form a spectacular display with different heights, shapes and textures.

Chimney pots in different colours or with exciting and attractive surface decoration add another dimension to aid the creation of interesting displays and designs.

Look out for the 'Bishop'-type pots, which have a tall column and a wider triangular castellated cowl at the top, with 'Halifax Little Bishop' and 'Halifax Big Bishop' making dramatic containers for fuchsias or fuchsias mixed with other plants. Some have a wider square base that improves the stability. The body of the chimney can be round, square or octagonal (as with the medium 'Pittsburgh Octagonal'), and is often enhanced by a surface pattern, being finished as natural terracotta or in a coloured glaze. Another good contender, with a wider planting area at the top, is the

Top: The 'Bishop' type of chimney pot has a wider castellated area at the top, which is ideal for planting up with fuchsias.

Right: A Bishop-type chimney pot planted with the cultivars 'Canny Bob', 'Lady Isobel Barnet' and 'Daniel Reynolds' against a background of lavender and *Aucuba japonica* (Japanese spotted laurel).

'Captain's Pot'. It has a long slender body, often decorated with patterns and flowers on a polygonal base, with a wider square castellated cowl at the top, usually finished in a cream glaze. Any of these pots look excellent planted with trailing fuchsias or uprights with a trailing edging plant.

Use the shorter chimney pots up to 30cm (12in) tall as a pot, filling them with potting compost (soil mix) while standing them on the ground, before planting the fuchsias and companion plants. Leave them undisturbed until the roots have filled the pot and hold the potting compost together.

CHIMNEY POTS AS STANDS

Use other tall tapering chimney pots such as the simple rolled top, 'Cannon Head' or 'Beehive' pots, by planting fuchsias in a plant pot that sits neatly in the top of the chimney, or use them as a stand for a basket planted with fuchsias. Using the thinner rolled-top pots as a stand for a basket also works extremely well, with the basket being less likely to be damaged by the wind than if suspended on chains, when it might hit the wall while being blown about. It also makes a nice feature with fuchsias gently cascading down the side of the pot.

Another interesting variation of the chimney pot is the H-pot, formed in the shape of a letter 'H'. The pot has a central pipe linked by horizontal tubes into the outside clay tubes forming the vertical sides

Below: A collection of reclaimed chimney pots, with the roll-top type in the foreground, some Bishop-type pots immediately behind them, and other designs in the background.

Above: A chimney pot planted with the fuchsias 'Royal Velvet' and 'Carmel Blue'. *Bacopa* 'Snowflake' has been planted with them, and is trailing over the edges of the pot.

of the H. These vertical tubes are excellent for placing suitable sized pots planted with fuchsias into the necks of the outside tubes.

SUCCESSIVE PLANTINGS

One advantage of using chimney pots to hold a planted basket or a pot inserted in the top is that you can raise a succession of plantings, placing each in the chimney when it is looking at its best. You could begin with winter pansies, heathers and spring bulbs, then bring some fuchsias into early flowering in the greenhouse, and finally put out your main planting of fuchsias when they are in full flower, to remain until the end of summer.

Other containers

Fuchsias are very adaptable plants, ideal for growing in a variety of containers. So why not try something different, such as a flower tube or wheelbarrow? With such a wide variety of growing habits, flower colour and shape, and overall plant size, it should be possible to find a fuchsia to suit most containers. A variety of different and unusual planting containers are available from garden centres and other retail outlets including novelty types made from many materials. There are many other items originally made for other uses which with some imagination and adaptation are suitable as interesting and unusual containers for growing fuchsias and other plants.

HANGING PLANTING BAGS

These simple black plastic hanging planting tubes, widely used for other types of trailing plants, are a very inexpensive way of creating a colourful display. Plant a tube with either several fuchsias of the same cultivar or a contrasting mixture of cultivars, insert a watering tube down the centre to reach approximately one-third of the length, hang it up and watch it grow.

Top: An unusual low pot planted with the fuchsia 'Gwen Dodge', *Lotus berthelotii* (parrot's bill) and *Cineraria maritima* 'Silverdust', with a seaside theme.

Green hanging bags are a good variation. Constructed from interwoven green polypropylene cloth, they include pre-made planting holes, and will last for several seasons, with careful handling. The best cultivars to use are smaller single or double-flowered cultivars, such as 'Claudia', 'Land van Beveren', 'Emma Louise' and 'Waveney Gem'.

Left: A hanging bag planted with several small plants of the trailing cultivar 'Emma Louise', just coming into full flower. This container looks great against the white wall.

FREE-STANDING FLOWER TUBES

These containers, made from rigid plastic with pre-made planting holes, can create an instant fuchsia column. Packed with several plants of just one cultivar, all having a stiff trailing or lax bushy habit, they will rapidly form an attractive column of flowers. Suitable cultivars include 'Border Queen', 'Harvey's Reward' and 'Waveney Gem'.

Above: This example of the fuchsia 'Major Heaphy' has been planted with *Abutilon* in a straw-filled hessian sack at the base of a tree fern. Tropical foliage fills the background.

Far left: A copper bowl planted with alpines and an Encliandra fuchsia, 'Lottie Hobby'. The broad shape of this pot, along with the gravel mulch, will help to prevent it from overheating.

Left: A wooden half barrel planted with a magnificent specimen fuchsia in full flower makes an inspiring centrepiece to any garden.

POT STANDS

A good alternative way of growing different cultivars together is in a heavy wire stand, which holds pots at different heights. It also helps you see the different cultivars clearly, enabling you to show off your favourite fuchsias. You can even swap and change, adding plants that are coming into flower and removing those that have just finished, maintaining the display over a long period.

FOUND CONTAINERS

With a bit of imagination, many other items can be used as containers. For example, old ridge tiles, either the half-round or V-shaped type, with wooden feet, can make interesting planters when filled with fuchsias or other plants. They can be sited anywhere around the garden to brighten up the corners. Also, try standing large-diameter ceramic drainpipes with a large connection collar on one end, fill them with compost (soil mix) and plant up with fuchsias.

Many metal items such as coalscuttles, buckets, and even smelting pots or milk churns can be used to plant fuchsias alone or mixed with other plants. Make plenty of drainage holes, and do not place metal containers in positions exposed to direct sun, as the conducted heat will cause root damage. Metal pots also give less protection against frost than other materials.

Right: *F. magellanica* var. *molinae variegata* growing in an unusual wall pot shaped like a head. This species variant is a sport from the parent, but with less vigorous growth and beautiful variegated gold and green foliage.

WOODEN CONTAINERS

Old oak wine barrels are ideal for planting large standard fuchsias or trained shapes because the weight and base area give extra stability. They are also excellent for planting large specimen fuchsias or mixed plantings of fuchsias, pelargoniums and other bedding plants. Wooden wheelbarrows are good for a mixed planting with one large fuchsia in the centre and trailing fuchsias around the edges, mixed with other plants. This will make a superb feature in the middle of a front lawn.

OTHER UNUSUAL CONTAINERS

Engineering bricks with three large holes through each brick can be used to grow three small fuchsia plants just by filling the holes with compost and small cuttings. They can be quite effective, but keep an eye on them because they do dry out very quickly. Keep the whole brick moist. Also, try filling hollow building blocks, commonly used in modern construction, with compost. Arranging fuchsias in unusual and stimulating ways can make your garden really special.

Putting containers together

A collection of containers containing fuchsias alone or with other plants can be a superb sight at the peak of their flowering season. Any arrangement of containers with fuchsias in flower will look beautiful and be very good value for money, flowering continuously for a long period, attracting bees and other beneficial insects. Planning your containers and flower colours beforehand is really worthwhile. Try some of the following ideas for displaying fuchsias in containers, planted out in the borders, and trained into different shapes. You may well find yourself in a fuchsia paradise, with waves of flowering fuchsias descending in tiers from each corner of your garden.

CREATIVE CONTAINERS

Use lots of different kinds of fuchsias with co-ordinating companion plants. Grow them in containers of various shapes, sizes and colours, creating different moods, using mauve, blue and white to give a cool, relaxing mood, or yellow, orange and red flowers to give an impression of warmth and cheerfulness.

ARRANGING CONTAINERS

For arrangements in corners with walls or other backdrops, create some tiers to increase the impression of height and show all the plants off really well. This can be a permanent structure, or a temporary one with stacks of breezeblocks, block pillars or slabs, but do ensure it is strong enough to support the containers safely. Start with simple small pots at the front and larger pots or containers behind, then add more containers on the tiers behind this. Setting a standard fuchsia at the back will raise the height still further.

For a free-standing display in the centre of an area of lawn or paving, follow a similar design, but check that you have considered the full 360-degree aspect to give an equally good view from any side. These central displays can look very effective in paved areas or on surfaces covered with decorative chippings.

PLACING POTS

Tiered staging set against a wall is a good way to display pot fuchsias, especially bonsai fuchsias. Another excellent way to show them off is on a post set in the ground, with crosspieces alternating at 90 degrees to each other, all the way up the post. On the end of each crosspiece fix a plastic pot, and then drop in fuchsias in pots of the same size to create a pillar of fuchsia flowers. If you keep some spare plants in the same-sized pots, you can exchange any fuchsias that are not flowering well.

Several types of commercial pot stands are available, varying from the simplest wire ring stand on a single leg that pushes into the soil, through those with three legs and a base, to more ornate cast iron versions, including semi-circular étagères. For specimen plants, you can obtain stone or cast concrete pillars or stands with matching pots that really display the plant well. These look splendid topped with specimen fuchsias on either side of a gate. There are also ornate cast iron pot stands that attach

Top left: A lovely weathered terracotta pot planted with the hardy fuchsia cultivar 'Alice Hoffman'. The semi-double to double flower has dark cerise sepals and a cerise-veined, fluffy white corolla, and the foliage – especially at the growing tips – is an attractive bronzy green. Regal and zonal pelargoniums are growing around it.

Left: An inspired collection of containers arranged together to create a beautiful garden vista. This grouping of containers and baskets consists of fuchsias, busy Lizzies and a colourful range of other summer bedding plants.

Above: An eye-catching arrangement of summer-flowering containers on a patio, including fuchsias and pelargoniums accompanied by cool hostas.

to a wall, or you can fix pot supports to a trellis or wood framework and fill them with fuchsias to make a wonderful display.

DISPLAYING HANGING BASKETS

Apart from fixing hanging baskets or pots to tree branches or wall brackets, an excellent way of displaying them is from a pergola, which allows you to walk underneath and see the beauty of the flowers from the best angle. This is especially good for the large double-flowered fuchsias. The other advantage of a pergola is that it is easy to add shade netting over the top of the pergola in very hot spells of weather, creating the additional shade that fuchsias love. Try placing standards and pots within the pergola, all along the edges, to create the visual effect of a tunnel of fuchsias.

You can also buy stands that allow you to place baskets of decreasing sizes on top of one another, and when planted with trailing fuchsias, begonias and pelargoniums these can look superb, forming a cascading fountain of colour.

Left: Pots of the fuchsia 'WALZ Jubelteen', a dark-leaved zonal pelargonium and dianthus enhance summer-flowering bedding plants by a gravel path.

Below: An antique mangle stand forms the framework for an attractive display against an old brick wall. Mixed containers filled with fuchsias, begonias, lobelia and other flowering plants are enveloping and trailing over the framework to give a wonderful cascade of colour.

THE INDOOR GARDEN

Fuchsias grown inside the house can be striking and beautiful flowering plants, although special care is necessary to adapt and protect them from the dry atmosphere in centrally heated modern homes. Tips are given in this chapter on how to raise indoor fuchsias, from the choice of varieties to their care and treatment.

A conservatory or sun room is an excellent place to grow fuchsias intermingled with other tender plants grown for their flowers, scent and foliage, creating an enjoyable spot in which to sit and relax in the winter sunshine. A greenhouse, an important resource for any serious gardener, is ideal for growing and propagating fuchsias, though they will always benefit from a spell growing outside in the summer. When growing standards and the larger trained structures, a greenhouse is essential to protect them through the winter in temperate climates. In areas of the world that have very hot and dry summer conditions, a shade or lath house is almost a requirement in order to maintain the cooler, more humid conditions that fuchsias love and thrive in.

Left: A display of many different fuchsia cultivars in a greenhouse on a staging table. Note the arrangement of heights of the different plants, giving a tiered effect.

Top left: The beautiful flared single flower of the fuchsia 'Caroline' is eye-catching, and this cultivar grows well in the greenhouse.

Top middle: The species *F. glazioviana* has unusual glossy foliage and pink/violet flowers, and is ideal to grow in a shadehouse.

Top right: 'Laura' is a strong-growing, spreading single-flowered fuchsia with a light orange tube and sepals, and a reddish-orange corolla.

Fuchsias inside the home

During the latter half of the 19th century, when the fuchsia was first imported to Britain from South America, species such as *F. coccinea* were commonly grown as houseplants. At that time, fuchsias were very expensive and therefore only available to the wealthiest households. Just before the start of the 20th century, most houses might have been cold and damp for the owners, but fuchsias thrived in these conditions. Modern houses are often double-glazed, centrally heated and rather dry inside, and not particularly fuchsia-friendly. However, if you provide the right conditions and acclimatize plants while they are small, it is possible to grow fuchsias successfully indoors.

HUMIDITY AND LIGHT

The first major requirement for growing fuchsias indoors is a boost in the immediate humidity levels. The easiest way to achieve this is to stand the pots on a tray of gravel, small pebbles, coarse sand or vermiculite, with water in the bottom of the tray but not touching the pots. Keep the water replenished, but it must never reach the level of the pots. They will still need to be watered in the usual way to keep the compost (soil mix) moist. Make sure that the trays are impervious and cannot leak, to prevent water damage to furnishings. Additionally, regularly mist the leaves with a small hand sprayer during the early parts of the day to help maintain the required humidity. Avoid growing the fuchsias too close to any heat source such as a radiator, as this will reduce the local humidity, causing leaf drop.

The second major requirement for indoor fuchsias is light. Fuchsias need good light to grow well, but not too much direct sunlight when grown indoors. Choose a windowsill that receives only early or late sun, and do not forget to turn the plants frequently. During winter, at latitudes more than 40 degrees north or south, move the plants to where they will receive as much sunlight as possible because of the shorter days and lower intensity of the sun.

GROWING FUCHSIAS INDOORS

One method involves rooting a cutting in a small propagator on a light windowsill that is out of direct sun. A pot propagator with a tall clear plastic cover is ideal. When the cutting has rooted – look for the fresh green growth at the tip – move the pot on to a gravel tray and gradually acclimatize the cutting to indoor conditions by slowly opening and then removing the cover over a few weeks to increase the amount of

Top left: The hardy cultivar 'Heidi Ann' has attractive cerise and lilac double flowers, and is a good one to try growing indoors.

Left: The fuchsias 'Bland's New Striped' (foreground) and 'Clair de Lune' can be grown successfully as colourful houseplants.

ventilation. Grow on the rooted fuchsia cutting, potting it on to a larger pot size as and when it needs it, training the growing plant into a shrub or a bush shape. It is very important to turn the plants frequently – ideally a quarter of a turn every day, to compensate for the one-directional light on the windowsill and keep the plant growing into a nice symmetric shape.

A second method involves moving a plant that has been growing in an outdoor pot into the house. Choose a small plant that is not in flower, or is just coming into bud, and keep it growing on the dry side by watering sparsely. Grow it in a shady position that is not too high in humidity for two to three weeks to help prepare the plant for the transition. Move the plant indoors, place it on a tray of wet gravel on a windowsill and mist it frequently with water in the first week indoors, while gradually increasing the watering. After a period of about two weeks, the plant will have adjusted to its new conditions.

Right: Planted in an unusual smelting pot together with a golden-leafed helichrysum, 'Kolding Perle' is a single-flowered fuchsia with waxy white sepals and a pink cerise corolla. This cultivar originated from Denmark.

Above: This group of young fuchsia plants, growing on a windowsill on a tray of wet gravel to provide extra humidity, will adapt to the drier conditions inside a house.

Right: Inside the house around the Christmas tree, this fuchsia 'Alice Hoffman' is sitting in a wicker basket decorated as a special gift, grouped among the other Christmas presents.

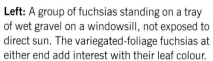
Left: A group of fuchsias standing on a tray of wet gravel on a windowsill, not exposed to direct sun. The variegated-foliage fuchsias at either end add interest with their leaf colour.

To grow a standard, take an indoor cutting using a short-jointed small-flowered cultivar. Grow the stem of the standard up a small split cane as a support and pinch out the growing tip when it is approximately 26–30cm (10–12in) tall. Leave the top three sets of side shoots, pinching them out at two pairs of leaves, and then twice again at one pair of leaves. At this point, leave the plant in the same-size pot, normally a 9cm (3½in) or 10cm (4in) container, because being rootbound will encourage it to bloom quickly and copiously.

A conical shape can be grown in a similar way, by rooting a cutting indoors, then growing it without removing any side shoots. When the cutting is about 13cm (5in) high, remove the growing tip and then remove the weaker of the two resulting side shoots, growing the strongest as the new leader with a split cane for support. When this is 5cm (2in) long, stop all the side shoots on the main stem at the growing tips and tie in the main stem. Continue this alternate stopping of the side shoots and the leader until the desired height is reached, then let the plant flower.

GROWING ON INDOORS

Once the plants are growing normally indoors and you have trained them to produce the desired shape and number of flowering shoots, keep them in the same size pot and let them flower. Containing the root system makes the plant feel threatened and causes it to produce more flowers. Continue to mist daily and feed twice a week, alternating between a general-purpose fertilizer and a high-potash one (such as tomato feed), to keep the plant healthy and encourage flowering while preventing it from putting on a lot of growth. Remember that restricting the roots in a small pot means it can dry out very quickly, so you should be extra careful to water it regularly.

TRAINED SHAPES INDOORS

As well as bush plants, some trained shapes can work well indoors. The best ones to grow in miniaturized form are a standard, conical or fan.

Left: A tray of small fuchsia plants growing in good light on wet gravel in front of French doors, next to a *Clivia miniata* (South African bush lily), with its clusters of bright orange flowers.

Right: This fuchsia, trained as a small standard, is growing indoors, placed inside an attractive ceramic pot holder.

Above: 'Tom West' is a fuchsia grown for its beautiful green-cream and cerise foliage. This example is growing well indoors, but it needs plenty of light to keep the variegated colouring of the leaves.

Right: The attractive red and mauve flowers of the hardy cultivar 'Tom Thumb'. With its small leaves and compact bushy growth, this type of fuchsia is well worth trying to grow as an indoor plant.

For a fan shape, grow on a single stem as described later in the book, supporting the plant on a frame of small split canes. The main side branch leaders will need stopping more frequently to obtain dense growth. Turn this structure so that the front or the back of the fan faces the window.

WHICH PLANTS TO CHOOSE?

Choose short-jointed self-branching varieties if possible because the lower light levels indoors will cause an increase in the internodal stem length. In general, hardy fuchsias seem to tolerate indoor conditions quite well, and single-flowered varieties manage better than doubles. If you would like to try a double, use a small-flowered one because it has more chance of keeping its flowers than a large-flowered one.

When growing a group of plants together, try to vary the sizes and heights to create interest or use a smaller trained shape, such as a miniature standard, fan or pillar. Use varieties that give an interesting

variation in flower colour, and those with variegated foliage, such as 'Tom West', to add different colours.

If you have a large picture window, or French or patio doors not used for access in the winter, then it is possible to grow some different fuchsias on stands of varying heights to create an interesting display, as they will continue to flower through the winter indoors. You can

also grow trailing fuchsias in pots on tall stands to add extra interest. Additionally, other foliage plants, such as *Tradescantia fluminensis* (wandering Jew), *Chlorophytum comosum* (spider plant), *Maranta leuconeura* (prayer plant) or even flowering orchids, such as *Phalaenopsis* (moth orchid), or perhaps *Paphiopedilum* (slipper orchid), can be mixed in to create an eye-catching display.

FUCHSIAS FOR GROWING INDOORS

The following is a list of cultivars noted as being suitable for growing indoors.

'April'	'Dollar Prinzessin'
'Baby Chang'	'Happy'
'Bambini'	'Heidi Ann'
'Beacon Rosa'	'Little Beauty'
'Chang'	'Minirose'
'Christmas Elf'	'Sandboy'
'Display'	'Tom West'

'Dollar Prinzessin'

Conservatory fuchsias

A conservatory is an area of transition between the house and the garden. Often used as both an extension of the living room and a space for growing plants, it is ideal for growing new fuchsias and for overwintering fuchsias and other plants, creating a warm and light atmosphere where it is very enjoyable to sit and relax on a cold day. The word 'conservatory' originates from the Italian *conservato* ('stored' or 'preserved') combined with the Latin suffix -ory ('a place for'), and originally meant a place for storing food. Wealthy gardeners who wished to grow the exotic and unusual specimens discovered in warmer regions by plant hunters first built conservatories as we know them today.

MODERN CONSERVATORIES

The costs of glass and winter heating originally made them prohibitive for all but the wealthiest families, but the production of cheaper glass and other materials gradually made them more accessible. In the modern age, construction in steel-reinforced PVC or hardwood, with double-glazed glass units, combined with advances such as solar reflecting and self-cleaning glass and under-floor heating, has made the conservatory a comfortable extension to the living space. Fuchsias will grow very well there providing you can keep up sufficient local humidity and make sure the inside is cool enough in the summer. If you feel comfortable in the conservatory, the fuchsias will probably be comfortable as well.

CONDITIONS IN THE CONSERVATORY

The humidity of the atmosphere is very important. It will be beneficial to use waterproof trays containing wet gravel, expanded clay beads or similar media on the floor and underneath the plants, combined with spray misting. Therefore, it is obviously a good idea to use robust furnishings and to keep anything easily spoiled by water away from the fuchsias. Similarly, the floor around them should be easy to clean as some dead leaves and flowers are bound to fall on it.

Top: Multiple plants of 'Eva Boerg' planted in a flower tower, growing in a conservatory. 'Eva Boerg' is a trailing fuchsia with semi-double flowers with pink-white sepals and a pinkish-purple corolla.

GROWING CONSERVATORY FUCHSIAS

There are two big advantages to growing fuchsias in a conservatory. The flowering period will be much longer, and it is possible to have fuchsias in flower for most of the year. Also, while most fuchsias would either be killed by winter frost, or die back to the ground, in the conservatory they can grow on from year to year, sometimes making very large, spectacular plants.

Fuchsias combined with other plants in the conservatory can extend the season of interest even further. Some good

Below: This conservatory is filled with tropical foliage plants and different varieties of fuchsia in terracotta pots supported by an ornamental plant stand.

companion plants are climbers such as *Jasminum polyanthum*, bougainvillea and plumbago, or shrubs such as *Hoya carnosa* (wax plant), *Gardenia jasminoides* and citrus. Use a mixture of fuchsias – singles, doubles, trailing and trained shapes like standards – to fit in with the surrounding plants. If the conservatory is very sunny, it will need blinds and good ventilation to prevent it becoming too hot in the summer; indeed, in any continuous hot spells of weather, it is worth giving the tenderest of plants a breather outside in a shady position.

CARING FOR CONSERVATORY FUCHSIAS

In a conservatory, the aim is to keep plants flowering throughout the year, so prune fuchsias in a similar way to plants growing in frost-free equatorial or tropical regions. Conservatory fuchsias need more gentle and partial pruning than those outdoors, mainly to shape and tidy them, leaving budding shoots intact to maintain flowering.

Above: 'Autumnale' growing in a moss-lined basket hanging in a conservatory. This is a spreading fuchsia that is grown mainly for its beautiful dark red, salmon and yellow-splashed foliage.

Unglazed terracotta (clay) pots are the best to use since they allow the compost (soil mix) to breathe, helping to cool the roots. This also helps to create more humidity.

Introduce plants into the conservatory in the autumn or winter so that they have a chance to acclimatize to the conditions before the stress of the summer heat. Fuchsias can usually be moved from the greenhouse to the conservatory directly, as the growing conditions are similar. You can put both new young plants and pruned old plants in the conservatory, but ensure you eradicate any pests and diseases before moving them in. Avoid using insecticides in the house. Turn the plants every so often to prevent them leaning over toward the light, and feed them regularly or use a slow-release fertilizer in the compost.

Left: 'Happy Wedding Day' is an Australian white double-flowered cultivar with lax growth. It is seen here growing with busy Lizzies among ferns in a conservatory.

Varieties for a conservatory

The choice of positioning of conservatories is normally where it catches the best of the sun and the maximum amount of winter light. Providing the conservatory atmosphere is maintained with a high humidity, growing fuchsias is easy, with heat-tolerant varieties being the top choice. Conservatories vary greatly in size and shape, and have different maximum temperatures depending on the amount of shading and ventilation they are given. When growing fuchsias in a conservatory, they are best intermingled with other plants for a display of foliage and flowers, stood on tables or plant stands and hung from the walls or roof bars in suitable containers.

SUITABLE TRIPHYLLAS

Fuchsias that can tolerate hot conditions thrive in conservatories, so Triphyllas are an obvious choice. Larger cultivars such as 'Coralle', 'Thalia' and 'Traudchen Bonstedt' are worth trying. 'Mary' excels on a pedestal because of its arching growth, velvety green leaves and clusters of brilliant red flowers. A similar but much smaller-growing Triphylla cultivar suitable for smaller conservatories is 'Bessie Kimberly', while others are 'Adinda' and 'Sparky'. 'Mantilla' and 'Chantry Park' are excellent for hanging or wall containers.

Top: The hardy cultivar 'Army Nurse' is a lovely semi-double with a carmine and bluish-violet flower, and grows very well in a conservatory.

SUITABLE SPECIES

Some of the species fuchsias are also a good choice for the conservatory, and they include *F. boliviana* or *F. boliviana* var. *alba* with their tropical appearance, large velvety green leaves and enormous clusters of red flowers for the former or white and red flowers for the latter. *F. arborescens* has leathery glossy leaves and upright panicles with first hundreds of tiny pink and mauve flowers, then later beautiful glossy blue-black berries. Try also *F. glazioviana*, *F. fulgens* and *F. lycioides*, which are recommended as heat-tolerant species.

Above: The beautiful species *F. boliviana* var. *alba* has clusters of long-tubed white and red flowers. It makes a large and very impressive conservatory plant.

DOUBLE-FLOWERED FUCHSIAS

There is not such a wide choice of heat-tolerant double-flowered fuchsia cultivars, but you should still find enough to create a good display, starting with 'Harbour Bridge', 'Nancy Lou', 'Phenomenal', 'Quasar', 'Royal Velvet', 'Shady Lady', 'Swingtime' and 'Voodoo'. 'Royal Velvet' is an excellent choice because of its beautiful red and deep purple flared double flowers and arching growth, with light to mid-green foliage. Suitable small- to medium-sized double-flowered cultivars include 'Blue Waves', 'Dollar Prinzessin', 'Heidi Ann', 'Pink Galore', 'Santa Claus' and 'Winston Churchill'. 'Heidi Ann' forms a very neat bush with its small dark green foliage and abundant flared red and lilac-purple blooms.

Right: 'Brutus' is a wiry-growing hardy cultivar with red and purple flowers. It is excellent for producing trained shapes when grown in the conservatory.

Above: 'Heidi Ann' is a hardy shrub with small to medium-sized cerise and lilac double flowers and grows well in the conservatory.

Above right: This cultivar is named 'Little Beauty' and what name could be more apt? It is highly floriferous, half hardy and very easy to grow in a conservatory.

Right: 'Nellie Nuttall' has been a 'show banker' for many years. With its plentiful semi-erect red and white flowers, it clamours for attention in the conservatory.

SINGLE AND SEMI-DOUBLE-FLOWERED FUCHSIAS

There is a much greater choice of heat-resistant single and semi-double cultivars. Good larger-flowered varieties – those with a (B) can be grown in baskets or hanging pots – include 'Amy Lye', 'Army Nurse', 'Aurora Superba', 'Bow Bells' (B), 'Brutus', 'Carmel Blue', 'Falling Stars' (B), 'Indian Maid' (B), 'Julie Horton' (B), 'Lena' (B), 'Lye's Unique', 'Mission Bells', 'Princessita' (B), 'Rufus', 'Swanley Gem' and 'Voltaire'. 'Aurora Superba' is a medium to large single with light apricot sepals and a deep orange corolla. It has lax upright growth, making it ideal as a half standard.

Small, single-flowered heat-resistant fuchsias are great for growing in pots placed around the conservatory to give points of colour. They include 'Baby Chang', 'Bambini', 'Caledonia', 'Christmas Elf', 'David', 'Derby Imp' (B), 'Fifi', 'Lindisfarne', 'Little Beauty', 'Little Jewel', 'Minirose', 'Mrs Marshall', 'Nellie Nuttall', 'Purperklokje', 'Red Rain', 'Sandboy' and 'Tom Thumb'. The pretty 'Bambini' stands out with its many very small crimson to mallow-purple flowers, while 'Sandboy' has small pink and dark mauve bell-shaped flowers with upright, bushy, short-jointed growth making an excellent small standard.

Some of the Encliandra hybrids are also heat resistant, especially 'Lottie Hobby', but 'Ariel', 'Artemis', 'Coral Baby', 'Hemsleyana', 'Marlies de Keijzer', 'Mikado' and 'Radings Mia' are well worth trying.

Right: 'Thalia' is one of the best-known of the Triphylla cultivars. Heat-resistant and very free-flowering, it is excellent as a striking centrepiece in the conservatory.

Greenhouse fuchsias

While it is perfectly possible to enjoy growing fuchsias without a greenhouse, you are certainly limited if you live in an area with freezing temperatures in winter. With a greenhouse, you can keep plants growing over winter, and thus grow large trained shapes such as fans, pyramids and standards, and even a climbing fuchsia if you wish, training the growth along the greenhouse ridge. You also have the perfect conditions for propagating new stock, which can be a highly rewarding process, as well as making it easy to fill your summer containers and bedding schemes with beautiful plants at very little cost, and having spares to give away.

BENEFITS OF A GREENHOUSE

One of the key features of any greenhouse is that it extends the growing season by creating a microclimate, insulating the fuchsias from the outside conditions. However, beware of overheating the greenhouse in winter because apart from the cost and environmental considerations, this causes long spindly growth when it is far better to keep your plants as compact and strong as possible.

Top: A floriferous basket hanging from a greenhouse roof, planted with the lovely fuchsia 'Swingtime'.

Below: The author's greenhouse, with six roof-vents, large doors to allow movement of tall plants, and water butts for a convenient, environmentally friendly water supply.

TYPES OF GREENHOUSE

There are many possible types and constructions of greenhouse. You can choose from aluminium or wood and glass or plastic, with brick or glass down to the ground. If you are going to use your greenhouse for growing fuchsias, make sure it is at least 2.9m x 2.2m (10ft x 7ft), preferably bigger if you have the space. Greenhouses with sufficient height for you to stand upright close to the edges are best. If you live in an area subject to strong winds, choose one with a heavyweight frame and a good glazing system. Plastic glazing is an alternative, especially the twin-wall type, which gives better insulation in the winter and more heat protection in summer. Add additional ventilation in the form of top vents and louvres, and ensure that at least one or two of the top vents have a manual opening, preferably with a screw thread.

POSITION OF THE GREENHOUSE

Ideally, the greenhouse should run from north to south lengthwise because this will give the most even distribution of sun. If possible, arrange for the minimum natural shade in winter, and some shade from a deciduous tree in summer. Avoid placing it in a dip, which may flood in heavy rain in winter, and try to avoid the windiest parts of the garden. Different bases are available, but for the best, build from bricks or blocks

Below: A commercial greenhouse filled with clearly labelled fuchsias on staging, with more fuchsias in hanging pots suspended from the roof structure.

and pave internally with concrete slabs or brick. Part of the floor could also be a layer of gravel on weed-suppression matting.

STAGING

You will need something on which to stand your plants. Most greenhouse manufacturers will supply aluminium staging, with a choice of open slats or aluminium trays, or you can build your own in wood. Ensure the staging is at a comfortable working height, and can easily be removed if you want the floor area for larger plants.

GROWING PLANTS

There is the temptation, when you buy a splendid new greenhouse, to fill it up by purchasing new plants, accepting gifts from friends, or propagating far too many plants. Try to avoid doing this, unless you know you can give many of your plants away in early spring. As a rule of thumb, the greenhouse should be one-half full in winter at most. One way to make yourself

adhere to this rule is to partition off about one-third of the space with a plastic sheet or bubble plastic, and only heat this section in winter.

The heated greenhouse allows you to grow cultivars and species that are more tender and difficult to grow. Good examples include *F. venusta*, a beautiful climbing fuchsia with orange-red flowers and wine-red stems, and *F. triphylla*, the parent of the modern Triphylla hybrids, which is small-growing in cultivation, with orange-red flowers. Some tender varieties are quite difficult to overwinter and grow better in a heated greenhouse. Such varieties include 'Citation', a beautiful American single fuchsia with rose-pink sepals and a white flared saucer-shaped corolla, and 'Constellation', a white American double.

Remember, you can also use the greenhouse to bring containers into flower before moving them outside for your summer display and, late next autumn, you can then take them back under cover to keep them safely inside over winter.

Above: A beautiful selection of trained standards and fan fuchsias growing in a commercial greenhouse.

Below: A collection of small fuchsia plants standing on a gravel bed in autumn. Centre front is the variegated cultivar 'Tom West'.

EARLY SPRING

In early spring, as the outside temperatures start to rise and the day length increases, the conditions inside the greenhouse promote rapid fuchsia growth. Make sure that you keep the plants well spaced out, turn them regularly, and pinch out the growth and pot them on as necessary. Conditions can be quite challenging at this time of year, as on bright sunny days the greenhouse can get quite hot, yet overnight frosts are still possible.

It is best to keep the greenhouse well ventilated on sunny days, and try to water or mist in the mornings, so that the plants do not sit in too much moisture overnight. When the days are warm enough and free of cold winds, the plants will benefit from a spell outside, hardening up the soft growth and keeping them growing in a compact way.

Early to mid-spring is a good time to start planting up hanging baskets, pots and containers, as many fuchsias and

companion plants start to become available from nurseries and garden centres. For the next few weeks, before you move them outside, control the watering in the greenhouse, keeping them on the dry side, so they will fill the compost (soil mix) with new roots. They will make plenty of growth and will already be in flower when moved outside in the late spring.

LATE SPRING

As the sun becomes brighter and the days longer, light shading will be necessary on the greenhouse roof and the sides receiving direct sun to prevent scorching of the young growth. Again, continue to move plants outside on suitable days to continue the hardening-up process and ensure the plants acclimatize to the outside conditions before you move them out for good. Space is often at a premium in the greenhouse at this time of year and you may need to move some plants outside permanently before they are completely

Left: A collection of fuchsia standards growing in a greenhouse over the winter. They were cut back in the autumn, started to grow again and are ticking over in green leaf.

ready. If so, be prepared to protect them with fleece if there is a late frost. Plant up any remaining baskets and containers with your chosen plants, and add full shading to the greenhouse glass if the weather gets very warm, with longer sunny days.

SUMMER

Throughout the summer months, fuchsias are better growing outside, but if you wish to continue growing some plants inside, ensure that you use maximum ventilation at all times, even to the extent of removing some glass panes and replacing them with fine netting. If you are growing plants for exhibition, place the same netting over all the vents and a detachable piece over the doors, as this will help to keep bees and other insects out, and prevent damage and marking of the flowers. Keep the floor and any gravel trays wet to increase the humidity; this will also help to cool the greenhouse. However, make sure the fuchsias are not sitting in water.

Top: Hanging baskets of fuchsias growing in a commercial greenhouse, suspended from a support rail in the roof. Note the green shading material fixed in the roof space.

Above: A large plant of the hardy cultivar 'Hawkshead' growing in a greenhouse. It has white single flowers, which stay white in the sun, and small bright green leaves.

Above: A staging table full of fuchsia plants in a commercial greenhouse, labelled and placed in groups ready for eager customers to buy. It is easy to find this environment very inspiring and tempting, but try not to buy more plants than you can actually grow.

Below: Pruned pot-grown fuchsias in green leaf, overwintering on the floor of the greenhouse underneath the staging. These plants will grow rapidly in the spring.

AUTUMN

During the late summer and early autumn, empty the greenhouse completely, clean all the glass, replacing any panes which were removed during the summer, sterilize all the benching and any other structures and check the heaters are working properly. Make sure that the whole structure is sound, replacing any cracked glass, and clean and if necessary lubricate the door slides or hinges and the vent openers. Now the greenhouse will be ready for its winter storage duties once more.

WINTER

Depending on the temperature you maintain through the winter months, the greenhouse can be used either to protect dormant plants, or to keep plants ticking over in green leaf. It is better not to overheat, since this will promote more rapid growth, which will become straggly and drawn owing to the low light levels in winter. A minimum temperature of 5°C (41°F) is ideal, not using too much energy, but protecting even the Triphylla hybrids. Keep the plants that are still in green leaf quite dry through the winter, removing any damaged or dying leaves, and give the greenhouse some ventilation on all but the coldest days. As the days start to lengthen in spring, the plants in green leaf will start to grow fresh green growth, which is ideal for early-season cuttings. It is important to turn the plants regularly to prevent them becoming one-sided, and to pinch them out to encourage bushiness, increasing the number of potential flowering shoots.

Ventilation, shading and heating

To grow fuchsias successfully in a greenhouse you will need to provide efficient shading and ventilation in summer, and heating and insulation in winter. The shading and ventilation prevent the temperatures becoming too high in the height of the summer. The heating will provide a minimum temperature at least a few degrees above freezing, while the insulation reduces heat loss and minimizes cold spots close to the glass. Your own requirements will very much depend on your local climate. The information on these pages relates to areas in USA weather zone 9 and below; for zone 10 and above, shading and ventilation are paramount if a greenhouse is used, while heating and insulation are less important.

HEATING

There are many different types of greenhouse heater and fuel available to the amateur grower. Probably one of the best is the electric fan heater, preferably with a remote thermostat rather than an internal type. This is the best because the fan generates a flow of air, thereby preventing stagnant zones in the greenhouse, and gives more even heating. Unfortunately, it is also usually the most expensive form of heating, because electricity is more expensive per unit of heat than other fuels.

The next best alternative is a heater running on bottled propane gas. Propane is better than butane, especially if the gas

Top: Louvre vents are an excellent way to get low-level ventilation into the greenhouse. Position them low at the opposite end to the door, or in the sides of the greenhouse.

bottles are stored outside the greenhouse where low temperature can reduce the cylinder pressure. Modern gas heaters have an accurate thermostat and a pilot light that allows the main burner to shut down when the greenhouse is warm enough. Some also have a catalytic converter to ensure the complete combustion of gas and minimize carbon monoxide production. For safety's sake, it is better to have two propane cylinders with an automatic changeover valve that will prevent the heater running out of gas in the middle of a cold night. Remember, though, that you need to exchange the empty cylinder for a full one.

A cheaper fuel option is to have mains gas professionally linked to your greenhouse. Alternatively, use an inexpensive heater that runs on paraffin, with the blue-flame type being best because they are cleaner

Above: Internal greenhouse shading blinds reduce the amount of direct sun hitting the plants during the warm summer months.

burning, though paraffin is not always available. Note that gas and paraffin heaters increase the level of carbon dioxide in the greenhouse, which aids plant growth, but they also increase the amount of water vapour, which can create ideal conditions for the fungal disease botrytis.

INSULATION

Twin-wall polycarbonate glazing gives excellent insulation without decreasing the amount of light significantly. If you are purchasing a new greenhouse, this is well worth considering. For standard greenhouses with single panes of glass, additional insulation will reduce the winter heating bills. UV stabilized bubble plastic

Left: Fuchsias standing on fired clay particles in trays inside a greenhouse. Note how the inside of the glass has been insulated with large bubble-plastic insulation.

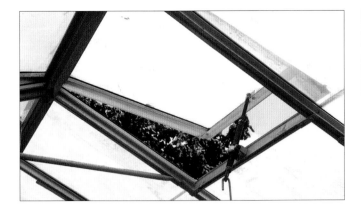

Above: A manual greenhouse vent with a screw thread opener. This firmly holds the vent open and is almost infinitely adjustable.

Above: An adjustable automatic greenhouse vent opener allows the vents to open automatically at a pre-set temperature of your choice.

sheets with large bubbles give the best insulation, but they will reduce the light levels. The best compromise is to insulate the sides with bubble plastic and the roof with clear plastic. Ensure you do not fix insulation over the roof vents because they will still need opening in winter to prevent the accumulation of stagnant air.

SHADING

In spring and summer, shading is essential to protect the plants from too much direct sun and help keep the temperature down. There are various solutions: the simplest is to paint white shading on the outside of the glass to reflect some of the sunlight and reduce the temperature in the greenhouse. You can also buy a special type of greenhouse shading that becomes transparent when wet, but opaque when dry, so increasing the light levels on dull wet days. The best solution is to fit automatic roller blinds with shade netting on the outside of the greenhouse, which extend in sunny conditions and roll away when it is dull. Whatever you use, though, it will make the greenhouse much cooler in summer.

VENTILATION

Good ventilation is important in summer. Install the maximum number of roof vents that you can afford in the greenhouse. Use automatic openers, but you will also need two, one at either end, which are manual, to maintain ventilation on cool days. Additionally, put in louvre windows at the far end of the greenhouse, opposite the doors, below the staging level to maintain good ventilation levels. Provide extra ventilation, if needed, by removing some glass in the roof apex opposite the door and replacing it with netting. An electric fan will also keep the air moving on dull, stagnant days.

Left: Double sliding doors at the front of the greenhouse allow a large opening, thus giving excellent access and allowing easy movement of large plants through the space.

Varieties for a greenhouse

Most fuchsias are easy to grow in a greenhouse during the cooler seasons, but during the summer only heat-tolerant varieties will grow well. Provided you follow the advice concerning greenhouse ventilation, maintaining humidity and shading, then growing certain heat-tolerant fuchsias over summer is possible in all but the hottest climates. Fuchsias which stand up to these hot conditions are in the Triphylla group, in the group of species which naturally grow in very hot climates in the central parts of South America and Mexico and a number of cultivars which have inherited these characteristics. By choosing the right varieties, you can create a stunning greenhouse display.

ADDITIONAL PRECAUTIONS

The use of porous terracotta clay pots will help keep the plants' roots cool by allowing the evaporation of water through the walls of the pot, and this also helps guard against the accidental over-watering of fuchsias in hot conditions. You can further improve a fuchsia's ability to cope with heat by planting directly or sinking the pots in the greenhouse borders. This will again help keep the roots cool. However, if the daytime temperatures in your area regularly exceeds 30°C, it may be difficult to grow greenhouse fuchsias through the hottest part of the year.

SUITABLE VARIETIES

Lists of heat-tolerant fuchsias exist in books and on the internet, and those compiled in the USA, Australia and southern Europe are the most valuable.

Above: The species variant *F. magellanica* var. *gracilis* is a large graceful plant when grown outside, but will also tolerate the hot conditions inside a greenhouse quite well.

The first group of varieties, which are very heat-tolerant, are the Triphylla and Triphylla-type cultivars. Most will grow quite well in the greenhouse over summer and flower continuously over a long period. 'Adinda', 'Billy Green', 'Bornemann's Beste', 'Coralle, 'Elfriede Ott', 'Jackqueline', 'Mary', 'Sparky', 'Thalia' and 'Traudchen Bonstedt' are among the best.

The second group contains the species, some of which are quite heat-tolerant. Try variants of *F. magellanica*, and also

F. magellanica var. *molinae*, *F. m.* var. *aurea*, *F. m.* var. *gracilis* and *F. m.* var. *gracilis* 'Tricolor'. Others reputed to be heat-resistant are *F. arborescens*, *F. boliviana*, *F. boliviana* var. *alba*, *F. glazioviana* and *F. lycioides*.

The third heat-tolerant group contains the Encliandras and their hybrids. Many in this group grow well in hot conditions, with 'Ariel', 'Hemsleyana' and 'Lottie Hobby' highly recommended.

The fourth group contains the double-flowered cultivars, but they are the most difficult to grow in the heat because the flowers are more demanding than the singles. The following are well worth a try:

Top left: The long pink Triphylla-like flowers of 'Billy Green' are very attractive. Strong, versatile and heat-resistant, this is well worth growing in the greenhouse.

Left: 'Adinda' is a small and compact-growing Triphylla. It has clusters of small salmon-pink flowers and green velvety leaves, and grows well in hot conditions.

'Blue Waves', 'Dancing Flame', 'Delta's KO', 'Easter Bonnet', 'Gay Fandango', 'Happy Wedding Day', 'Harbour Bridge', 'Irene van Zoeren', 'Kevin Heinz', 'King's Ransom', 'Molesworth', 'Nancy Lou', Novella', 'Phenomenal', 'R.A.F.', 'Red Ace', 'Red Devil', 'Red Rum', 'Royal Velvet', 'Swingtime', 'Voodoo', 'White Ann' and 'Winston Churchill'.

The final group contains the single and semi-double cultivars, which are often slightly easier to grow in the heat than the doubles. Try 'Abbé Farges', 'Abundance', 'Accent', 'Achievement', 'Ambassador', 'Amigo', 'Amy Lye', 'Anna', 'Aurora Superba', 'Autumnale', 'Beauty of Exeter', 'Beauty of Swanley', 'Blands New Striped', 'Blue Sleigh Bells', 'Brutus', 'California', 'Carmel Blue', 'Checkerboard', 'City of Leicester', 'Clair de Lune', 'Derby Imp', 'Display', 'Evening Star', 'Falling Stars', 'Flash', 'Graf Witte', 'Grasmere', 'Happy Fellow', 'Hidcote Beauty', 'Ice Maiden', 'Joan Cooper', 'Joy Patmore', 'Kwintet', 'La Campanella', 'Les Hobbs', 'Little Beauty', 'Lord Byron', 'Marinka', 'Nicis Findling', 'Orange Flare', 'Papoose', 'Pixie', 'Rufus', 'Tom Thumb', 'Tom West' and 'Whiteknights Pearl'.

RED SPIDER MITE

Heat is not the only potential problem. You need to look out for greenhouse pests, particularly red spider mite, which thrives in hot dry conditions. To minimize the chances of an outbreak, keep the

greenhouse as humid as possible by regularly hose-spraying or splashing the floor. Even better, if you live in a soft water area or have an adequate supply of stored rainwater you can install a misting system to maintain consistently high humidity levels. Electronically controlled systems give bursts of misting when required by using an internal moisture or humidity sensor. This monitors the amount of water moisture in the greenhouse atmosphere, and only activates the system when required.

Above: 'R.A.F.' has beautiful large red and rose-pink double flowers and a lax habit of growth. It looks stunning hanging from the greenhouse roof.

Below left: The Encliandra cultivar 'Lottie Hobby' has vigorous and wiry growth with tiny leaves that give it a fern-like appearance, and plentiful tiny light crimson flowers.

Below: 'Dancing Flame' has a medium-sized orange and orange-carmine double flower and a lax habit. It is well-suited to growing in a greenhouse basket.

Shadehouse fuchsias

In hotter climates, a shadehouse is an essential item to ensure that fuchsias will thrive through the heat of the summer months. In areas where the summer temperatures regularly reach the high 30s Celsius (over 100°F), such as Australia, New Zealand and the southern USA, fuchsias in pots will not easily survive outside in the garden. The shadehouse creates ideal natural growing conditions for fuchsias in summer, and mimics the natural conditions of some of the species that grow in shady forest margins with high cloud humidity. In the height of summer, it is also possible to provide shading for some plants growing in the ground outside the shadehouse by using netting on poles.

TYPES OF SHADEHOUSE

The oldest kind of shadehouse, still used in some parts of the world, is the lath house. The simplest kind is a box frame with strong corner posts and crosspieces, which are large enough for you to stand up inside and to hang up various containers from the roof. The roof consists of thin strips of wood (laths), typically 2.5–3 cm (1–1¼in) wide, equally spaced out. This effectively filters out approximately half the direct sunlight. The sides are open, or may be covered if protection is needed from the wind or sun. An interesting alternative, once used in California, is a pitched roof covered with closely spaced old fluorescent tubes. These disperse and diffuse the light very effectively.

The modern shadehouse is made from a tubular frame that is easy to erect and is covered with polypropylene shade netting, which is usually green. Shade netting is available in a range of sun-shading densities, with 50 per cent being the most common. It is also possible to make a wooden frame and cover it with shade netting, or to erect a pergola that can be shaded with netting in the hottest parts of the year.

USING A SHADEHOUSE

Enthusiasts may wish to use shadehouses in the far northern or southern latitudes, where the day length is very long, but the summers can vary between long periods of clear sky and equal periods of heavy cloud and rain. Here, use a cover with 30 per cent shade factor, with an additional overlaying removable top cover with 30 per cent shade factor used in the hottest spells.

When it comes to frost, shadehouses do not provide anything but the lightest protection, so do not move any plants into them until all danger of frost is past.

TYPES OF FLOOR

There are many different types of floor, but whichever one you choose it must provide a sound surface on which to stand potted fuchsias. Drainage is important in times of heavy rain, so if you use paving, lay it with

Top left: The cultivar 'Marin Glow', with its white and imperial-purple single flowers, easily bleaches in the sun, as in this picture, and benefits from a shadehouse.

Left: A view through the doorway of a shadehouse in midsummer. Inside are many pot-grown fuchsias in flower, standing on beds of moist gravel. Note the green shading material on the sides and roof.

Left: A magnificent fuchsia fan growing in a shadehouse, surrounded by other fuchsias in pots. This cultivar is 'Waveney Gem', a medium-sized single-flowered fuchsia with white sepals and a mauve corolla flushed pink. It has light green foliage and makes a vigorous lax bush. It is very adaptable, and excels as a basket plant, a small standard or a fan.

Below: A shadehouse, constructed from a wood frame and shade netting, filled with fuchsias. The central post strengthens the ridge, allowing pots and baskets to hang.

a high point in the centre sloping away to the outsides of the shadehouse. Another popular solution is to cover the floor with a heavyweight grade of weed-suppressant matting, which is porous, preventing the growth of weeds while allowing water to drain away. When it is very hot, you will need to wet the floor regularly, as you would in a greenhouse; a layer of gravel, chippings or shale will help hold moisture and maintain humidity throughout the day.

ADVANTAGES OF SHADEHOUSES

As well as heat regulation, shadehouses provide some protection from the wind, helping to stop plants from blowing over. Those made of shade netting also break up heavy drops of rain into the kind of fine mist that fuchsias love. Hot places in the world may not get much rain but, when it does rain, it is often torrential, and this is a real extra benefit.

Another advantage, for exhibitors, is that the houses limit the access of bees, which can damage and mark the flowers when they try to reach the nectar, and moths, whose caterpillars can be very destructive.

Left: These green net shading covers on cold frames will protect young fuchsia plants from direct sun, helping in the hardening-off process prior to moving them outside.

GROWING IN A SHADEHOUSE

Providing there is side protection, free-standing pot plants on the floor in a shadehouse will stay upright on all but the windiest days but taller structures, such as standards or fans, do need support to prevent them blowing over. You can use wall wires strung along one side or a vertical framework from the roof to the floor. Cement rings or other types of stand made to fit different pot sizes are another way of keeping pots upright on windy days. If the roof is high and strong enough, hanging containers, hanging baskets and pots grow exceptionally well hung from the roof, but be aware this will create extra shade for any plants below them. You must also check that there is sufficient space for turning and maintaining the pots, for wetting the floor to maintain decent humidity levels and for watering, Although the fuchsias are shaded from the sun in hot windy weather, pots will dry out very quickly and may need watering twice a day.

Also, look out for pests. While the humid conditions and the protection of the shade netting will minimize attacks from red spider mite, other pests, such as aphids, whitefly and capsid bugs, can still attack the plants. For that reason, pick the plants up when watering and thoroughly check under the leaves for any early signs of attack. Early detection makes the control of pests much easier.

FUCHSIAS FOR THE SHADEHOUSE

The shaded environment is an excellent place for growing fuchsia cultivars whose flowers change colour when exposed to direct sunlight. This phenomenon is very common with white flowers, which often tend to turn pink, such as 'Countess of Aberdeen', 'Midwinter, 'Shelford' and 'Trudi Davro'. Similarly, the shadehouse can help protect the colours of the pastel-coloured flowering fuchsias, for example 'Blush o' Dawn', 'Eleanor Clark', 'Flirtation Waltz', 'Lilian' and 'Shady Lady', where the pale

Above: A flower bud of the cultivar 'Shelford' just prior to opening. Grown in the protection of a shadehouse, blooms of 'Shelford' will maintain their pure white colour.

Above: 'Trudi Davro' is a lovely small white double, excellent for growing in hanging pots. The flowers should stay pure white when grown in a shadehouse.

Right: Ferns, such as this collection in a shadehouse made from thin wooden laths, would make attractive foliage companions for fuchsias that like similar conditions.

sepals become pinker and the dark corolla may bleach. Some dark-coloured fuchsia flowers also tend to bleach in the sun, while in a shadehouse they will keep their pure, deep colours – good examples are 'Golden Anniversary', 'Hot Coals', 'Marin Glow', 'Ortenburger Festival', 'Preston Guild', 'Tamworth' and 'Zulu Queen'.

Another group of fuchsias ideal for a shadehouse are the species originating from tropical cloud forests, especially those in central South America, where they have similar warm, shady conditions. Good ones include *F. boliviana* and its variants, *F. denticulata*, *F. dependens*, *F. fulgens*, *F. macrostigma*, *F. sessifolia*, *F. splendens* and *F. venusta*. Remember, though, that many of the species can grow to a significant size and have large leaves. In latitudes more than 45 degrees north or south of the equator, the tropical species often flower best during spring and autumn, as the day length more closely matches that of their natural habitat.

You can grow Triphyllas in a shadehouse, but as most of them are happy in full sun, this is not necessary – and they can tend to grow a little long-jointed, develop too much foliage and not enough flowers. Variegated leaf cultivars can often benefit from the shelter of a shadehouse, but the leaf colours develop best in maximum light, so it is often better to find a lightly shaded outside position.

When visiting an enthusiast's shadehouse for the first time, it can be an impressive experience. You feel the change in temperature and humidity as you walk in; then comes the enthralling vision of rows of pot plants, standards and baskets, all in flower. Often it is the sight of the more unusual cultivars and species which flourish in these conditions – many of which would be difficult to grow otherwise – that inspires gardeners to invest in a shadehouse for themselves.

Above: *F. splendens* is easy to grow, has beautiful red and green flowers, and does very well in the shadehouse.

Left: *F. boliviana* var. *alba* has clusters of long white and red flowers and large velvety leaves, and enjoys shadehouse conditions.

GARDENING TECHNIQUES

Growing fuchsias is an enjoyable and rewarding pastime, whether you have only a few plants or whole collections of many different varieties. There are so many exciting colours, shapes and sizes of flowers and types of growth to choose from, and different ways to use them. Some fuchsias are hardy and can be grown as permanent shrubs, even in parts of the world with quite cold winters. This chapter contains tips and techniques on how to plant and grow them in this way. It also describes the best way to grow the more tender varieties. There is advice about buying and choosing fuchsias, propagating them, and growing and training them into beautiful shapes such as standards, pyramids and fans. There is information about the different types of growing medium and their suitability for growing fuchsias, and practical guidance on how to plant large containers and hanging baskets, and their subsequent care.

Left: You do not need many specialist tools to grow fuchsias. Simple basic items such as a pair of secateurs, a selection of plant pots and labels, a garden trowel and a small hoe will suffice.

Top left: There are many different types of baskets suitable for growing fuchsias. This type is a wicker construction lined with polyethylene to protect the willow.

Top middle: A large terracotta (clay) pot surrounded by fuchsias, pelargoniums and other companion plants ready for planting. This picture is from the start of a planting sequence, shown in full within this chapter.

Top right: Many sorts of different propagators are available to take fuchsia cuttings. For small quantities, homemade versions using a cover on a pot are quite suitable for windowsills.

Selecting and buying fuchsias

One of the most enjoyable parts of growing fuchsias as a hobby is the selection of new plants. The inspiration can come from seeing them in other people's gardens, or from looking at nursery catalogues. There is a tremendous sense of excitement in waiting for those first buds of your new acquisitions to open and reveal the hidden inner flower secrets. A fuchsia enthusiast should try to support the specialist fuchsia nurseries as much as possible, since this will help to keep a large range of unusual varieties in cultivation. The owners are usually enthusiasts themselves and will often be able to give very useful help and advice with problems you have, or suggestions of varieties.

ORDERING FUCHSIAS

Browse the catalogues and decide on the varieties you want to try. Most of the specialist fuchsia nurseries will accept orders for rooted cuttings or plants in small pots to be supplied in the late winter or early spring, and this is the best way to be sure you get the varieties you want. Getting together with friends, putting in and collecting a large order together, is one way to make this more economically viable.

Some growers will send an order by post, and while this is probably a good

Top: 'Display' is an excellent hardy cultivar for a beginner. It is very adaptable in its growth and is easy to grow as a standard or pyramid. It has dark foliage and almost self-coloured pink flowers with a flared corolla.

solution if you live a long way from the nursery, the best way to ensure that you start with healthy plants is to collect them yourself. Expect to come away with more plants than you ordered, though!

WHAT TO LOOK FOR

The first thing to do is to look carefully at the plant you are thinking of buying.
- Does it look strong and healthy?
- Are there any signs of disease?
- Is the growth even and balanced?

Next, look at the plant from above.
- Are the leaves growing evenly?
- Are the side shoots growing evenly? Often when the leaves are bigger on one side of the plant, the side shoots will be stronger as well.

If you want to take cuttings from the plant when you get home, pick one without the main growing tip removed (unstopped). If you are considering growing a standard, look for an unstopped plant or a rooted cutting that is growing strongly, with a straight stem.

CARING FOR NEW PLANTS

When you have bought rooted cuttings or small plants from a nursery early in the season, remember they have probably been growing in more heat than you will be able to provide. If you want to take cuttings from them, do so straight away, as these will go directly into your propagator, with no check in growth. When you bring new plants into your greenhouse, try to place them in the warmest position you can find

CHOOSING PLANTS FOR CUTTINGS

1 Look for plants with shoots pinched out evenly and growing in a balanced way. Try to choose plants not recently stopped, with growing tips.

2 This is an ideal shoot to take a tip cutting from. It is healthy, growing strongly and evenly, and there is a pair of leaves and a small growing tip.

POTTING UP STANDARD CUTTINGS

1 Choose cuttings with a balanced and even growth for growing on as a standard. You can see the healthy and well-developed root systems that will give rapid growth.

2 Pot up into 6cm (2½in) pots, centring the cutting in the pot. Keep them separate from your other plants so you remember not to pinch out the growing tips.

and gradually get them used to the growing conditions over about a week. When they are ready for potting up or potting on, move them into the next size pot and settle them in with an overhead spray, but do not soak the compost (soil mix).

LARGER PLANTS

If you do not have the facilities to raise small plants in a greenhouse early in the season, simply buy larger plants later on, and grow them on outside, following the previous guidelines for stopping and potting on. The plant cost will be higher, but there are no costs for heating.

POTTING UP ROOTED CUTTINGS

1 Pot up a rooted fuchsia cutting in a 6cm (2½in) pot, taking care not to disturb or damage the fine root system.

2 Water the fuchsia cutting in its new pot with a fine rose or an overhead spray. Use just enough water to settle the cutting in its pot.

POTTING UP MAIL-ORDER PLANTS

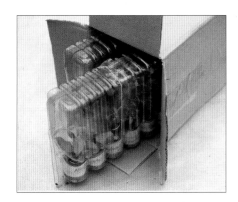

1 When the cuttings arrive, they should be potted up as soon as possible. If you cannot do it immediately, cut off the top of the plastic case and keep them well watered.

2 When you are ready to pot the plants up, open the plastic case. There should be a label identifying each plant. If the root balls are dry, soak them immediately.

3 Remove the elastic band and label from the plant root ball and place the cutting in a suitably sized small pot such as a 6cm (2½in). Write a plastic label with the cultivar name.

4 Complete the potting-up of the cutting by gently adding compost (soil mix) and tapping the pot to settle the contents. This cultivar is the Triphylla 'Chantry Park'.

5 Water the cuttings into their pots, using an overhead spray. Do not overwater at this time, but use enough water to settle and moisten the compost, allowing the roots to grow.

Composts and feeds

The quality of the compost (soil mix) used in containers is very important for growing fuchsias. It is the anchor for the roots and the reservoir for water and plant nutrients. Its structure is equally important, as this will allow the passage of air, vital for the health of the plants. There are many types of commercial potting compost prepared from various base materials. They contain some nutrients, but these are soon used up by strongly growing plants, especially if they are crowded into a small container, since they cannot put their roots down into the ground. It is therefore crucial to feed the plants by mixing in slow-release fertilizer granules or watering regularly with a suitable diluted liquid fertilizer.

TYPES OF COMPOST

Lawrence and Newell, two scientists at the John Innes Institute, developed the first standardized and reproducible potting composts during the 1930s. These mixes are known as John Innes formula composts, and consist of seven parts loam, three parts peat and two parts gritty sand (by volume) with increasing amounts of fertilizer to make the number one, two and three grades.

Soil-less compost (growing medium) was developed at the University of California, and is known as UC compost. It consists of 75 per cent sphagnum moss peat and 25 per cent coarse sand with

Top: A strip of fuchsia cuttings rooted in seed and cutting compost (soil mix), ready for potting up in potting compost.

added fertilizers. There have been many variations on this mixture, including the use of other additives such as vermiculite and water-retention granules. However, for many years concern has been growing about the unsustainable use of sphagnum moss peat, which destroys sites of special scientific interest and we are being urged as gardeners to go complete peat-free if we can. Luckily, today there are many perfectly acceptable completely peat-free multi-purpose composts available.

COMPOST FOR FUCHSIAS

Fuchsias will grow well in most good-quality, peat-free, general-purpose composts, preferably an open free-draining mixture. In terracotta (clay) pots, use mixes containing 50 per cent or more loam as soil-less

composts can dry out very quickly, and are difficult to re-wet when completely dry. For plastic pots, the soil-free types work well, but aim to add up to 20 per cent loam.

ADDITIVES

These are non-fertilizing materials mixed into the compost before use. Vermiculite, a thermally expanded mica, and perlite, another expanded mineral, open up the texture, and improve the drainage and water-retention abilities of the compost. Use them at a ratio of about one part vermiculite or perlite to six parts compost (by volume). Coarse sand and grit function purely as structure and drainage aids, but they will also add some weight to the compost mix, improving the stability of pot plants, especially when they dry out. Use

Above: Some different composts (soil mixes) and additives. At the back from left to right are: peat-free multi-purpose compost and a loam-based compost. At the front from left to right are: water retention granules, vermiculite and coarse grit.

Above: Some fertilizers and equipment used for growing fuchsias in the greenhouse, including a hand pressure sprayer, liquid fertilizer concentrate, slow-release fertilizer granules and a small watering can. In the background are overwintered fuchsia cuttings in 6cm (2½in) pots.

them at a ratio of about one volume part to six volume parts compost. When using multiple additives together, reduce the proportions accordingly. Water retention gel has become very popular mixed in with compost in hanging baskets, which often dry out very quickly. It will both improve the retention of water in the basket, and make re-wetting dry compost easier.

FERTILIZERS AND FEEDS

Useful supplements, fertilizers are solid materials mixed into the compost before use. Commercial compost normally contains sufficient fertilizer for a few months of growing. Feeds are liquid fertilizers, normally a liquid concentrate or soluble powder applied during watering or sprayed on as a foliar feed. Fuchsias, like all plants, need three major elements: nitrogen (N), phosphorus (P) and potassium (K) (commonly known as potash from its horticultural origin in wood ash). Nitrogen promotes leafy growth, root growth requires phosphorus, and potash promotes hardening of the wood, and flower and fruit formation. In addition, there are a number of trace elements and minor components needed for healthy growth of the plants. Fertilizers are labelled with their N:P:K contents, measured in weight per cent. For example, a high-nitrogen soluble powder feed could be 30:15:15, a balanced feed would be 20:20:20 and a high-potash feed 15:15:30.

One simple option is to use slow-release fertilizer granules. These contain concentrated fertilizer encapsulated in a polymer shell, which will not start to release the fertilizer until the compost reaches a certain temperature. The rate of release is dependent on the temperature and, to an extent, the moisture content. Alternatively, use liquid concentrate or soluble powder fertilizers mixed with water to give the correct strength. Fuchsias like a high-nitrogen feed early in the season, and a balanced feed for the rest of the season. You can use a high-potash feed at flowering time, preferably alternated with a balanced feed. Frequent feeding with a weak solution – maybe even a quarter of the recommended strength – is better than infrequent, stronger doses.

MIXING COMPOST AND ADDITIVES

1 Sift 12 parts of good-quality peat-free potting compost (soil mix) through a 5mm (¼in) sieve into a strong plastic bag.

2 After sifting, the larger lumps of wood, bark etc. are retained in the sieve. Use this coarse material above pot crocks.

3 Add a measure (one part) of a suitable coarse grit or sand to the mixture. Here 3–5mm (⅛–¼in) Cornish Grit is used.

4 Add a measure (one part) of horticultural grade perlite or vermiculite to the mixture. This improves the drainage and texture.

5 Grip the neck of the bag to close it, leaving plenty of air space, and roll and invert the bag to mix the ingredients together.

6 The final mixture spread out in a tray. The light colours of the grit and vermiculite additives show the effective mixing.

Hybridization techniques

There are more than 10,000 recorded cultivars, of which about 5,000 are still in cultivation. Many fuchsia flower colours exist, with only yellow and deep royal blue evading the plant breeders so far, but even these may be achieved one day. Modern cultivars are created by hybridizing two fuchsias and growing the resultant seed. If a seedling looks commercially promising, new plants are produced by vegetative propagation (cuttings). The natural phenomenon of mutation known as 'sporting' has produced many other new fuchsias, including variegated-leaf cultivars such as 'Golden Marinka' from 'Marinka', and different flower colours, such as 'Lady Thumb' and 'Son of Thumb' from 'Tom Thumb'.

HISTORY OF HYBRIDIZATION

Since gardeners began their attempts at hybridization early in the 19th century, many different fuchsias have been produced, with varying shapes and sizes of leaf and flower and new flower colours. After the surge of new cultivars in the 19th century, fuchsias lost some of their popularity in the early part of the 20th century. The revival of interest in fuchsias was in part due to the formation of national fuchsia societies and the realization that the fuchsia was not just a greenhouse plant, but many varieties could also be grown in the garden as a hardy shrub.

Top: The fuchsia 'Alan Titchmarsh' is named in honour of the well-known British gardening celebrity. This bushy vigorous plant has plentiful semi-double flowers with rose sepals and a pale lilac-pink corolla.

PARTS OF THE FUCHSIA FLOWER
The fuchsia flower is formed of insect-attracting parts (including the colourful sepals and petals) and reproductive parts.

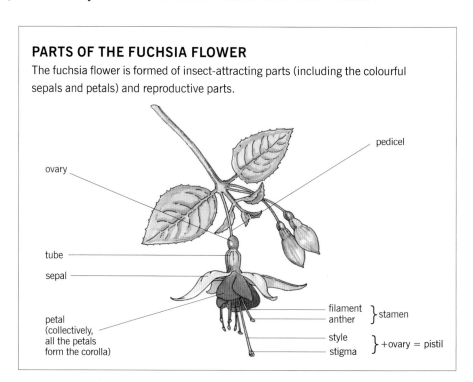

HYBRIDIZING PLANTS

1 Select a suitable flower bud in the seed parent. Remove any other buds growing from the same leaf axil. Pop it open one or two days before it would normally open.

2 Emasculate the flower by carefully cutting away all the anthers (pollen-bearing organs) with scissors. Protect the flower in a polythene or muslin (cheesecloth) bag.

3 After about a week, when the stigma is receptive (sticky), pollinate the stigma by transferring pollen from the anthers of the selected male parent flower.

4 Reseal the flower in the bag to protect it from further pollen, and label. Remove the bag in 5–6 days, when the flower has died. Allow the berry to form and ripen before harvesting the seed.

In the 1930s a group of enthusiasts from the recently formed British Fuchsia Society collected 100 of the best cultivars available in Europe and took them to California at the request of the American Fuchsia Society. American growers then applied scientific methods to further hybridization and soon started to produce new cultivars with unusual colour combinations, as well as the range of large double-flowered fuchsias for which they are famous. In Europe, the focus was more on producing hardy cultivars with a better range of flower colours and sizes. In the last decade, there has been a huge increase in the production of cultivars with new and exciting flower colours and shapes.

MAKING YOUR OWN HYBRID

If you wish to produce a new fuchsia, you must first make a selected hybridization cross between two cultivars or species, or a combination of the two. The first step is to select the two separate cultivars or species to use as the pollen parent and the seed parent. Experienced hybridizers have their preferences for these, knowing the previous parentage of cultivars and the viability of their seed production. For example, the cultivars 'La Campanella' and 'String of Pearls' have been used quite extensively as seed parents. It's best to do some research, by consulting reference books and talking to other growers, before you make your choice.

GROWING ON HYBRID SEEDLINGS

Once your hybridized seeds have germinated – which may take up to six weeks, so be patient – let them grow until they are large enough to handle. Prick them out (holding them by the leaves, to avoid damaging the stems or roots) into individual pots and grow them on without stopping, potting on as necessary, or in the summer you can plant them out into a trial bed. Judge the growth habit and the flower as objectively as you can, if possible bringing in some other growers to help with the assessment.

Take cuttings from the best candidates and try growing them for a few more years. If you have anything that looks really interesting, contact one of your local fuchsia nurseries, as the growers are always interested in new cultivars.

COLLECTING AND PLANTING SEEDS

1 Carefully squash the ripe fuchsia berry in a small dish of water, breaking the skin and opening the flesh.

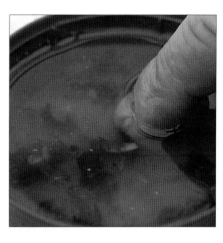

2 Break up the flesh as much as possible into a pulp suspended in water, releasing the seeds into the water.

3 Filter the mixture through a fine strainer, washing through the berry debris separating the pulp form the seeds.

4 Carefully pick out the fuchsia seeds and place them on a paper towel, drying them as much as possible.

5 Transfer the dried seeds into a pot or tray of good-quality seed compost, pressing them into the surface and carefully moistening.

6 Place a transparent plastic or glass cover on the pot and germinate at 15.5–18°C (60–65°F). Germination may take six weeks.

Propagating fuchsias

Taking cuttings is a really simple and rewarding way of propagating fuchsias to increase or replace stock. It is the only way to increase the stock of a specific fuchsia cultivar as plants propagated from collected seed will not come true except for the fuchsia species. You can take cuttings at almost any time of the year: soft cuttings in the late winter and spring; semi-ripe cuttings in the summer; and woody cuttings in the autumn. You can also take soft cuttings in the autumn by cutting back plants in the late summer and allowing them to shoot again. Ensure all cutting material used is short-jointed and free from any disease or infestation, and comes from strongly growing plants.

SOFT CUTTINGS

Depending on your location, climate and greenhouse conditions, take soft cuttings in the late winter or spring when plants are growing strongly. Different parts of the shoot can be used as cuttings, but it is always best to use a tip cutting, if you have

Top: A set of late summer cuttings that are well rooted and showing fresh tip growth eight weeks after planting. Spring cuttings would root in five to six weeks.

enough material. The tip cutting contains the highest concentration of natural growth hormones and it will root more quickly. It also gives a more symmetrical cutting, with the flexibility to be trained and grown on in different ways.

Before you start, ensure the parent plant is well watered and the growth is turgid (the plant has had time to take up the water). Look for growing tips where the growth is symmetrical, and cut just

below a node with a razor-sharp knife to give a cutting with two sets of leaves and a growing tip. Try to avoid handling the stem, as you could damage the delicate tissues. Remove the bottom set of leaves and immediately place the cutting into the rooting medium. Add a label with the variety name and the date, water with a fine spray and place in a propagator. You may use rooting powder, but it is not really necessary. Keep the propagator with a bottom temperature of 15.5–21°C (60–70°F), in good light, but not in direct sunlight, and the cuttings will root in 14–28 days. When rooted the cuttings take on a fresher, brighter appearance and start to make new tip growth. At this point, gradually increase the ventilation in the propagator to acclimatize the cuttings to the drier outside air and harden them off.

SEMI-RIPE CUTTINGS

In the summer, most plants are flowering and the stems have started to ripen. You can now take longer cuttings with a 'heel', the bit of bark that comes away when you tear off a whole side shoot from the parent plant. The cuttings can have up to five pairs of leaves and the growing tip. Remove all flower buds, treat the bottom node and stem with fresh rooting powder or gel, and then treat as soft cuttings.

HARDWOOD CUTTINGS

In the late summer and autumn, when the wood is ripe, you can take hardwood cuttings, again with a heel, as described for semi-ripe cuttings. Remove any flowers or

TYPES OF CUTTING

A semi-ripe cutting (left), consisting of a side shoot removed with a strip of bark from the parent stem, is similar to a hardwood cutting. On the right is a long semi-ripe cutting split into different types of cutting that could be used if propagation material is limited for an individual variety.

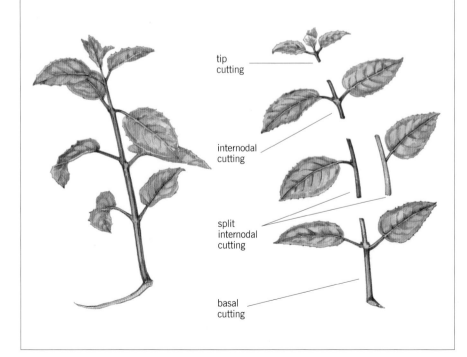

tip cutting

internodal cutting

split internodal cutting

basal cutting

buds, and treat similarly to soft cuttings. This type of cutting will also often root if inserted into sandy soil in a shady spot outside.

CUTTING COMPOST

Use commercial cutting compost (soil mix), or even better, try two parts of sifted peat-free compost mixed with one part of washed sharp sand or 2–3mm (½–⅛in) grit and one part of vermiculite or perlite. This gives an open, free-draining mixture with few nutrients, which will encourage rapid root formation.

PROPAGATORS

Commercial nurseries use heated propagating benches with overhead misting, and often root directly into sand. Amateur growers can rarely invest in anything quite as elaborate, but there are a number of other solutions:

- Electrically heated, gravel tray-sized propagators with vented plastic lids.
- Similar unheated ones, placed over a greenhouse heater.
- Plastic covers that fit on to seed trays or pots.
- Cut-off plastic bottles, or plastic bags fixed above pots with rubber bands.

CONTAINERS

There are many choices for cutting containers, including seed trays, plug trays and small shallow pots. Trays with individual compartments are an excellent choice. The trays with 60 small cells that fit into a standard seed tray, and split into strips of 12, are very good. They keep each cutting separate, with its own label, prevent the roots intermingling, and make

TAKING CUTTINGS

1 Using a sharp knife, remove a suitable cutting from its parent plant. A small disposable modelling knife with a retractable stainless blade, as shown here, is ideal.

2 If making your own cutting medium, mix together two parts of sifted peat-free compost, one part of horticultural grit or coarse sand and one part of vermiculite or perlite.

3 Fill a cell strip with cutting medium. Cut the lower leaves off the stem and insert into a prepared hole in the cutting medium. Add a label to each cell.

4 Moisten the cell strip with cuttings with an overhead spray of water, before being placed in the propagator with a bottom heat of 60°F (15.5°C).

it easier to pot up the cuttings later. If you treat them carefully, they can be reused a few times. It is easy to cut out a single cell from the strip to give away a cutting.

Below left: Some commercial and home-recycled propagators for fuchsias.

Below: Commercial propagation with heated benches, lights and misting.

Potting on

While building the structure of the plant, fuchsias need potting on into larger pots stepwise as they grow. If you allow a plant to become pot-bound, it will feel its survival is threatened and this will trigger flowering and production of seed. Potting on gradually instead of moving the plant from a small pot to a large pot will make it easier to water correctly because there is less compost (soil mix) that will stay wet and start to go stale. The roots will also use the smaller amount of new compost more efficiently rather than going straight down through the compost to the bottom of the new pot but not using the bulk of the compost until the formation of branching roots.

POTTING ON SINGLE PLANTS

As a general guideline, a rooted cutting can be potted up into a 6cm (2½in) pot. The next move could be into a 7.5cm (3in) pot, followed by a 9cm (3½in), 11cm (4¼in), 13cm (5in) and finally a 15cm (6in) pot. This sequence will give approximately the same percentage increase in compost volume at each potting-on stage. If you wish to go beyond a 15cm (6in) pot, you can continue to an 18cm (7in) pot and onwards in 5cm (2in) steps. If a plant is growing very strongly then it may be possible to miss out one pot size in the sequence, but water it very sparsely for the next two weeks, forcing the roots to search out new compost. Use of the technique shown in the step-by-step sequence will ensure that there is minimal disturbance of the root system and few air pockets, if any, in the compost.

POTTING SEVERAL PLANTS INTO A LARGE CONTAINER

Take similar care when planting up a large pot with fuchsias, or fuchsias with other container plants. In this case it will be impossible to increase the pot sizes gradually. You might use a few plants from 13cm (5in) pots and the rest from 9cm (3½in) pots. This will lead to the problems of over-potting just described, so water with great care. In other words, give enough water to settle the plants in but do not

Top: A small flowering plant of the Triphylla cultivar 'Thalia' in a terracotta (clay) pot, with a collection of other old pots.

POTTING UP TO A 6CM (2½IN) POT

1 Carefully remove the rooted cutting from its rooting cell with the minimum possible root disturbance. Note the good formation of its root system in the cell.

2 Add compost (soil mix) into the bottom of a clean 5cm (2in) pot, adjusting the amount to ensure the cutting is at the same level as when in the rooting cell.

3 Add compost to fill the rest of the space in the pot, tapping it on a solid surface to ensure the contents settle and fill any voids, preventing air pockets in the pot.

4 Water in the cutting with an overhead spray and place the pot in a warm position out of draughts and direct sun until the cutting adjusts to its new surroundings.

POTTING ON TO A 7.5CM (3IN) POT

1 Add compost (soil mix) so that the smaller pot sits inside the new larger one, its top level with the rim. Fill the gap between the two pots with compost. Then carefully remove the inner pot, taking care not to disturb the compost.

2 Remove the plant from its smaller pot and drop it into the hollow, taking care not to disturb the mould.

3 Tap the new pot to settle the plant, and top up with more compost. Keep the plant moist by using an overhead spray.

Above: This quarter standard of 'Katrina Thompsen' is flowering for the first time, standing on a lawn. Note the PVC tape ties anchoring the stem firmly to the cane.

completely soak the compost. Then keep the pot as dry as possible for a period of three to four weeks in early spring, or two to three weeks in late spring, to encourage the roots to penetrate right through the pot. When the roots are short of water they will spread out in search of it. This helps reduce the problem of unused compost becoming stale because of a lack of air, and the roots will penetrate this just moist compost much quicker. Fuchsias will very quickly show when they are starting to get thirsty because the leaves become dull and slightly less turgid, and then start to droop. After this period, increase the watering and treat the plants as normal.

POTTING ON STANDARDS

Use the same techniques as described above, but remember to loosen the ties holding the main stem to the supporting cane, and push the latter down to the base of the new pot. Mixing in washed sharp sand to the top 2.5cm (1in) of compost helps to anchor the cane in the top of the pot by forming a very solid, compact but free-draining layer, and prevents it loosening as it moves in the wind.

WATERING

To keep the compost and roots healthy, it is important to use a cycle of wetting, drying out and rewetting. This cycle sucks in air to the compost every time it dries out, which is important for the health of both the roots and the compost. The gradual increase in pot size also means that the compost fills more evenly with roots using the water more quickly, thus keeping the cycle going, and allowing the plant to make the best use of the limited space. There is evidence that fuchsias grow quickest just before the roots dry out, producing larger plants more quickly.

Multi-planting

An easy way of producing large fuchsia pot plants in a single season is to use 'multiple planting'. It is a common practice with commercial growers of chrysanthemums, where a number of cuttings are rooted, packed close together in one pot – producing the popular 'Pot Mums'. Multi-planting is particularly useful if you do not have the facilities for keeping fuchsias over winter. There are three main techniques, categorized by the size of the planting material used. Although the first two methods ideally need a heated greenhouse, you can also try these techniques inside a house on a bright windowsill if you have suitable plants from which to take cuttings.

MULTI-PLANTS FROM TIP CUTTINGS

The first method is to root many cuttings together in a single pot. It is the most difficult method and needs great care to prevent botrytis because of the crowding of green stems and leaves. For this reason, it is best to avoid varieties that are more prone to the disease.

Start by rooting six or seven tip cuttings in a 9cm (3½in) half pot, one in the centre and the rest equally spaced around the

Top: This cascading cultivar 'President Margaret Slater' is multi-planted in a hanging pot, its growth trailing down the pot with flowers on the ends of the branches.

edge. Alternatively, use a larger half pot and more cuttings, arranging them in concentric rings around the centre, staggering the placing of cuttings in adjacent rings to fill the pot evenly. When the cuttings have rooted and adjusted to conditions outside the propagator, stop all the cuttings at a maximum of two pairs of leaves. As the plants start to grow, remove any overlapping lower leaves with nail scissors, allowing more air into the base of the plant. If any of the cuttings do succumb to botrytis, cut them back to soil level to prevent the problem from spreading to adjacent cuttings. Continue stopping the side branches at one or two pairs of leaves,

and pot on as necessary using standard pots. Once the bottom stems have started to harden and form bark, then grow on, treating the plant in the normal way.

MULTI-PLANTS FROM ROOTED CUTTINGS

The second method involves cuttings, raised individually, ideally rooted in trays with separate compartments. Pot several of them together in a single pot, arranging them with one in the centre, then one or more rings around the outside. You can use cuttings all of the same variety, or a mixture, but if you use cuttings of different cultivars, remember that they will grow at

GROWING MULTI-PLANTS FROM TIP CUTTINGS

1 Choose a parent plant with plenty of cutting material. Take cuttings in the normal way. If the bottom leaves are large, cut them in half.

2 Fill a 9cm (3½in) pot with cutting compost (soil mix). Place one cutting in the centre and another six in a ring around the outside.

3 Add a label, water in with an overhead mist spray and place in a propagator or add a transparent cover to the pot.

different rates and there might be different degrees of self-branching with flowering at different times, especially if single, semi-double and double-flowered varieties are mixed. Pinch out the growing tips at two or three pairs of leaves, and then the resultant side branches at two pairs of leaves, potting on as necessary. Continue pinching until you achieve about 60 per cent of the size desired, then allow them to become pot bound to increase the flowering.

MULTI-PLANTS FROM LARGER PLANTS

The final method involves the use of larger plants growing in 7.5cm (3in) or 9cm (3½in) pots, and putting five or more of them into a 20cm (8in) pot with one in the centre and the rest in a circle around it. If you wish to use many more plants or want to buy plants in larger pots than 9cm, then use a correspondingly bigger pot for planting that greater size of plants in.

This method is much easier for those who do not have good propagating facilities because you can use nursery-bought plants and harden them off in your own conditions, planting them up into a large pot after the last of the frosts. With the proper attention, these pots will be spectacular in late summer. Take great care to avoid over-watering, until the plants are established, and see the earlier advice on potting up into large containers.

GROWING MULTI-PLANTS FROM ROOTED CUTTINGS

1 Part fill a 9cm (3½in) pot with compost (soil mix). Place a rooted cutting into the centre so the compost surface is just below the rim.

2 Add another four cuttings of the same variety spaced equally around the edge of the pot. Remove all the small growing tips.

3 Add compost, filling the gaps between the rooted cuttings, tapping the pot to settle them in. Water them in with an overhead spray.

4 As the individual cuttings start to grow together, remove any overlapping lower leaves. Continue to stop side shoots.

Far left: It is easy to grow an excellent multi-planted hanging pot from the single-flowered cultivar 'Hermiena'. It will reward you with prolific flowers.

Left: The beautiful pink-flushed-white flowers of the cultivar 'Shelford'. This flexible and vigorous fuchsia responds well to multi-planting.

Training shrub and bush fuchsias

Most fuchsias seen in gardens, whether in large containers or planted in the ground, are growing naturally as shrubs, and they form beautiful, graceful plants with little or no deliberate training. When a fuchsia grows from seed or from a cutting without any stopping, the natural form is rather like a Christmas tree, although this depends on how self-branching and upright the variety naturally is. In outdoor conditions, however, the central growing stem will often be damaged by the wind, frost or other physical damage, and this leads to new shoots growing up from the base to create the shrub shape. Our intervention will create the desired shape right from the beginning.

SHAPE DIFFERENCES

Though the terms 'shrub' and 'bush' are usually synonymous, for fuchsia growers a shrub has a central growth and shoots which grow up from underneath the soil around the centre, while a bush grows on a short single stem.

SHRUB TRAINING

Start with a rooted cutting. If you have taken this yourself, use one that you originally cut just below a node, since this will encourage growths from below the surface. Pot the cutting into a 6cm (2½in) pot and remove the growing tip once the cutting has grown to four pairs of leaves. This will encourage the formation of side shoots. Check the growth of the roots and when the main roots start to curl around the bottom of the pot, move it on to a 7.5cm (3in) pot, lowering the plant slightly in the pot, and water in gently. Give the plant a 90-degree turn every two to three days, or more frequently if you are growing it on a windowsill indoors.

When the resultant side shoots have grown to two pairs of leaves, stop them by pinching out the growing tips again. You often find that certain varieties will grow additional side shoots between the junction of the first side shoot and the main stem, especially at the point of removal of the main growing tip. This is a bonus, so just

Top: This shrub of 'Genii', photographed two months after the last picture in the shrub sequence (right), has now made a nice shape and is growing on outside to harden the growth and flower for the first time.

SHRUB AND BUSH STRUCTURES

In a shrub structure (left), a number of main stems grow from the ground, self-branching above to form the structure. A bush structure (right) is grown from a single central stem growing from the ground with side branches forming the structure.

STOPPING TO CREATE A SHRUB

1 Pot up a selected fuchsia cutting into a 6cm (2½in) pot and grow it on until it has four pairs of leaves and a distinct growing tip.

2 Remove the growing tip and allow the side shoots to develop. Later on, after potting, the lowest shoots will be below the soil level.

3 When the side shoots have grown to two to three pairs of leaves remove the tips again. Repeat after every one to two pairs of leaves.

Above: This large shrub fuchsia, growing in a tub as a central feature in the middle of a lawn, has been well trained to produce a dense plant with plenty of flowers.

treat them in the same way as the other side shoots and they will add to the density and number of flowers.

Continue to pot the plant on as it grows, before hardening it off to plant in the garden as a permanent shrub. If you wish, continue to stop every one or two pairs of leaves to create a more dense, bushy and floriferous specimen plant, but remember that every stop made delays flowering by approximately three weeks.

BUSH TRAINING

A fuchsia bush grows on a single stem, which for exhibition purposes should not exceed 4cm (1½in). For garden use, this may be longer, but still not more than 7.5cm (3in). Take a fuchsia cutting and remove the lowest side shoots and leaves so that the cutting has a clear stem of 4cm (1½in) showing above the compost (soil mix) and three pairs of leaves. Place the cutting in a 6cm (2½in) pot and stop the growth by removing the growing tip. When the side shoots have started to form, stop the bottom two sets at two pairs of leaves and the upper set at one pair of leaves. Grow on as for shrub training above.

When the resultant side shoots have grown to one pair of leaves, stop them by pinching out the growing tips again. Treat all the side shoots in the same way and continue the process until the plant is in a 13cm (5in) pot, lowering the plant slightly if the basal stem has grown too long.

STOPPING TO CREATE A BUSH

1 Pot up the fuchsia cutting into a 6cm (2½in) pot. Grow it on until it has five pairs of leaves and a distinct growing tip.

2 Remove the growing tip and the bottom two pairs of leaves and side shoots to leave a clear, short stem.

3 When there are two to three pairs of leaves, remove the tips again. Repeat every one to two pairs of leaves.

POTTING ON A SHRUB FROM A TERRACOTTA POT

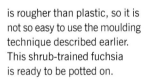

1 Unless the plant is pot-bound, the root ball will not usually keep its shape when removed from a terracotta (clay) pot, since the surface is rougher than plastic, so it is not so easy to use the moulding technique described earlier. This shrub-trained fuchsia is ready to be potted on.

2 Add a few pieces of broken terracotta pot over the drainage hole to ensure it is not blocked, and to keep the new compost (soil mix) in the pot.

3 Add soil-based compost to the pot, covering the broken pot at the base, so that the plant will sit at the same level or slightly lower than before.

4 Place the plant in the pot and add more compost around the sides, filling all air voids and tapping the pot to settle the contents.

5 Press the compost down gently, but take care not to compact it too much. Finally, water the plant in sparingly, to settle the plant in the pot.

Growing standard fuchsias

A fuchsia grown as a standard is an excellent way to display the spectacular beauty of the flowers. To be in proportion, the head of a mature flowering standard fuchsia should be approximately one-third of the overall height, and if grown in a pot, a 1.8m (6ft) full standard needs one that is 30cm (12in) in diameter. Of the different large trained shapes, a standard fuchsia is the easiest form to grow. A lot of attention and consideration must be paid to the support cane and the ties to support the stem and head, especially in the early stages. Choose a suitable vigorous, upright variety such as 'Checkerboard', 'Display' or 'Snowcap', and follow the instructions below.

STARTING THE PROCESS

Start as early in the season as possible, or grow from a late summer/autumn cutting over the winter indoors on a windowsill, in a heated greenhouse, or in a conservatory. Either take a cutting yourself, or buy a suitable young plant from a nursery. Make sure it is unstopped, with the growing tip intact, and look for a variety

Top: A first-year full standard fuchsia 'Snowcap' placed on a lawn in a 20cm (8in) pot. The red and white flowers stand out beautifully against the green foliage and against the large *Fatsia japonica* visible in the background.

with leaves in sets of three instead of pairs as this gives an extra branch in each set in the head, allowing it to fill more quickly. If you wish to avoid the stem-growing stage, you can buy a ready-grown whip from a specialist nursery.

GROWING THE WHIP (STEM)

Pot the cutting up into a 6–7.5cm (2½–3in) pot and, looking down from above, insert a split cane as close to the main stem as possible between the leaves. Make sure the cane is straight, as this is the guide for the growing stem. As the plant begins to grow, start to remove the lowest side

shoots, which are very easy to snap out. Leave the top three sets and the growing tip in place, but do not remove the main leaves on the stem. Turn the plant one-quarter of a turn every two days (every day on a windowsill) to keep it growing evenly. As the stem starts to develop, fix it to the cane in several places using suitable ties. Check the ties regularly, because they will quickly cut into the soft stem if they are too tight.

As soon as the roots have reached the bottom of the pot and started to coil around, pot on to the next pot size. Make sure you loosen the ties and push the cane to the bottom of the new pot before re-tightening them. It is essential not to let the roots become pot-bound while growing the stem as this often initiates flower buds, which means the plant will not produce the side shoots needed to make the head. Feed regularly with a quarter-strength high-nitrogen feed, and mist the plant frequently.

FORMING THE HEAD

When the whip has reached the desired height, take out the growing tip, leaving sufficient side shoots to make the head. A guide is 2–3 sets for a mini standard, 3 sets for a quarter standard, 3–4 sets for a half standard and 4 sets for a full standard, but it will depend on the variety, and also on the stem length between the leaves. Pinch out the side shoots on the lower sets at two pairs of leaves and on the upper set at one pair of leaves. Often, additional side shoots will form at each break, especially

STANDARD STRUCTURE

The stages of growing a standard fuchsia (from left to right). The first picture shows growing the stem – notice the leaves and top side shoots left on the plant. In the centre, the standard has nearly reached the desired height and removal of the main growing tip is imminent. The last picture shows the dormant structure of the finished standard without leaves.

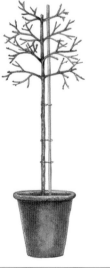

TRAINING A HALF STANDARD

1 Choose a young plant, ideally with leaves in sets of three, and grow it without stopping, potting on as soon as roots start to appear at the bottom of the pot.

2 Insert a split cane and tie to the stem. Remove the side shoots, leaving the top three sets. Do not remove the leaves. When flower buds appear, pinch out below them.

3 Stop the resulting sets of side shoots at two or three sets of leaves, to form the head. Do not remove the leaves from the main stem at this stage.

4 When a good, bushy head has formed, carefully remove the leaves from the main stem. Stop pinching out the growing tips, to allow the plant to flower.

CHANGING A STANDARD CANE

1 A half standard 'whip' grown from the cultivar 'John Bartlett'. After removal of the growing tip the head is forming, but the existing cane is not long enough.

2 Remove the ties to the existing cane, taking care not to damage the stem or small branches. Remove the existing cane while supporting the stem.

3 Insert a longer cane and replace the ties, ensuring the stem is straight against the cane. Pay attention to the ties supporting the developing head.

4 The standard is complete with a new cane. Note the regular ties and the length of the cane above the head. This disappears when the full head grows to its final size.

with the top set. Treat these in the same way. Stop all resulting side shoots once again at one pair of leaves, and then once more. Gradually remove the leaves from the stem and tie the standard stem in well, especially within the head itself, to prevent the risk of the whole head snapping off in the wind.

ALLOWING THE STANDARD TO FLOWER

For the final tying of the stem, PVC adhesive insulating tape is excellent, since it stretches and is waterproof. Another good alternative is green self-adhesive fabric tape. The young standard will benefit from a spell outside to strengthen it up and form the wood necessary in the main structure. Do not pot it on again at this stage, as being root-bound helps to give more flowers. It is important to ensure any standards are well supported to prevent them being blown over and damaged.

Growing pillars and pyramids

If you want a different challenge in fuchsia training, try growing a pillar or a pyramid. These can grow to more than 3m (10ft) tall, making a very impressive sight. A pillar is simply a tall column, as the name implies, and is the easier form to grow. The shape commonly described as a pyramid is actually a cone, with the height approximately one and half times the width at the base. It is possible to grow a small one of either in a single season if you choose a fast-growing variety, but a large specimen will take three years or more. For this, you will need enough space in a heated greenhouse to keep the plant over the winter, unless you live in an area free from winter frosts.

PILLARS

The first thing to consider is how the plant should look when the pillar is completed. The aim is to make a graceful column with proportions of about 4:1 height to diameter, covered in flower. The easiest way to do this is to use the twin stem approach, described below, which will allow your pillar to grow up to 1.5m (5ft) in one season.

Take a cutting of a vigorous self-branching variety and grow it up to three pairs of leaves before removing the growing

Top: A first-year pillar grown from the fuchsia 'Katie Susan'. It will need further pruning and shaping to reach the final goal.

tip. Allow two laterals from just below the stop to form, and remove all others. Then start to train the laterals upward, supported by two canes close together or one cane with longer ties. Decide on the final height of the pillar, and grow one stem like a stretched bush to half this height, and the other like a standard to the full height. For the stretched bush side, leave all the lateral growths and stop them at one or two pairs of leaves, and for the standard side, remove all the lateral growths except the top three or four sets. Pot on as soon as the roots start to curl round the pot. As early as you can, put in the final cane, as replacing the ties becomes more difficult later.

When the bush side reaches half the final desired height, remove the growing tip and continue to stop at one or two pairs of leaves. When the standard stem reaches half the desired height, allow the laterals to stay on and pinch them at one or two pairs of leaves. From now on, stop the shoots at alternately one or two sets of leaves to maintain the shape.

When the standard stem side reaches the desired height, pinch out the growing tip, and also pinch out the laterals to complete the desired shape. Continue to pinch to build the shape. When you achieve your target plant shape, stop pinching the shoots and allow it to come into flower.

PILLAR STRUCTURE

This twin-stem pillar has been grown on two growths from a single central stem, one trained as a tall narrow bush and the other as a stretched standard to form a single structure.

GROWING A TWIN-STEM PILLAR

1 Pot up a fuchsia cutting into a 6cm (2½in) pot and grow on until it has three pairs of leaves and a growing tip. A vigorous growing culitvar is needed for this; the variety used here is 'Katie Susan'.

2 The growing tip is removed to leave two or three pairs of leaves, depending on how long you wish the main stem to be. After the stop, allow only the two side shoots from the top of the plant to grow on.

3 Continue to grow the two stems trained up the central cane, removing the side shoots of the tall standard and leaving them on the stretched bush. At half the final height, stop the bush stem.

4 From this point on, leave the side shoots on the standard side, stopping all side growths to give the desired shape. When the standard side reaches the desired height, remove the growing tip.

PYRAMIDS

When fully grown, this should look like a Christmas tree, with approximate proportions of 3:2 overall height to diameter at the base, the diameter decreasing steadily toward the top to form a pyramid or cone shape. The best growing technique for a pyramid is as a single plant, and it can take two or three years to grow.

Take a cutting of a vigorous growing variety with strong, stiff lateral growths. Grow it upward to a height of 25cm (10in) with a cane to support it, and then remove the growing tip. This stop will result in a surge of growth to the laterals, which is important for the shape. Remove the lowest pair of laterals to give a short single stem at the base. When the two new shoots start to develop from the point where you removed the growing tip, decide which has the stronger growth and remove the other. Now you will be growing the stronger shoot on up as the new leader. When it has grown 7–10cm (3–4in), stop all the laterals on the first part of the stem. The leader will have a new surge of growth. When the growth has the same number of joints as the first part of the stem, pinch out the growing tip again. However, this time remove the opposite shoot to the first stem stop, so the growth goes in the opposite direction to the previous stem and the same as the first.

Continue growing in this way, potting on, changing the support cane, adjusting ties and feeding with high-nitrogen fertilizer, alternately stopping the leader and the laterals to form the desired shape. If the laterals are growing too weakly on one side of the plant, simply lay the plant down horizontally with the weak leaders positioned vertically for a few days, and the resultant change in the flow of sap will boost the growth. Note that you will need to create special supports or hangers to do this. Grow on until the desired height is reached, then allow the pyramid to flower and enjoy the lovely display. Trim it back to retain the shape in the late summer or early autumn, and keep the plant ticking over in green leaf through the winter, as this will ensure that all parts of the structure stay alive until the next season.

PYRAMID STRUCTURE

When training a fuchsia pyramid, the alternate stopping of the leader and the branches creates the desired shape. Continue the process until you attain the desired height for the specimen.

new leader growing on the opposite side to the leader from the first stop

second stop of leader

first stop of leader

GROWING A PYRAMID

1 Start to grow the structure with a suitable cutting of a strong-growing wiry variety; in this case it is the semi-double 'Little Beauty'.

2 Grow the plant on without check, potting on as required, removing the lowest side shoots to leave a short clear stem at the base.

3 When the main stem reaches a height of 25cm (10in), remove the growing tip. Later, remove the weaker new side shoot.

4 After removing the weaker side shoot, grow the strong one as the new leader, tying into the cane and periodically stopping the side shoots.

5 When the height has doubled again, remove the tip of the leader again, but this time select the opposite growing shoot to grow on.

6 This growing structure has been allowed to flower, but in the late summer it will be trimmed to shape and overwintered in green leaf.

Growing espaliers and fans

One spectacular variation of the many shapes that you can achieve with fuchsias is a flat shape in one plane, for example an espalier or fan. The training of both shapes is to display their flowers to the front, which makes them a terrific way of brightening up a wall or fence. Fuchsias grown into these shapes require suitable winter protection in colder climates and it is best to cut them back in the late summer or early autumn, allow them to make new growth, then overwinter them in green leaf. This minimizes the chances of part of the structure suffering from die-back. Start by training an easier shape, such as a standard, before attempting either of these challenges.

ESPALIERS

A fuchsia espalier needs to be grown over a framework of canes, fixed to a wall or fence for support while the plant is outside, to prevent it being blown over. Choose a suitable variety that is vigorous and strong growing, preferably with a degree of laxness or wiriness, but strong enough to make sturdy, horizontal branches. Examples include 'Brutus', 'Phyllis' and 'Swingtime'. If you want to grow a smaller version of this shape, use small-flowered varieties such as 'Alice Hoffman' and 'Janice Ann'.

Top: A close-up photograph of the flowers and growth on a large fan of 'Lillian Annetts'. Note the density of the growth and the sheer number of double flowers produced.

Start by choosing a suitable, strong, two-leaf cutting and grow it on without stopping, removing at least every other set of side shoots, so that the laterals grow in one plane only. The natural tendency of the laterals is to grow upwards at an angle of 40–60 degrees to the main stem. With a fuchsia espalier, it is important to start training these laterals horizontally as soon as possible, while the stems are soft and green. As soon as the plant is big enough, insert a central, vertical cane and firmly attach horizontal canes to it at the level of each set of laterals, and then start to tie the laterals to it, pulling them down to the horizontal. Some angled canes pushed into the pot and tied to the horizontal canes will help keep them in the correct position.

ESPALIER STRUCTURE

An espalier is formed from a central stem and a series of strong horizontal laterals supported by a framework. The lateral side growths are tied in and carry the flowers.

TRAINING AN ESPALIER

1 Choose a vigorous-growing healthy cutting with only pairs of leaves. A three-leafed cutting cannot be used for this form as it will not grow in one plane.

2 Decide the plane of growth for the espalier. Choose the bottom set of side shoots you will use and remove every other pair as you go up the main stem.

3 Insert a cane to support the main growth and tie it up. You can now see four of the side growths that will form the espalier structure when mature.

4 Replace the main cane with a strong cane, and tie horizontal canes to it to support the growth. Tie the growths to the horizontal canes with suitable soft ties.

Pot on the moment the roots have reached the bottom of the pot, and then start feeding with high-nitrogen fertilizer to promote lots of new growth. When the plant has made six sets of laterals, remove the main growing tip, and select the strongest side shoot to continue growing upward. When the plant has reached the desired height, stop the main stem and remove any further shoots that grow from the top. Continue allowing the laterals to grow, tying them in, and pinch any side shoots from the main laterals. As the laterals grow longer, they may start to produce flowers. Allow this flowering to take place and side shoots should appear in the leaf axils once the flowers have finished.

FANS

You can grow a fan using either a single plant or three plants of the same variety. It is essential to have all the main growth and stems growing in the same plane, so it is best to pick a cutting of a strong-growing but slightly lax variety such as 'Waveney Gem'. Stop the cutting when it has made four pairs of leaves and remove the first and third sets of side shoots so that, again, all the side shoots are growing in the same plane.

Pot on as soon as roots start to coil around the bottom of the pot. Construct the support structure by inserting five to seven canes in a fan shape with the central one

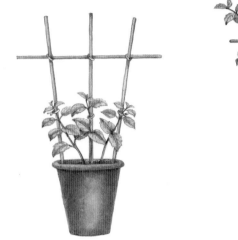

FAN STRUCTURE

When beginning a fan (left), the main shoots of the initial growth should be in the same plane. Later (right), the fan growths have been stopped and the side shoots now cover more of the frame.

pointing vertically upwards, and fix horizontal canes to them to make the framework rigid. Grow the laterals to cover the framework, tying them in as necessary, and periodically stop them to increase the number of leaders covering the structure. Pull any side shoots growing towards the back through to the front, tie them in and stop them. When the main leaders are close to the edge of the frame, stop them again and allow the fan to flower.

This is the most labour-intensive structure because of the amount of pulling through and tying in of the side growths needed. The fan structure needs a lot of support to keep it in the correct shape, which is why it is best to tie the framework to a wall or fence. If you do not have much space, you can keep it small by pruning it and restricting the pot size; alternatively pot it on regularly and allow it to grow bigger from year to year, until it reaches the desired size.

TRAINING A FAN

1 Stop the cutting at three pairs of leaves. Remove the middle set of side shoots, so there are two pairs left, growing in the same plane. These will form the structure.

2 Stop the side shoots at approximately three pairs of leaves. Remove any side shoots that are not growing aligned with the plane of the fan.

3 Insert five canes to form the fan with two horizontal canes to brace the structure. Tie the growing side shoots to the cane frame, spreading them to form the fan.

4 Complete the frame structure with two more horizontal canes. This growth has reached the top of the frame and is starting to flower. Ensure you tie in the growth well.

Bonsais and fuchsia topiary

Growing fuchsias as bonsai or novelty shapes is an exciting way of training fuchsias when you have limited space. They are fiddly and intricate, but lots of fun. Bonsais take a long time to grow well – firstly, because of the length of time to get the aged woody appearance to the growth; secondly, the task of miniaturizing the growth; and thirdly, persuading the branches to take on the form you desire. Growing fuchsias as novelty shapes is easier to achieve quickly, especially when employing the quick-growing Encliandra hybrids. These will fill the frame of a three-dimensional (3D) mesh former very rapidly, but are still amenable to clipping to shape.

BONSAI FUCHSIAS

Growing fuchsias as bonsai specimens is a long-term project, as with any bonsai training. It is best to choose a variety with small, single flowers, since although the leaves are dwarfed by the training, the flowers remain the same size, and large flowers would look out of proportion. To start, you need a plant grown deliberately with a bonsai in mind or an older plant with a sound, woody structure. An older plant can be either a pot plant with a suitable shape or an old, hardy plant growing in the garden that can be dug up and used. To prepare it for its move into a bonsai container, pot it back into decreasing pot sizes over 6 months in 1cm (½in) steps. This will involve some root pruning of the tap and major roots and reducing the top growth by approximately 40 per cent, removing any unwanted laterals and leaves.

Meanwhile, shape the branches gently to the desired position with loose wire ties.

Top: A wonderful old bonsai specimen of the cultivar 'Pink Rain', with a beautiful gnarled trunk. This lax fuchsia has very pretty small pink flowers, which makes it highly suitable to bonsai.

Right: 'Lottie Hobby' is an Encliandra hybrid with quite strong and vigorous wiry growth, small leaves and tiny red flowers. It is an excellent cultivar for creating topiary sculptures around a 3D wire shape.

PLANTING A BONSAI USING AN ESTABLISHED HARDY FUCHSIA

1 Dig up the plant (in this case the hardy 'Genii') while it is dormant, and prune the roots so that it fits into your bonsai container. When dormant, the plant survives this.

2 Prune the top growth back to a number of short growths. Further pruning will be needed later when growth starts. Remove any remaining old foliage.

3 Pot up in a gritty compost (soil mix) containing charcoal and blended to contain a lower level of nutrients than usual. This prevents too much rapid growth.

4 Gently water to settle the fuchsia into the container. Allow the plant to settle down for a few weeks, then start misting the wood to encourage it into growth.

TRAINING A TOPIARY SQUIRREL

 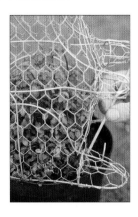 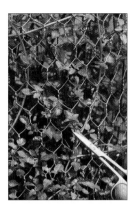  

1 Plant three fuchsias of the same variety (in this case 'Lottie Hobby') in a pot with a wide, stable base. Place a 3D mesh former of a squirrel over them and wire it to the pot.

2 Tease out some of the long wiry growths with a cane and move them to the desired position, filling areas of the shape that need extra growth, such as the feet and the tail.

3 Clip back the side growths that try to grow through the mesh with a pair of nail scissors. This will make them develop more side growths to fill the surface structure.

4 After some weeks, the growth reaches the top of the structure. Stop the growing tips and cut back a bit further to encourage side shoots to fill the structure at the top.

5 The growth has now filled the structure completely. Keep the structure clipped to maintain the shape but leave enough growth to enjoy the tiny flowers.

Also gradually expose the top of the uppermost roots (the nebari) by scraping away the top layer of compost (soil mix), and when inserting the fuchsia in a smaller pot, raise the height of the plant in its new container by putting more compost beneath it. When the plant is ready to move into a bonsai container, use special bonsai compost or seed compost with low nutrient levels mixed with some grit and charcoal. Prune the roots further, as necessary, and try to run the uppermost roots over a suitable smooth stone to add to the bonsai effect.

As soon as the danger of frosts has passed, grow the plant outside, protected from excessive direct sun either by artificial or natural shading. Feed with a quarter-strength balanced fertilizer once a week, keeping it moist but not saturated, and continue to shape the plant by removing large leaves and unwanted strong growth.

NOVELTY SHAPES

Commercially made wire mesh formers are readily available in many different shapes, but you can easily make one yourself if you want to try something different, with a spiral being the easiest shape. The best varieties for the job come from the Encliandra group and include 'Lottie Hobby', *F. microphylla* subsp. *hemsleyana*, *F. microphylla* subsp. *hidalgensis* and *F.* x *bacillaris*. These

fuchsias have tiny leaves and grow quickly, filling and covering the structure in a season. They also have tiny flowers, and still produce them even when you clip the main shoots tightly to keep the shape. If you use a vigorous Encliandra cultivar, for example 'Lottie Hobby', it is quite possible to create a 60–100cm (2–3ft) tall figure in a season, starting from small plants in late winter or early spring.

Start by planting up to five fuchsia plants of the same variety, the number depending on the size and shape of the wire frame. Then secure the former to the pot, using wire. Ideally, you should stop the plants twice when young to initiate low branching,

and they should at first be kept on the dry side to encourage rapid rooting through the pot. When the top growth reaches the edge of the wire shape, start to train and twist it along the wire, cutting back hard any growth that tries to grow straight outwards from the mesh.

If one part of the surface has a hole or a lack of growth, try to move some branches to this area, cutting back to increase branching and positioning the structure on its side for a few days if necessary, so that this part faces upright to increase the sap flow and therefore the growth. Direct the growths to fill the whole surface of the shape and keep the plants clipped regularly to maintain the shape.

Left: A novelty chicken shape created by growing the fuchsia 'Lottie Hobby' and variegated thyme around a wire frame, bedding in moss and potting compost. Note the use of flowering tips of other fuchsias to represent the comb and wattle.

Planting in containers

Many gardens now have extensive patios, terraces and other paved or gravelled areas, and of course many have no exposed soil at all. With an imaginative choice of containers, and a careful selection of fuchsias and other plants, you can create all kinds of different moods, ambiences and garden styles in these areas. A tremendous variety of different containers in many materials and colours are available from nurseries, garden centres, DIY superstores and specialist potteries. When choosing a container, remember that fuchsias like to keep their roots cool. Porous terracotta (clay) pots are the perfect choice, as the evaporation cools them down and they also help keep the compost (soil mix) aerated.

DRAINAGE

The most important requirement for fuchsias is good drainage, because although they love moisture, they detest waterlogging of the growing medium. Therefore, it is vital to ensure the provision of good drainage holes and to increase the number or size of the holes if they are not good enough for the purpose.

To protect the pot's drainage, especially in large containers where a soil-based compost is used, it is important to add drainage material to the bottom of the container to ensure the holes stay open. An ideal way is to place curved pieces of broken clay pots over the holes, followed by a layer of stones of various sizes, broken polystyrene (Styrofoam) or similar materials. When you add the compost on top of these pieces, they will stop most of it reaching the bottom of the pot and potentially blocking the drainage holes. To further improve drainage, you can stand large clay or stone pots on special feet which raise the pot approximately 2.5cm (1in) off the ground.

PLANTING LARGE CONTAINERS

The best time to plant up large containers with fuchsias is in the spring, when the plants are growing strongly and the roots will rapidly expand and penetrate the compost. A good range of plants are

Top: Standing on steps, this large mixed pot is planted with busy Lizzie, helichrysum, pelargoniums and the fuchsias 'Coralle', 'Seventh Heaven', 'Cambridge Louie' and 'Happy Wedding Day'.

PLANTING A LARGE POT

1 Assemble all the plants you wish to use with the large pot, in this case, a terracotta (clay) bell pot. Add crocks over the drainage holes and additional material such as broken polystyrene to improve drainage.

2 Part-fill the pot with compost (soil mix) so the plants may be stood in the pot. Arrange them putting the trailing plants around the edges. Lift the plants out and replace with the same sized empty pot.

3 Add more compost to the large pot, working it around the edges of the empty pots. Remove the empty pots one by one and plant the chosen plants into their correct positions.

4 Add more potting compost to fill depressions and voids. Gently lift and drop the pot on to a soft surface to settle the contents. Water in sparingly and grow on in a sheltered area.

available in the spring, since the garden centres and nurseries expect and prepare for the demand. Plan in advance the plants you would like to use and either grow them yourself or purchase them. The actual week of planting will depend on your local climate and what extra protection, such as a greenhouse, you have available to protect from them late frosts.

You can apply the planting technique described in the pictorial sequences for the planting of any large container. Additionally, use this technique for any type of plant grown or purchased in a smaller pot when you transfer it to a larger one, as it minimizes the damage to the plants and makes it easier to fill all of the spaces with compost, not leaving any empty spaces. You can choose to add slow-release fertilizer to the compost or feed regularly with liquid fertilizers, but be careful to do either one or the other, or you may risk over-feeding or starving the plants. There is sufficient fertilizer in the new compost to last for about four to six weeks after planting, so do not start adding either type before this time has elapsed.

It is also very important to control the watering for the first weeks, keeping the container rather dry until plants have become established and made good root growth through the container. Therefore, if you are growing newly planted containers outside, take the precaution of keeping them under cover when heavy rain is likely, to prevent them becoming too wet, as this will slow down the growth.

Right: An informal arrangement of terracotta (clay) urn pots piled on stones, with flowering fuchsia plants growing among them.

Far right: This large specimen fuchsia plant is growing in a decorative plastic pot and just coming into flower. Beside it is a variegated ivy, and behind it a small statue surrounded by a *Fatsia japonica*.

PLANTING A CHIMNEY POT

1 Use a 'Bishop' type of chimney pot as an ideal planter. Cut a piece of heavy wire mesh to fit as a support. Add a piece of finer mesh on to the top.

2 Add a layer of coarse stone chipping to act as a bed for the compost (soil mix), to prevent it from washing through before the roots have established.

3 Add a layer of compost on to the support. Choose the plants you want to use and find empty plastic pots of the same size they are planted in.

4 Set the empty pots in evenly and add compost until it is up to the lowest parts of the cowl, working in well around the pots.

5 Knock a small plant out of its pot, lift its corresponding empty pot out and drop the plant into the empty hole. Repeat with the other plants.

6 Add more potting compost to fill any voids. Settle the contents, then water them in sparingly. Grow on in a sheltered position.

Planting in hanging baskets

Fuchsias are a natural choice for hanging baskets. The variety and profusion of fuchsia flowers and their amenable growing habits make them ideal plants in this situation, particularly the double-flowered cultivars. Fuchsias look wonderful both on their own and mixed with companion foliage and flowering plants. Look around in your own neighbourhood, or at nurseries and garden centres, at the types of fuchsia cultivars and companion plants grown in baskets. This should help you decide what combinations to try in your own baskets. Remember that they come with different habits, some have almost upright growth but big double flowers weigh down the branches, while others cascade.

BASKETS AND LINERS

There are many different types of basket to choose from, constructed from PVC wire, plastic, wicker, metal strips and other materials. The baskets usually hang by chains from a support, and it is important to ensure that these chains are strong enough to hold up a fully watered basket with a lot of plant growth, blowing about in the wind.

If you wish to have plants growing through the sides, pick an open-mesh type of basket. This type needs lining before planting: choices for the lining include sphagnum moss, pre-formed liners or plastic. The pre-formed liners are available in different sizes, and are made of many different fibres, such as coconut, jute and

Top: A mixed hanging basket planted with the fuchsias 'Ruth King', 'Golden Marinka', 'Harry Grey' and 'Auntie Jinks'.

sisal, some lined with plastic inside. A cheap solution is to make plastic liners out of empty PVC compost bags, remembering to place the black side facing outward. It is better to line the wicker type of basket with plastic, to reduce the wetting of the wicker and retain the compost (soil mix).

PLANTING

The best time to plant up a summer basket is early to mid-spring. Gather the plants you want to use and ensure they are well watered. Use a mixture of multi-purpose compost and vermiculite or perlite, as described earlier. You may want to add water-retaining gel, and/or slow-release fertilizer.

The step sequence opposite shows how to plant a basket with plants only on the upper surface; this is often all you need for

a good display, especially if you are using plants with long trailing stems around the edge, such as ivy or petunias. However, if you want to have plants coming out of the sides, you should begin by cutting small crosses in the liner. (Cutting is not necessary if the basket is only lined with moss.) Insert the plants from outside the basket, before you start filling it with compost.

GROWING ON

Once you have planted the basket, if frosts are still threatened, leave the basket in the greenhouse at night, taking it outside on suitable warm days to harden off. Keep the basket on the dry side to encourage the roots to penetrate and spread through

Below: Hanging baskets come in a wide variety of shapes and sizes. This one is a long cone-shaped wicker basket.

Above: A range of wire baskets displayed with different liners. Clockwise from the front: a 30cm (12in) basket with a pre-formed felt liner; a 36cm (14in) basket lined with sphagnum moss; a 40cm (16in) basket with a liner made from an old compost bag.

the compost. Turn the basket a quarter of a turn every one to two days. If you wish, you can pinch out the fuchsia growing tips one more time to increase the number of flowering shoots, but remember this will delay flowering by a few weeks. Increase the watering as the plants grow and their roots fill the basket.

When all danger of frosts has passed, hang the basket in its final position, making sure that the hook is strong and sturdy enough to take the weight. Water when necessary, remembering to increase the watering as the plants grow, the day length increases and the temperatures rise. Baskets will dry out very quickly on warm, dry and windy days, and may need watering more than once a day.

Left: A hanging basket suspended from a tree branch, planted with multiple plants of the old French cultivar 'Marinka'. This beautiful cultivar has single bright red flowers, and the sepals cup the corolla. Take care when moving this fuchsia from the greenhouse as the leaves often mark with rapid temperature changes.

PLANTING A HANGING BASKET

1 Assemble the plants you will use together with the basket and the liner or lining material and a suitable multi-purpose compost (soil mix) mixed with additives.

2 Stand the basket on a large pot to keep it upright. Line the basket using a preformed liner, cut plastic such as old compost bags, or sphagnum moss, as in this case.

3 Add the compost, pushing it well to compress the moss into the basket wire frame. Add enough compost to ensure the plants will sit at a level slightly below the basket rim.

4 Begin inserting the plants, with the largest and upright plants in the centre. Plant the trailing plants at the edge, angling them outwards.

5 Add the rest of the plants and fill any voids with compost. Leave the surface higher at the edges. This will make watering easier.

6 Settle the contents and water in sparingly. The fuchsias used here were the cultivars 'Claudia', 'Postiljon' and 'Swingtime'.

Planting in borders

Fuchsias make excellent plants for all kind of borders and beds as temporary summer residents. You can use them within bedding schemes, for edging and even in the rockery. They are a great way to add extra height to the border and create an eye-catching feature. They can be used throughout the summer, then either discarded in the autumn or potted up and overwintered for use the next year, using the techniques described later. If you are growing standard fuchsias or other trained fuchsia shapes in large pots with a view to overwintering them in the greenhouse, you can sink the pots in the border, so that it is easy to lift them at the end of the season.

SOIL PREPARATION

Fuchsias are quite tolerant of different soil types, but they do not like being waterlogged and they are quite greedy feeders. They will benefit from extra organic matter, such as leaf mould, well-rotted manure, garden compost or any equivalent materials, which will improve both fertility and texture. If the soil is very heavy, you could also dig in some horticultural grit. The best time to dig over the border is in the winter or early spring, so that you can leave it a while to settle.

TEMPORARY BEDDING

Any fuchsias bedded out in a border as temporary residents should be planted normally, with the plant crown (the soil level in the pot) at ground level. If you are planting out any double-flowering types with heavy blooms where the growths are a little soft or lax, stake and tie the main branches to give some additional support. They still benefit from a good addition of organic material in the soil, but drainage is not as critical in summer as in winter. Use a good general fertilizer when planting, and

feed again during the summer following the manufacturer's instructions.

Plant out fuchsias with a sufficient distance between the plants, for them to fill up the spaces by the middle of the summer. The actual planting distance depends on the size of the plant when first planted out, and the typical growth of the variety. As an example, you might be planting out the Triphylla cultivar 'Thalia' from 12cm (5in) pots, each plant having about 20–30cm (8–12in) of growth. They will need to be spaced with about 30cm (12in) between

Top left: This half standard of the cultivar 'Thalia' is in full flower, with clusters of orange-red flowers standing out from the dark leaves. It is growing in a pot sunk into the ground and is supported against a wall with wire stays.

Left: This collection of hardy fuchsias is flowering beautifully in an oval bed in the middle of a lawn. Behind are more hardy fuchsias in a straight border at the edge of the lawn, protected by a hedge.

the centres of each plant. One of the best ways to do this if you want blocks of the same variety is in a triangular layout. Space two plants 30cm (12in) apart, and put the next one at a point halfway between and 26cm (10in) behind the first two, forming an equilateral triangle. Extend this to a three-by-three triangle with three more plants, then a four-by-four with four more and so on. Using this arrangement of plants, you can create different shapes, ensuring the plants are always the correct distance apart. Of course, if you prefer a more natural look, you can just mix and match the plants as you wish.

Small, compact-growing fuchsias are excellent for use as edging, planted as shown in the step sequence above. Fuchsias that typically only grow to 30–45cm (12–18in), such as 'Tom Thumb' and 'Happy', or fuchsias with variegated or light foliage, such as 'Tom West', 'Abigail Reine' and 'Sunray', are good choices for edging plants.

PLANTING OUT STANDARDS

Standards are very useful to raise the height of a planting scheme, but they are tender even when grown from a hardy variety, and need returning to the greenhouse for frost protection during the winter. Before

planting out, harden them up by standing them outside during the day for two weeks, then finally overnight as well for another few days, with support to prevent them from falling over. Either plant them directly into the ground or sink their pots in the ground with their rims just above soil level.

The major additional requirement when planting out standard fuchsias is to ensure proper support for the head. Tie in the trunk and head well to a strong cane; some

Above: This pretty 'Mercurius', covered with masses of flowers, is growing in a beautiful dome shape in a border of bulbs.

additional support is a good idea, especially with younger standards that have not developed heavy wood. When planting close to a wall or fence, fix some horizontal struts and tie them to the main cane, or alternatively use a strong stake behind the plant with similar horizontal struts.

PLANTING FUCHSIAS AS EDGING PLANTS

1 Compact fuchsias, especially those with a light foliage colour, make excellent edging plants. Place the plants out first to find the correct positions.

2 Dig a suitable hole the correct size for the root ball, then knock the plant out of its pot, loosen the coiled roots and place it in the hole and firm the soil around it.

3 Repeat the process for all the other plants, spacing them out in such a way they will quickly grow together and form a pretty, uniform edging to the border.

4 When they are all planted, dress the soil with a general fertilizer and hoe it in carefully around the plants. Water in with a watering can fitted with a fine rose.

Planting a hardy fuchsia bed

Permanent planting of hardy fuchsias in the garden is a wonderful way to get a superb display of flowers from early summer to late autumn, with very little maintenance needed. There is a wide range of hardy fuchsias available, most of which can grow anything from 30cm (12in) up to 1.6m (5ft) in one season in a typical Zone 8–9 climate. There is also a good range of colours, varying from the common red-and-purple, through red-and-white, pink, pink-and-white to pure white. When you are planning to create a hardy fuchsia bed, a certain amount of preparation is advisable; as usual in gardening, careful planning in advance will give better and more long-lasting results.

THE SITE

It is important to look long and hard at the area you are going to use for planting your hardy fuchsias.

- Good drainage should be at the top of your list. Waterlogged soil in the winter will kill the fuchsias, so avoid low-lying areas likely to flood. Heavy soils need improvement with organic matter and anything else to improve drainage, such as grit or sand.
- Wind exposure, especially in an area with very cold winter temperatures, will mean you can only use the hardiest varieties.
- Fuchsias prefer partial shade, but hardy ones planted in the ground will tolerate the sun quite well as long as they are watered in long dry spells. If you can provide some shade from the midday and early afternoon sun, that will help to avoid stress on hot days.

SOIL PREPARATION

The area you have chosen to plant your hardy bed needs preparation. The preparation depends on the soil type: sandy soils need extra organic material, and heavy clay types need both organic material and coarse sand and grit to improve drainage. Dig it over and remove any perennial weeds. Ideally do this in the autumn so that the area can settle and weather in the winter.

Top: A hardy fuchsia bed contrasting with the long thin stems of the purple-flowered *Verbena bonariensis* in the background.

Right: An established bed full of hardy fuchsias, their stems entwining and reaching heights of more than 2m (6ft).

PLANNING

Read the directory in this and other books, and obtain catalogues from different nurseries. In these, you will find descriptions and illustrations of different hardy fuchsias, with their flowers and colours, their growth habits and the heights to which they will grow in a typical season. Note that these are average measurements, and are based on areas where winter frosts

will cut them down to the ground. If you are lucky enough to live in a milder area, they will continue to grow from toward the top of the previous year's growth and will reach greater heights each year.

Make a list of the varieties you want, and plan how to plant them, thinking about the heights, colours and any other types of plants you will interplant. Generally, the larger plants should be at the back and the smaller ones at the front.

OBTAINING PLANTS

If you have a greenhouse, you can probably get some cuttings of hardy fuchsias from friends and neighbours and grow them on over the winter. If you wish to order from a nursery, do so in good time, as ideally you should have well-developed plants in 13–

Right: This fuchsia plant of the Triphylla 'Thalia' is in full flower alongside a leafy canna, with other vividly yellow and orange flowering cannas in the background.

15cm (5–6in) pots by planting-out time in the late spring or early summer. Place the plants outside on suitable days in mid-spring to harden them off, and finally leave them outside in their pots for a few days before planting out.

PLANTING

First place the plants you are going to use, still in their pots, in their final positions on the bed to get the spacing correct. Mark the positions with canes and remove the plants. For each position, scoop out a shallow depression over a diameter of four to five times the pot diameter and to

PLANTING A HARDY FUCHSIA

1 Scoop a shallow depression 65cm (26in) wide and 10cm (4in) deep. The cane shows the level of the soil surrounding the depression.

2 Dig a hole large enough at the centre to take the root ball of the plant, forking in some general fertilizer at the bottom.

3 Place the hardy fuchsia plant in the hole so that the surface of the soil around the plant is level with the base of the depression.

4 Firm the soil, then, as the plant grows through the summer, gradually pull back the soil around the plant to fill the depression.

a depth of 7.5–10cm (3–4in) at the centre. Then make a hole at the centre of the depression slightly larger than the pot, dig in some fertilizer and plant the fuchsia. The soil surface around the plant should be at the level of the bottom of the depression. Firm the soil and water the plant in well. The crown of the plant is now 7.5–10cm (3–4in) lower than the general soil level in the bed. Repeat this procedure for all the other plantings.

As the fuchsias grow and establish through the summer, gradually pull back the soil, filling the depression around each plant back to its original level, so that you cover the plant crown by 7.5–10cm (3–4in) of soil, watering in dry periods. This added protection of the crown is essential for winter survival, and the first year is the most critical. Most hardy fuchsias, if they survive the first year of planting, will probably last for many years.

Planting a fuchsia hedge

In milder areas, it is possible to grow hardy fuchsias as exotic and eye-catching hedges. Hedges of the hardy cultivar 'Riccartonii' are a beautiful sight and quite common in the south-west of England and Ireland. In gardens, these make a good dividing hedge or an attractive low hedge grown against a fence. It is not a good idea to use fuchsias as boundary hedges except in very mild areas. Grow fuchsia hedges only in parts of the garden where the average winter conditions will not kill the wood down to the ground, so that you can easily maintain the structure of the hedge. If an extreme winter does occur, it is still possible to re-grow the hedge from the base.

USING FUCHSIAS FOR HEDGES

Grow the hedge from a row of plants of the same variety, as different plants develop at different rates and it would be difficult to keep them all in shape as a hedge. Since the hedge will be in flower from midsummer until the end of the autumn, opportunities to clip and shape the hedge

Top: This low *Fuchsia magellanica* hedge, which is dripping with flower in the summer, delineates the edge of a sloping driveway from a neighbouring property.

are quite limited unless you are willing to sacrifice some flowers, so do not expect an ultra-smooth, neat surface – the result will be informal, but full of colour.

PREPARATION

Plant fuchsia hedges in a shallow trench to give the maximum protection to the crowns of the plants. You will be expecting your hedge to last for some years, so good preparation of the ground is important. Avoid any areas that are prone to waterlogging in the winter,

or provide some additional drainage by digging in a coarse horticultural grit or sharp sand, in addition to incorporating plenty of organic material such as leaf mould or rotted manure. Finish the preparation by making a shallow trench 15cm (6in) deep, and 45cm (18in) wider than the desired width of the hedge.

Below: A vigorous hardy fuchsia growing more than 2.5m (8ft) tall alongside a brick wall and over a doorway in a garden in the south-west of England. This demonstrates how high a fuchsia hedge can grow in the right conditions.

PLANTING

Decide how tall and wide you wish the hedge to be, and select a suitable variety. If you want extra thickness, you can plant in a double staggered row. The plants should be spaced about 45cm (18in) apart, unless you are making a low hedge with a dwarf variety, when a spacing of 30cm (12in) is more appropriate. Estimate how many plants you will need and add a further 10 per cent as a safety margin.

The plants need to be healthy, growing well in 13cm (5in) pots, hardened off and ready for planting in the late spring. If you cannot grow these plants yourself, order them in good time from a reputable fuchsia nursery, making it clear that you are going to use them for a hedge. They will be glad to give you advice on suitable varieties. Plant the ready plants into the trench in a row, or a staggered double row, making sure that the top of the compost (soil mix) in the pot comes level with the base of the trench. Dress the row with a suitable balanced fertilizer and water the plants in well.

GROWING ON

Grow the plants on with the absolute minimum of pruning, just trimming any wayward branches and enjoying the flowering. Water the hedge well in any dry periods and give it an occasional foliar feed to boost the growth. Gradually pull the earth back into the trench so that the crowns of the plants are 15cm (6in) below soil level.

In mid-autumn, when the growth subsides, trim the shape of the hedge by removing any long straggly growth. Protect the plants with a mulch of leaves or other organic material. During the first winter, protect the hedge with fleece in any very cold frosty periods. In the next spring, when the new growths have started to appear, remove any dead branches and give the live growth another trim to get the desired shape. It is well worth propagating or overwintering spare plants of your chosen variety ready to replace any which may have succumbed to the first winter.

Right: A *Fuchsia magellanica* hedge, bordering a path in Guernsey. It was clipped well early in the year but is now dripping with flowers, and still has a good shape.

PLANTING A HEDGE

1 When planting a hedge alongside a fence, set out the plants on the prepared soil, staggering them 30cm (12in) apart.

2 Dig a hole in the soil deeper than the depth of the pot. This ensures the crown of the plant will be well below the soil surface.

3 Knock the plant out of its pot, and loosen any long roots. Plant the fuchsia at the bottom of the hole and cover with soil.

4 Water in well, and add a mulch of composted bark or similar material to help reduce weed growth and retain moisture.

Pruning fuchsias

Fuchsias need pruning at different times of the year for various reasons. It can be simply a need to remove some wayward branches that have grown across a pathway. It may be part of re-invigorating a plant to create numerous new flowering shoots, or the pruning of a hedge after you have enjoyed the flowers through the summer. The first and most important point to consider before pruning a fuchsia is that the tools you will use – secateurs, pruners, saws and other implements – are clean and sharp. A clean cut heals more quickly and is less likely to die back or become diseased. Try to prune fuchsias when they are dormant, but when that is impossible try to ensure the soil is dry by withholding water.

REQUIRED PRUNING

Fuchsias are very amenable to hard pruning, quickly sprouting new growth. Trained structures need annual pruning to maintain the desired size and flowering density. Older plants in large pots may need some root pruning during potting down.

PRUNING PRINCIPLES

Although some of these points may be obvious, it is worth considering them before undertaking fuchsia pruning. Secateurs and other implements are – or should be – very sharp, so you should always wear gloves and exercise care when using this type of cutting equipment. Cut back fuchsias, like most shrubs, to a pair of buds so that when hard pruned, they will always shoot from close to the cut. When using bypass pruners or secateurs to cut a side branch back to the main stem, use them so the cutting blade is closest to the main stem. This sometimes means reversing them in your hand but allows a closer cut. When cutting the stems, cut them at an angle rather than horizontally, then if they do bleed the sap is more likely to drip off. Use a proprietary sealing compound if cuts are large and bleed sap profusely.

HEDGES

Fuchsia hedges should be left to grow freely through the summer and autumn, apart from the tidying of any very wayward branches, so the production of flowers continues unabated. This means you carry out most of the cutting and shaping of the hedge in the autumn and winter.

In the autumn, cut the hedge to return it to its basic height and width, leaving some extra growth to help protect it through the winter. Then in the late winter, as the buds are beginning to break, cut it back to the actual required shape, removing any damaged and diseased branches. Look carefully for any gaps, especially low down, then manipulate and prune suitable growths to fill them. In the case of a large gap at the base, consider planting another plant of the same variety later in the year.

Top left: 'Constance' is a reliable hardy cultivar, easily pruned as a standard. It has double flowers with a pink tube, green-tipped pink sepals and a rose-mauve corolla.

HARDY FUCHSIAS

All hardy fuchsias should have soft growth removed in the autumn after the frosts have blackened the foliage. This normally means removing about one-third of the growth. It helps to minimize dieback and prevents the plant loosening in the ground, blown about by the wind.

The time to prune hardy fuchsias depends on the winter conditions in your garden and which varieties you are growing. If the frosts kill the plants down to the ground each year, prune in the early spring as the fuchsias start to send shoots up from the base. Cut all of the dead stems back hard down to 5–15 cm (2–6in) of the

PRUNING CUTS

1 Use sharp secateurs to prune back a fuchsia stem as close as possible to new buds without damaging them. This ensures a minimum of dead wood, which may become diseased.

2 This is a pot plant of *F. denticulata*, pruned back hard to the new growth, which is now shooting well. When potted on, it will grow to a large shrub by the end of the summer.

Above: A superb plant of the hardy cultivar 'Genii' in full flower, planted in a growing space created when building a stone wall. This plant is cut back hard every year and grows vigorously again.

ground and the fresh growths will make a new shrub. If the wood above ground survives through the winter, prune them when they are as dormant as possible, normally late winter, watching for excessive sap bleeding from the cuts. You can cut back hard, or very lightly, depending what size you want to maintain the plants.

WARMER CLIMATES

In frost-free areas, fuchsias will grow throughout the year, without the seasonally enforced winter rest common in far northern or southern latitudes. Fuchsias growing in these conditions need pruning to give the plants a resting period. During the winter, when the plants are growing more slowly, they are pruned to tidy up the growth and invigorate the plant again by encouraging strong growth from lower down in the plant structure. In these areas, fuchsias tend to be at their best in the late spring and early summer, then will often suffer with the midsummer heat before reviving in the late summer and autumn. A light pruning in the summer tidies up the plant and creates fresh growth, giving another good flowering display in the late summer and autumn.

ROOT PRUNING A FUCHSIA

1 Cut the old growth back to a healthy pair of shoots, then prune the plant structure to get a nice evenly shaped plant.

2 Take the plant out of its pot and remove as much of the compost (soil mix) from the root ball as possible, with a cane or plant label.

3 Cut any long woody tap roots that will prevent the fuchsia from being moved into the pot of the desired size.

4 Re-pot the pruned fuchsia into the smaller pot with fresh compost, and then tap the pot on a hard surface to settle the contents.

PRUNING A HARDY FUCHSIA

1 A hardy fuchsia has had last year's growth killed back to the ground by the winter frosts. In early spring, when the first shoots start to appear at the base, prune back to the ground.

2 In a few weeks, several new shoots are growing from the base of the plant and by midsummer the plant will be flowering heavily again as a nicely shaped shrub.

Overwintering fuchsias

Gardeners living in the colder parts of the world, where there are periods of the year when the temperature is below freezing, can keep non-hardy fuchsias alive through the winter using various techniques depending on the facilities available. A lot depends on how you wish to grow fuchsias, and the type and size of your plants. A greenhouse, especially a heated one, is probably the best facility for overwintering fuchsias, but there are many other possibilities. You can use a frost-free garage or cellar, a conservatory, a spare room in the house kept cool with minimum heating, or even bury the plants in a prepared site in the garden. Any of these methods can allow fuchsias to survive cold winters.

HARDY FUCHSIAS

With the benefit of proper planting and a little extra care, hardy fuchsias will survive even quite cold winters where they are planted in the garden. The first year for a newly planted hardy fuchsia is always the most challenging, but by using the recommended planting method and pulling back the soil around the plant so the crown is 7.5–10cm (3–4in) below the surface, you will give it a good chance of survival. After the first frosts have killed the leaves, cut back the plants by about one-third to ensure removal of most of the soft growth and reduce the chances of wind-rock loosening the plant. Further, protect the crown with a layer of leaves, straw, or a similar material, and renew the coverage whenever necessary throughout the winter.

Top: Fuchsias cut back and stored underneath the staging on the floor of a frost-free greenhouse over the winter. The plants will quickly come back to life in the early spring.

Right: The view inside a heated greenhouse in the winter. Fuchsia plants are growing on the staging at the back and back left, kept in green leaf with minimum heat.

PROTECTING A HARDY FUCHSIA

1 Add a mulch of leaves or straw over the crown of a hardy fuchsia to give it some extra protection to survive the winter frosts.

2 Other mulching materials, such as moss peat, dry bracken or chipped bark, will also help to protect the plant.

PREPARING TENDER FUCHSIAS

Allowing tender fuchsias in pots to stay outside through one or two light frosts can be beneficial to help to induce dormancy. However, if you have a lot of plants, or if the weather can change suddenly in your area to severe frosty conditions, you can induce dormancy by drying and pruning.

Allow the pots to dry out as much as possible, then cut the plants back by two-thirds, remove all the remaining leaves and give the wood a spray of insecticide to kill any overwintering insects, if these have been causing problems. Leave the plants on their sides for a few days to ensure the cuts heal and avoid any sap bleeding from the cuts running down the stems and causing future dieback problems. Large mixed containers and baskets can be broken up, the plants separated and potted up, then treated in the same way. Tender plants in beds can be left until the first frosts kill the foliage, then they should be lifted, the loose soil shaken off, potted up and again treated like pot plants.

WINTER STORAGE

In a frost-free or heated greenhouse, place plants on the floor or on the staging, keeping the compost (soil mix) just slightly moist. Open the manual greenhouse vents whenever possible on warmer days to improve ventilation and decrease humidity. A fan in the greenhouse will also help stop the atmosphere becoming stagnant. The plants in a heated greenhouse will start growing new shoots in mid- to late winter, while in a frost-free greenhouse they will shoot from late winter to early spring.

Storage in an unheated greenhouse will depend on your local weather conditions. In milder areas, they might survive with just a covering of fleece on the few frosty nights, but in colder areas, they may need burying in trenches in the greenhouse border, lying them down on their sides. In areas with extremely long, cold winters, it is not possible to use an unheated greenhouse to overwinter fuchsias.

You can store plants with the compost just moist in a frost-free cellar or garage by leaving them in trays covered by fleece, or wrapped in paper and stacked on their sides in boxes. Inspect them periodically (once a month should be sufficient) to make sure they have not dried out, and remove any long white shoots from the wood to prevent them removing nutrients and vigour from the plant.

Storage in a cool conservatory or spare room is a little trickier, since the temperature will be more than 5°C (41°F) and the plants will continue to grow. Therefore, they need as much light as possible, occasional watering and regular turning. If by the spring they have made too much spindly weak growth, simply cut back this new growth quite hard before placing them back outside, where they will soon start growing normally with strong growth and short internodal joints.

OVERWINTERING A TENDER FUCHSIA

1 Dig out a tender fuchsia, planted out over the summer in a border. Take care to lift most of the main roots with the plant.

2 Clean all the loose soil off the plants and carefully pot up in dry potting compost (soil mix). Tap the pot to settle in the compost.

3 Remove the leaves and trim back the branches by one-half. Spray the wood with a combined insecticide and fungicide.

4 When the spray has dried, water it sparingly and put it away in the greenhouse or other chosen storage area.

STORING POT PLANTS IN BOXES

1 After drying off pot plants that are ready for storage, wrap them up in newspaper and place them in a storage box, with the pots stacked on their sides.

2 Pack the gaps with straw or more newspaper as insulation and put the box away in a cool frost-free area over the winter. Straw is better as it allows more ventilation.

Pests and diseases

Fuchsias are quite robust and strong-growing plants, generally free from serious diseases. If you give them the right conditions and care, you should not have any problems. Slugs and snails, often among the worst pests in the garden, tend not to attack fuchsias. Keep an eye out for any signs of damage – this should be done at night in some cases, but mostly can be a part of your normal routine, especially with pot-grown plants, which you water and turn regularly. In the next pages there is a comprehensive list of the main pests and diseases that affect fuchsias, with some suggestions of techniques and treatments for keeping them under control.

APHIDS (*Aphis*)

These sap-sucking insects belonging to many different species are normally green, red or black. Adults appear in spring, under the leaves and on the stems and growing tips; heavy infestations can distort the latter. The aphids also excrete a sweet, sticky fluid (loved by ants, which sometimes 'farm' the aphids) on which small, black fungal spots known as sooty moulds can grow. Often the damage is slight and control unnecessary, but you can squash them between finger and thumb, or remove them with a jet of water. In severe cases, spray with insecticidal soap or an aphid-specific insecticide.

Top: A honeybee visiting a flower of 'Alan Titchmarsh' to collect nectar. A serious exhibitor would discourage bees because of the damage they cause to the flowers.

CAPSID BUG
(*Lygocoris pabulinus*)

This small, green, fast-moving insect can cause a lot of damage to fuchsias, especially those grown outside. They are difficult to see and as a defence mechanism, they fall to the ground and play dead. If your garden has many shrubs, hedges or overhanging trees, you are more likely to have capsid bugs. They are sap-sucking insects and make small holes in the leaves, especially in the growing tips, around which the tissue dies. Then as the growth of the leaves continues, these dead areas tear into small holes with distortion of the growing tips and loss of flower buds. This can severely delay flowering because the growth has to restart from lower leaf joints. Spray with a systemic insecticide or insecticidal soap at the first sign of damage.

ELEPHANT HAWK MOTH
(*Deilephila elpenor*)

The brown caterpillar of this impressive moth is nearly 7.5cm (3in) long, and feeds on fuchsias, *Chamerion angustifolium* (formerly *Epilobium angustifolium*) (rosebay willowherb or fireweed) or *Galium* (bedstraw). The adult feeds on nectar. It lays its eggs singly under the leaves, mainly in the months either side of midsummer, and the best control is to remove the eggs before hatching. The caterpillar feeds at night and is voracious, eating flower buds and leaves. In the day, they hide down in the plant, well camouflaged. At this stage they are hard to control, but if you find one on a specimen plant, you can move it to a fireweed, or even a less precious fuchsia that you do not mind it eating.

aphids

capsid bug

capsid bug damage

elephant hawk moth

elephant hawk moth caterpillar

froghopper

FROGHOPPER
(*Philaenus spumarius*)

This insect, which can jump remarkable distances as an adult, is easy to recognize in its sap-sucking nymph phase, when it covers itself in a protective froth commonly known as cuckoo spit. Froghoppers do not cause serious damage but are easy to control by washing away the protective froth and killing the nymph.

FUCHSIA GALL MITE
(*Aculops fuchsiae*)

This is a very serious pest first identified in South America in the early 1970s, and in the southern USA in 1981. It was identified in France in 2003, the Channel Islands in 2006 and the first confirmed case in the UK was in 2007. It is not yet present in Australia or New Zealand. It is an eriophyoid mite 0.2–0.25mm ($\frac{1}{125}$–$\frac{1}{100}$in) long with a white to pale yellow wormlike body invisible to the naked eye. On the fuchsia, the symptoms start with a reddening of the leaves followed by thickening, fusing and galling of the growth, especially at the growing tips where growth stops. Current opinion is that large insects moving from plant to plant spread it, along with gardeners' fingers and tools. Treatments are being researched, but the best advice with severe infestations is to cut down and dispose of affected growth and spray with a suitable acaricide.

FUCHSIA RUST
(*Pucciniastrum epilobii*)

This is the most serious fungal disease affecting fuchsias. In the wild it needs both the *Chamerion angustifolium* (formerly *Epilobium angustifolium*) (rosebay willowherb or fireweed) and *Abies* (fir) to complete its life cycle, and because the former belongs to the same family as the fuchsia, it is sensible to remove it in your own garden and surroundings. The ripe spores, which can be carried by insects or on the wind, spread over large distances. The worst outbreaks tend to be in the late summer and autumn, but with a very wet spring and summer, it can be earlier. The affected leaves typically have pale or dark spots on the top, while underneath there are corresponding spots of orange pustules containing the growing fungal spores. When ripe, the spores shake off like a dust and are easily spread to other plants. As the leaves become more affected, they turn yellow and die. Once the rust becomes established, it is difficult to control. The best solution is to pick off and dispose of the infected leaves, and then spray the plant alternatively with a systemic insecticide followed by a protective fungicide. It is important to eradicate this before bringing in plants for winter storage, or the problem will persist into next year.

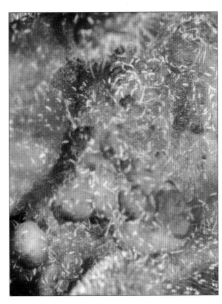

fuchsia gall mite

fuchsia rust

GREY MOULD
(*Botrytis cinerea*)

This fungal disease is most likely to occur in damp, stagnant conditions, and is usually at its worst over winter. The affected plant parts are covered in a grey, furry layer of fungus and the plant tissue rots. The spores have the ability to lie dormant until the right conditions occur. The best control is cleanliness, removing any diseased or dying leaves, especially those that fall into the joints between the branches and green stems. If they stay there then botrytis often sets in and migrates up the stems, killing them. In the greenhouse provide as much ventilation as possible all year round, even using fans when necessary.

RED SPIDER MITE
(*Tetranychus urticae*)

This microscopic arachnid loves the hot, dry conditions hated by fuchsias. Despite the name, only in autumn do the overwintering females take on this colour. The normal adult colour varies between white and green, with two spots on its back. Being minuscule, the mites are hard to see with the naked eye, and you are more likely to find their fine webs. The mites live on the backs of leaves and suck sap from the leaf cells, making the foliage turn brown and die. A severe infestation can result in considerable defoliation. Attacks are most likely to occur inside the

grey mould

greenhouse, but can occur outside in hot conditions. Suitable preventive measures are increasing the shading and humidity, and using a biological control or spraying with a pesticide (but not the two together). It is also important to sterilize the greenhouse in autumn because the mites will linger over winter in nooks and crannies. A new control based on a networked polymer system sprayed on to the back of the leaves works by covering the mites and eggs and killing them.

TORTRIX MOTH (*Tortricoidea*)

These small moths lay large clusters of greenish-white eggs on the underside of fuchsia leaves in spring and early summer. The small caterpillars emerge and eat about halfway through the leaf from underneath, which gradually dies. Later they move from leaf to leaf on small silk strands, and even roll up one or two leaves and live inside them. The best control is to remove the eggs before hatching, and spray with a systemic insecticide.

red spider mite

tortrix moth caterpillars

VINE WEEVIL
(*Otiorhynchus sulcatus*)

This small beetle has a dull black body 8–9mm (½in) long, is nocturnal and eats small, semi-circular shaped pieces out of the leaves. This is irritating rather than serious, with the real damage coming after it lays its eggs in the surface of the compost (soil mix), because the resultant white grubs (about the same size as the adult) feed on the roots. This happens from late summer through autumn and winter, into early spring. The plant will start to look distressed, with the leaves turning yellow and limp. The roots may also become slightly loose in the pot, and dormant winter plants might die if grubs remain undetected, because they can eat the entire root system.

Search for the adult weevils at night with a torch and kill on sight. They are quite slow moving and frequently play dead if you find them during the day-time. They have a very hard exoskeleton and need a lot of force to squash them. You can also water in the systemic neonicotinoid insecticide acetamiprid in late summer, but only use with ornamental plants, not edible crops. A biological nematode is also available.

WHITEFLY
(*Trialeurodes vaporariorum*)

Also called the 'ghostfly', this is a white 1.5mm (¹⁄₁₆in) long flying insect that lives mainly under leaves, where it sucks the

Left: 'Tom Thumb', a dwarf-growing hardy cultivar is shown here with its red and purple single flowers dripping with water after heavy rain. When fuchsias are continuously wet, they are much more prone to fungal diseases – especially botrytis, but also rust.

sap and leaves its scale-like nymphs. Whitefly nymphs damage the foliage, and their sugary excretions encourage the growth of sooty mould. Infestations are more likely in the greenhouse, but they can also occur outside. Growing French marigolds (*Tagetes patula*) in the greenhouse will deter the pests, but will not help if they are already present.

Check regularly under the leaves and kill any individuals you find. Yellow sticky strips trap the adults and act as an alert. When a plant is disturbed, the pests immediately fly up, resulting in mini-clouds in the case of severe infestations. Control whitefly using the predatory wasp *Encarsia formosa*, which feeds on the nymphs, or an insecticide spray, but not both.

vine weevil grubs and root damage

whitefly

DIRECTORY OF FUCHSIAS

More than 10,000 fuchsia cultivars have been introduced since the work of the first fuchsia hybridizers started in the early 19th century. Many of these have been lost over the years, but some have been continuously in commerce for more than 100 years, which is a good indicator that there is something special about them. Fuchsia nurseries introduce more than 300 new cultivars worldwide every year.

This directory lists and describes over 500 fuchsia varieties, organized into groups recommended for different purposes, and accompanied by many identification photographs. Each entry includes details about the fuchsia's origin, flower type, size and colour, growth habit and foliage colour, as well as its hardiness and how much sun it will tolerate. This is an excellent resource for anyone new to growing fuchsias, as well as keen collectors who would like to grow some of the more unusual varieties.

Left: 'Dark Eyes' is a lovely double cultivar from the USA, with a deep red tube and sepals and a full violet-blue corolla. It is quite a strong upright bush and makes a good temporary resident in the border.

Top left: 'President Margaret Slater' is a true cascading fuchsia with vigorous growth and plentiful white and mauve single flowers.

Top middle: 'WALZ Jubelteen' is a lovely single Dutch cultivar with erect pink flowers. It is a strong-growing fuchsia and will make a good standard, a superb garden border plant or a specimen plant.

Top right: 'Red Spider' is an ideal cultivar for a mixed basket, with its medium-sized single crimson and rose flowers.

Standard fuchsias

Please note that standards, even when grown from hardy cultivars, are not frost proof, so treat them as tender subjects, giving them shelter from the frost in the winter. Keeping them ticking over in green leaf is the best way to ensure they survive the winter.

'Alan Titchmarsh'

This has small to medium-sized single or sometimes semi-double flowers. The tube and sepals are rose and the corolla pale lilac-pink. This vigorous, upright cultivar – named after a British celebrity gardener – makes a very nice quarter or half standard. It is a strong grower, covered with flower, but when grown as a pot plant looks untidy in a smaller pot, therefore better grown as a large pot plant. The foliage is mid-green and small to medium-sized. Its introduction was as part of the diamond anniversary celebrations of the British Fuchsia Society. Half hardy; Zones 9–10. Weston, UK, 1998.

'Alf Thornley'

This is well covered in medium-sized double flowers with a pink tube, neyron-rose sepals and a creamy white full corolla, which stand out well against the

'Alan Titchmarsh'

medium-sized, mid-green foliage. The flowers have a beautiful overall shape and the plant usually produces two at each leaf axil. It is a vigorous, strong growing, upright, self-branching cultivar and makes a terrific half standard. Better grown outside than under glass and enjoys cool shade. Half hardy; Zones 9–10. Clark, UK, 1981.

'Amelie Aubin'

This is an excellent old German cultivar with a strong growing and self-branching, if rather lax habit. It has medium to large single flowers with a long, fat, waxy-white tube, waxy-white horizontal sepals and a rosy-carmine corolla. The foliage is medium to large, mid-green and slightly serrated. It makes an excellent full or half standard, which is slightly weeping, and is good for trained shapes, especially a pyramid. Half hardy; Zones 9–10. Eggbrecht, Germany, 1884.

'Annabel'

This cultivar has medium to large double flowers with a white-striped pink tube, white sepals with pink tips and a full white corolla veined with pink. Growth is upright and self-branching but slightly lax when flowering. It makes a beautiful half standard with its flowers standing out

'Annabel'

'Ballet Girl'

among the large, light-green serrated leaves. Also try as a full or quarter standard, in baskets and as a pot plant. Various nurseries call it hardy, but treat with caution. Hardy; Zones 7–8. Ryle, UK, 1977.

'Baby Bright'

The small to medium single flowers have a white tube with a pink blush, white sepals blushed pink and a white corolla blushed pink. The flowers are white when grown in shade but turn pink in sun, and they sit beautifully on the small to medium-sized bright mid-green foliage. It has an upright bushy habit and is excellent grown as a mini or small quarter standard. It also makes an effective small pot plant. Half hardy; Zones 9–10. Bright, UK, 1992.

'Ballet Girl'

This very old but excellent strong-growing bushy cultivar has stood the test of time. The medium to large double flowers have a bright cerise tube and sepals, and a white corolla with red veining. Its strong upright growth habit with attractive mid- to dark green foliage suits training as a half or full standard. Half hardy; Zones 9–10. Veich, UK, 1894.

'Barbara'

The flowers of this fuchsia are medium-sized singles with a pale pink tube and sepals, and tangerine-pink corolla. It is a strong, upright grower and the flowers stand out well against the medium-sized light to mid-green foliage. It will make a good quarter or half standard, and grows strongly enough to make a full standard. It tolerates the full sun quite well, so try it as a patio plant or in a summer bedding scheme. It will survive in milder areas planted as a shrub. Frost hardy; Zones 7–8, Tolley, UK, 1971.

'Bicentennial'

This US cultivar has medium-sized double flowers with a white tube flushed orange, orange sepals and a corolla with magenta centre and orange outside petals. Its lax trailing habit makes it effective in a hanging basket or as a weeping standard, but its weeping habit and flower size means it might be best as a half or full standard. The unusual coloured flowers are spectacular among the light to mid-green leaves. Half hardy; Zones 9–10. Paskesen, USA, 1976.

'Caroline'

This is one of a group of fuchsias with very flared, bell-shaped corollas that make a striking sight. The flowers are medium-sized singles with a pink tube, cream-flushed pink sepals and a flared violet corolla. It has strong, upright, self-branching growth

'Celia Smedley'

'Barbara'

with medium-sized mid-green foliage. It makes an excellent eye-catching half standard and grows very well as a pot plant. Half hardy; Zones 9–10. Miller, UK, 1967.

'Celia Smedley'

This cultivar has medium to large single flowers with a neyron-rose tube, neyron-rose sepals and a currant-red corolla. It is very quick growing and vigorous, and becomes a large plant in a single season. It makes a spectacular full standard and a good half standard. If it has a fault, it makes a lot of wood and can be difficult to get back into growth again after pruning back. The large vivid flowers contrast well with the large mid-green leaves. Because of its rapid growth, it also makes a very good specimen patio or container plant. Some growers have success with it as a permanently planted shrub in milder areas. Frost hardy; Zone 8. Bellamy, UK, 1970.

'Checkerboard'

If you have not grown a standard before, this cultivar is an excellent one to choose. It has medium-sized long single flowers with a red tube, red sepals sharply changing to white, and a red corolla

'Checkerboard'

turning white at the base. The flowers stand out and sparkle against the mid-green finely serrated foliage. It makes a very nice full or half standard, and grown in this way it resembles a Christmas tree with all its decorations and lights on. Flowering starts early in the season and it blooms continuously until the autumn. Use this cultivar to try a variety of trained shapes, as it is very adaptable. It is one of those cultivars that should be a part of everyone's collection. Half hardy; Zones 9–10. Walker and Jones, USA, 1948.

'Derby Imp'

This small-flowered cultivar with wiry stems is useful for creating many different trained shapes including standards. The prolific single flowers have a crimson tube and sepals and a violet-blue corolla that is pink at the base of the petals. The small, mid-green foliage complements the flowers very well, and this cultivar can be used as a basket, bush, hanging pot, fan or quarter standard. It only reached the commercial world because of the interest shown by a fuchsia enthusiast, who when visiting Cliff Gadsby's garden took a liking to this seedling among many others that were growing there. Half hardy; Zones 9–10. Gadsby, UK, 1974.

'Doreen Redfern'

'Ernie '

'Doreen Redfern'

The medium-sized single flowers of this fuchsia have a white tube, white sepals tipped green with pale lilac underneath and a violet corolla, maturing to violet-purple, which contrasts well with the small to medium-sized dark green foliage. Grow it as a quarter or half standard, but make sure to grow it in a shady position because it likes cool conditions and dislikes direct sun. It resulted from a cross between 'Cloverdale Pearl' and 'Marin Glow'. Half hardy; Zones 9–10. Redfern, UK, 1984.

'Dusky Beauty'

This has small single flowers with neyron-rose tube and sepals, and pale purple petals with darker picotee edges. This very floriferous fuchsia with mid- to dark green foliage and bushy, self-branching growth is very useful for training as a standard, especially a quarter standard. It makes an attractive pot plant and was used widely as an exhibition cultivar in the 1990s. Half hardy; Zones 9–10. Ryle, UK, 1981.

'Elaine Margaret'

This Australian cultivar has medium to large double flowers with a white tube, long white sepals tinged magenta, and a three-quarter flared white corolla. The buds are long and pointed, with mid-green

foliage. The growth is somewhat lax but it will make a good weeping half or full standard. It is also suitable for baskets and containers. Half hardy; Zones 9–10. Richardson, Australia, 1988.

'Ernie'

This recent cultivar has small to medium-sized single flowers with a red tube, red sepals and a white corolla with red veining. The red colour is rather bright, almost iridescent, and the short corolla has an attractive semi-flared shape. It has

vigorous, upright, self-branching growth with medium to dark green, small narrow leaves, and grows easily as a quarter or half standard. It is also very good as a pot or outdoor container plant. This cultivar is protected by plant breeder's rights. Half hardy; Zones 9–10. Götz, Germany, 2004.

'Ernie Bromley'

This wonderful, adaptable cultivar could be placed in almost any section of this directory. It is hardy with vigorous, slightly lax self-branching growth, and its attractive yellow-green foliage provides the perfect foil to the abundant, intensely coloured flowers. They are medium-sized singles with a pink tube and sepals, and a deep violet, flared corolla. It makes a superb slightly weeping half or full standard, but can also be used for hanging baskets, training as pillars and fans, or as a hardy plant in the border. Hardy; Zone 8. Growth 1m (3ft). Goulding, UK, 1988.

'Evensong'

This is a strong upright that is well suited to growing as a quarter or half standard. It has medium-sized single flowers with a white tube blushed with pink, fully reflexed white sepals with a pink blush at the base, and a white, flared corolla. The growth is quite vigorous and the small to medium-sized foliage is light green. Half hardy; Zones 9–10. Colville, UK, 1967.

'Ernie Bromley'

'Fascination'

This was named 'Emile de Wildeman' when first released but is now commonly known as 'Fascination'. It has very full medium to large double flowers; the tube and sepals are carmine-red and the corolla pink with cerise veining. It is a strong, upright, vigorous grower and can be trained as a superb half or even full standard with its attractive mid-green foliage. It also makes a good pyramid and is happy as a summer bedding plant. This is perhaps one of the best of Lemoine's many introductions. Half hardy; Zones 9–10. Lemoine, France, 1905.

'Flirtation Waltz'

This cultivar from the Waltz stable makes a superb half standard. It has medium double flowers with a creamy white tube, sepals flushed pink and a shell-pink corolla with startling red anthers. The growth is upright and bushy with light to mid-green foliage. It flowers early in the season, but the blooms mark easily when allowed to get wet. Half hardy; Zones 9–10. Waltz, USA, 1962.

'Flying Scotsman'

This is a strong-growing upright with attractive medium-sized double flowers set against the medium-sized mid-green foliage. The flowers have a short white tube with a pink flush turning red on maturity, pink sepals and a full corolla with rosy red petals streaked white. It is easily trained as an excellent half standard and also good as a pot plant or in summer bedding schemes. It is one of a series of cultivars named after famous trains, introduced by Edwin Goulding. Half hardy; Zones 9–10. Goulding, UK, 1985.

'Gay Parasol'

The name describes the flowers of this cultivar very aptly – they open to a rather flat shape, just like a parasol. They are a medium-sized double with an ivory-green tube, pinkish-white sepals and a burgundy-red, flat rosette-shaped corolla. The plant has strong upright growth with mid-green foliage and makes a very nice half standard, or is equally good as a pot

'Flirtation Waltz'

plant. It is one of many excellent introductions by the US hybridist Annabelle Stubbs. Half hardy; Zones 9–10. Stubbs, USA, 1979.

'Grandma Sinton'

This double-flowered cultivar has medium-sized flowers with a pale pink tube striped red, pale pink sepals with green tips

'Gay Parasol'

'Grandma Sinton'

touched red near the base, and a full white to pale pink corolla. It is very free-flowering for a double with rather stiff, wiry lax growth and medium-sized mid-green foliage. Grow it as a slightly weeping half standard or use in hanging baskets, although some weighting might be required to bend down the branches. Half hardy; Zones 9–10. Sinton, UK, 1986.

'Gruss aus dem Bodenthal'

This old German fuchsia (the name means 'Greetings from the Bode Valley') is synonymous with 'Black Prince' and is also known as the 'black fuchsia'. An upright self-branching fuchsia packed with flowers from early to late in the season. Grown as a pot plant it needs very little pinching after the first stop and can easily be grown as a smallish standard; it is not vigorous enough to make a full standard. The small to medium-sized single flowers have a short, rich crimson tube, rich crimson sepals held horizontally and a dark violet-purple corolla, almost black on opening, with small mid-green foliage. Take care when watering it in a pot because it is easy to drown the root system, especially early in the season. Half hardy; Zones 9–10. Sattler and Bethge, Germany, 1893.

'Hampshire Blue'

This strongly upright-growing cultivar with semi-double flowers was a sport from the cultivar 'Carmel Blue'. The flowers are medium in size, semi-double or sometimes single with a cream-flushed pink tube, semi-reflexed cream-flushed pink sepals and a powder blue corolla, with white at the base of the petals. The strong upright growth with medium to large mid-green foliage lends itself to training as a half or full standard. Half hardy; Zones 9–10. Clark, UK, 1983.

'Harbour Bridge'

This double-flowered Australian cultivar is named after the famous Sydney Harbour Bridge. The medium to large double flowers have a short rose tube, rose sepals tipped green and a lavender-blue corolla with pink blotches on the petals. With strong upright growth and mid-green foliage, it is easy to grow as a large standard. Half hardy; Zones 9–10. Lockerbie, Australia, 1971.

'Hazel'

This slightly lax cultivar has large double, rather round flowers with a neyron-rose tube and sepals, and a violet and neyron-rose corolla with purple edges, splashed with white. The flowers contrast well with

'Irene van Zoeren'

the large red-veined, lettuce-green foliage. It is excellent when grown as a weeping full or half standard, used in a hanging basket or as a pot plant with support. Half hardy; Zones 9–10. Richardson, Australia, 1985.

'Ingelore'

This cultivar is quite floriferous and grows well in a sunny position. The small to medium-sized single flowers have a red

tube, horizontal red sepals and a rose-purple corolla with scalloped edges to the petals. The medium-sized ovate leaves are mid-green. Grows well as a quarter or half standard, and is effective in summer bedding schemes or in a pot. Half hardy; Zones 9–10. Strümper, Germany, 1986.

'Irene van Zoeren'

This bushy cultivar has medium double flowers with a light orange tube, rose-red sepals with yellow-green tips and a lilac-rose corolla with a darker red border to the petals. It has a bushy habit with strongly upright growth and makes a nice quarter or half standard, or a good pot plant or specimen plant. It has mid- to dark green foliage and tolerates full sun. Half hardy; Zones 9–10. Beije, Netherlands, 1989.

'Iris Amer'

This compact double cultivar responds well to pinching, forming a tight shape. The medium-sized double flowers have a white tube, white pink-flushed sepals with green tips, and a tight rose-magenta corolla with lighter splashes. The medium-sized foliage is dark green and the growth suits a quarter or half standard. It inherited its free-flowering habit from one of its parents, 'Empress of Prussia'. Half hardy; Zones 9–10. Amer, UK, 1966.

'Hazel'

'Iris Amer'

'Joy Patmore'

'Kolding Perle'

'Jack Acland'

This cultivar has very vigorous stiff trailing growth, with long arched branches and mid-green foliage. It has medium to large single flowers with a medium pink tube, slightly recurving pink sepals and a bell-shaped corolla that opens rose-red and fades to dark pink. It makes a good weeping half or full standard, and is also excellent in a hanging basket. The incorrect spelling of the name as 'Jack Ackland' is often seen and it is also sometimes confused with 'Jack Shaan'. Half hardy; Zones 9–10. Haag and Son, USA, 1952.

'Joan Pacey'

This is an upright, strong-growing cultivar with self-branching growth and mid-green leaves. It flowers over a long period and will happily take full sun. The single flowers are medium-sized with a long white tube blushed pink, pink sepals with green tips and a phlox-pink corolla with red veining. It grows well when trained as a half or full standard, or various trained shapes, including an espalier. Half hardy; Zones 9–10. Gadsby, UK, 1977.

'Joy Patmore'

This striking cultivar has medium-sized single flowers with a white tube, waxy white sepals tipped green and a flared carmine corolla. The colour combination of the flowers is very vivid and they stand out well from the mid-green foliage. It has very strong upright growth and will make an

excellent quarter, half or full standard. It will also make a splendid specimen plant, and because of the way it displays its flowers, it will also excel as a summer bedding plant. This cultivar deserves a place in everyone's collection. Half hardy; Zones 9–10. Turner, UK, 1961.

'Katrina Thompsen'

This exhibition-class cultivar bears small to medium single flowers but it compensates for their small size by the sheer number. The flowers have a white-green tube, white sepals and a white corolla. In common with many of the whites, the flower colour will stay white in shade but if exposed to full sun it acquires pink hues. It grows as a vigorous, self-branching and slightly lax bush, excellent as a beautiful quarter standard covered in flowers that stand out against the small, dark green foliage. It is very adaptable and can be trained into various shapes, including a pyramid or column, or simply grown as a pot plant. Beware of fuchsia rust on this cultivar. Half hardy; Zones 9–10. Wilkinson, UK, 1991.

'Kolding Perle'

This is a very vigorous and strong-growing cultivar originating from the Copenhagen area, easy to grow to a large standard in a short space of time. It has quite long inter-nodal joints and is therefore better grown as a full or perhaps a half standard. The medium-sized single flowers have a waxy white tube and sepals, and a pink corolla

shaded with cerise and salmon. The flowers are reminiscent of the Lye cultivars, and it is sometimes confused with 'Lye's Unique'. The leaves are large and light to mid-green. Half hardy; Zones 9–10. Unknown raiser, Denmark, unknown release date.

'Kwintet'

This attractive Dutch cultivar has strong upright, bushy growth with medium-sized light to mid-green foliage that is slightly serrated. The attractive medium-sized and almost self-coloured single flowers have a long, dark rose-red tube, reflexed rose-red sepals and a flared rose-red corolla. Very free-flowering, it makes excellent standards, probably best as a half but strong enough for a full standard. Half hardy; Zones 9–10. van Wieringen, Netherlands, 1970.

'Kwintet'

'Love's Reward'

'Margaret Brown'

'Love's Reward'

The name of this cultivar is very apt – the particularly beautiful flowers caused a huge stir among fuchsia growers when it was first released. It has small to medium single flowers that are almost semi-erect and held off the mid-green foliage. The flower has a pink tube, pink sepals and a violet-blue corolla with red stamens. The growth is short, bushy and self-branching, and it makes a very striking quarter standard. You will need to remove any dead foliage quickly, since this cultivar is prone to botrytis in the branches caused by rotting leaves. You should also be sparing with watering, as it hates water-logging. Half hardy; Zones 9–10. Bambridge, UK, 1986.

'Loeky'

This upright self-branching Dutch cultivar (named after the hybridizer's wife) makes an excellent quarter or half standard. The medium-sized single flowers are very distinctive, with the corolla opening flat like a saucer, rather similar to 'Citation'. The tube and sepals are rose-red, the flat corolla is dark mallow-purple, and it has a very long pistil and long, crimson stamens. The leaves are dark green with a serrated edge. Half hardy; Zones 9–10. de Graaff, Netherlands, 1985.

'Lye's Unique'

This is a very old cultivar and perhaps one of the best-known varieties developed by James Lye. The flower is a hanging,

medium-sized single with a waxy white tube and sepals (both being a trademark of the Lye varieties) and a salmon-orange corolla. It has upright vigorous growth with mid-green leaves, and flowers early, continuing right through the season. Grows easily and quickly to make an impressive half or full standard. Half hardy; Zones 9–10. Lye, UK, 1886.

'Margaret Brown'

This hardy cultivar is probably one of the best fuchsias there is. It has small single flowers with a rose-pink tube and sepals, and a light rose-bengal corolla with light veining. Its growth is vigorous and upright,

'Lye's Unique'

with light green foliage. It makes a splendid quarter or half standard, or you can grow it as a permanently planted shrub in the garden where it will give years of pleasure with its continuous summer and autumn flowering. It was awarded an RHS Highly Commended Certificate for hardiness in 1965. Hardy; Zone 6. Growth 1m (3ft). Wood, UK, 1939.

'Miss California'

This introduction from the USA has medium to large semi-double flowers with a pink tube, long narrow pink sepals and a flared corolla with white, pink-veined petals. It has reasonably vigorous growth with thin wiry stems and a slightly lax habit. The long flowers show up well against the small to medium and rather narrow mid-green leaves, and it is easy to grow to a quarter or half standard. Half hardy; Zones 9–10. Hodges, USA, 1950.

'Mrs Lovell Swisher'

This is an easy and rewarding fuchsia to grow, recommended for beginners. The small to medium single flowers have a long pink tube, green and pinkish-white sepals held just above the horizontal, and a deep rose corolla. The growth is vigorous and upright with mid-green leaves. The tremendous number of flowers produced over a long season makes up for their smaller size. It is easy to grow to a quarter, half or full standard, although it is probably at its best as a half. Half hardy; Zones 9–10. Evans and Reeves, USA, 1942.

'Nancy Lou'

This has beautiful medium to large double flowers with a pink tube, fully reflexed pink sepals with green tips and a very full, brilliant white corolla. The growth is strongly upright with large mid- to dark green serrated leaves, but it needs some pinching to encourage branching. It is well suited to training as a half or even full standard and makes a striking patio pot plant. Half hardy; Zones 9–10. Stubbs, USA, 1971.

'Nellie Nuttall'

This small, showy cultivar is widely used for exhibitions, and when you see it you can understand why. It has small to medium-sized single flowers that are semi-erect and held out from the mid-green foliage. The tube is small and red, the horizontal sepals crimson and the corolla white with red veining. The growth is upright and very bushy, and it makes a superb edging plant, miniature or quarter standard. The growth is probably not vigorous enough to make a larger standard unless you have a lot of patience and can grow it for a few years. It was hybridized from 'Khada' x 'Icecap'. Half hardy; Zones 9–10. Roe, UK, 1977.

'Norfolk Ivor'

This is a strong-growing upright and self-branching cultivar with mid-green foliage and medium to large, semi-double – sometimes fully double – flowers. The buds are fat and pointed, and the flowers

'Nancy Lou'

have a white tube, white sepals with a hint of pink, and a lavender-blue corolla. It is an excellent cultivar to grow as a larger standard and good as a summer bedding plant. Half hardy; Zones 9–10. Goulding, UK, 1984.

'Olive Smith'

This cultivar has small single flowers held semi-erect from the mid-green foliage, with a carmine tube, carmine sepals that curve upward and a crimson corolla. It has vigorous upright self-branching growth, and the sheer number of flowers produced compensates for their small size. It makes

a superb quarter, half or full standard and is often seen at exhibitions trained this way. It also makes a good summer bedding plant. Half hardy; Zones 9–10. Smith, UK, 1991.

'Orwell'

This is a small, compact fuchsia with mid-green foliage that is excellent as a quarter standard or smaller pot plant. The small to medium double flowers have a short tangerine tube and sepals, and a ruffled, darker tangerine-orange corolla. The colour combination is unusual and striking. Half hardy; Zones 9–10. Goulding, UK, 1987.

'Ortenburger Festival'

This cultivar has very striking flowers that really catch the eye, especially when grown as a standard. It has medium-sized bell-shaped single flowers with a short, thick red tube, deep red sepals held just below the horizontal and a violet-blue corolla turning reddish on maturity. The growth is upright, bushy and self-branching, and the leaves are dark green with serrated edges. A very impressive half or full standard, and older specimens have attractive peeling bark. Half hardy; Zones 9–10. Töpperwein, Germany, 1973.

'Nellie Nuttall'

'Olive Smith'

'Paula Jane'

'Paula Jane'

The medium-sized semi-double flowers of this fuchsia have a pink tube, carmine-rose sepals and a beetroot-purple corolla that matures to ruby red and flares open. The flowers stand out against the shiny light to mid-green foliage. It has strong, upright bushy growth, makes an excellent bush and is easy to train as a standard. It is best as a half standard, but can also be grown as a quarter or a full standard. The freely produced pollen deposits on the leaves, which can look messy, and the firmly attached berries need to be cut off to ensure continued flowering. Half hardy; Zones 9–10. Tite, UK, 1975.

'Peppermint Stick'

This cultivar has a rather unusual flower, as suggested by its name. It has medium-sized double hanging flowers with a carmine-rose tube, carmine sepals with a white stripe and a corolla with purple centre petals and light carmine outer petals with a purple edge. It is very floriferous for the size of the flower, and the growth is strongly upright with mid-green foliage. The two-tone flowers display well when growing it as a half standard. It is also a good choice for a pot or bedding plant. Half hardy; Zones 9–10. Walker and Jones, USA, 1950.

'Perky Pink'

This is a strong upright US cultivar that is bushy and very floriferous with rather narrow, slightly serrated mid-green leaves. The medium-sized double flowers have a short pale pink tube, short broad pink sepals with green tips and a white corolla flushed pale pink and pink veining. It is easy to grow as an excellent half standard. Half hardy; Zones 9–10. Erickson and Lewis, USA, 1959.

'Perry Park'

This British cultivar is a strong-growing and self-branching bush that is excellent as a quarter, half or even full standard. The flower is a medium-sized single with a pale pink tube, pink sepals with green tips and a bright rose corolla, the petals becoming paler at the base. The mid-green foliage is of medium size and the cultivar does well as a pot plant or as a summer bedder in the garden. Half hardy; Zones 9–10. Handley, UK, 1977.

'Ridestar'

This fuchsia is excellent when grown as a quarter or half standard. Strong upright and self-branching growth with mid-green oval leaves with a lighter central vein. The flower is a medium to large double with a short red tube, broad red sepals with reflexed tips and a full lavender-blue corolla which fades to a rosy pink on maturity. The buds are very fat and round before they open adding to the attraction. Half hardy; Zones 9–10. Blackwell, UK, 1965.

'Rigoletto'

This cultivar has rather unusually shaped flowers, quite freely produced, given their size. They are medium to large doubles with a short, deep red tube and sepals, and a light purple corolla with petals that have frilled edges and are lighter at the base. The whole flower has an attractive triangular shape, which displays beautifully among the light to mid-green foliage. The upright growth is self-branching, making a good half or full standard. Half hardy; Zones 9–10. Blackwell, UK, 1965.

'Ron Ewart'

This beautiful cultivar, named after a British fuchsia enthusiast and author, is a good upright grower with a self-branching habit. The abundant small single flowers are carried semi-erect and have a white tube and sepals, and a rose-bengal corolla shading to white at the base of the petals. The mid-green foliage is small to medium-sized and a lovely foil for the flower. It excels when grown as any of the smaller sized standards, especially as a quarter standard, and is also good for summer bedding or as a pot plant. Half hardy; Zones 9–10. Roe, UK, 1981.

'Rigoletto'

'Royal Velvet'

'Shelford'

'Royal Velvet'

This cultivar has medium to large double flowers with a crimson red tube and sepals, and a deep purple corolla splashed with red, which flares very widely open on maturity. The growth is vigorous and upright, with bright light to mid-green foliage. It makes an excellent half or even full standard, but needs pinching well to create branching early in the season. A period grown outside to harden up the growth ensures that the branches are strong enough to support the flowers. It really rewards you when you display the flowers at eye level, but also does well as a summer bedder. This is probably one of Waltz's best introductions, although it has some stiff competition. Half hardy; Zones 9–10. Waltz, USA, 1962.

'Schneeball'

This old German cultivar has an upright and bushy, albeit small, growing habit. The semi-double flowers are medium-sized with a reddish-pink tube, long reddish-pink fully reflexed sepals and a white corolla with pink veining, semi-flared with attractive ruffed petals. The small to medium foliage is light to mid-green. It responds well to standard training and is excellent as a quarter standard. Half hardy; Zones 9–10. Twrdy, Germany, 1874.

'Shelford'

This vigorous and very adaptable cultivar has medium-sized single flowers with a baby pink tube, baby pink sepals shading to white and tipped green, and a white corolla. The amount of pink depends on how much sun it receives; kept in the shade it is almost white. It is vigorous, self-branching and upright and makes an excellent quarter or half standard with very little effort. The flowers stand out well from the medium-sized mid- to dark green foliage. In all ways this is an excellent cultivar, which can be used in baskets and as a summer bedding plant. Half hardy; Zones 9–10. Roe, UK, 1986.

'Sleigh Bells'

This is one of the almost pure white cultivars and has medium-sized single flowers with a white tube, white sepals with green tips and a white corolla. The growth is upright and bushy, with mid- to dark green serrated leaves that contrast beautifully with the flowers. It makes a very good half standard and is excellent trained as a pyramid or espalier. Half hardy; Zones 9–10. Schnabel, USA, 1954.

'Sophie Louise'

This is a compact, attractive and floriferous cultivar introduced by Mel Wilkinson. It has small single flowers with a greenish-white tube, white sepals and a vivid dark purple corolla, which hold themselves semi-erect, contrasting well with the small mid-green foliage. It has a bushy, self-branching habit and grows quite well, but will not make a big plant quickly. Grow as a miniature or quarter standard and it will reward you with a tremendous show of flowers. Half hardy; Zones 9–10. Wilkinson, UK, 1999.

'Sophie Louise'

'Tom Thumb'

Introduced over 150 years ago, this small hardy fuchsia is still very popular, having proved itself reliable and easy to grow. It has small single or semi-double flowers with a carmine tube and sepals, and a mauve-carmine veined corolla. The flowers hang down among the small, dark green leaves. It has compact, upright bushy growth and makes a superb miniature or quarter standard. It is equally at home in the rockery or for edging borders. It was awarded an RHS First Class Certificate for hardiness in 1962. Hardy; Zone 6. Growth 46cm (18in). Baudinat, France, 1850.

'Torvill and Dean'

This is a strong, upright growing cultivar named after the famous British ice-dancing couple. It has large double flowers with a pale cerise tube, pale cerise sepals tipped green and a full white corolla flushed cerise with pale cerise veining. The attractive dark green foliage is a perfect foil for the flowers, which stand out beautifully. It makes an impressive sight when trained as a half or full standard, but you need to ensure that the trunk and stems have developed hard wood, otherwise the weight of the flowers can cause branches to break in strong wind and rain. Half hardy; Zones 9–10. Pacey, UK, 1985.

'Tom Thumb'

'Tsjiep'

This Dutch fuchsia, hybridized by Herman de Graaff and named after his son, is a delightful floriferous cultivar for training as a small standard, excelling as a miniature or quarter standard. The small single flowers have a longish cream tube, cream sepals blushed rose and a blood-red corolla maturing to claret. It has attractive light to mid-green foliage, while the growth is upright and bushy. Half hardy; Zones 9–10. de Graaff, Netherlands, 1981.

'Ullswater'

'Ullswater'

With its bushy and upright growth, this makes a good half standard. It has medium to large double flowers with a long pale pink tube, long pale pink sepals and a compact orchid-blue corolla fading to orchid-purple. The medium to large leaves are mid-green, and contrast well against the attractive pastel-coloured flowers. Half hardy; Zones 9–10. Travis, UK, 1958.

'Vanessa Jackson'

This cultivar has long, large single flowers with a salmon-red tube, long salmon-orange sepals and a trumpet-shaped salmon-orange and red corolla. The trailing, self-branching growth, with large mid-green leaves, makes a lovely weeping standard, and it is also ideal for hanging baskets and pots. Half hardy; Zones 9–10. Handley, UK, 1980.

'Vivien Harris'

This strong upright and bushy fuchsia with light to mid-green foliage is easy to train as a standard, excelling as a half standard. It resulted from a cross between 'Rufus' and 'Leverhulme', and inherited characteristics from both parents. The medium-sized Triphylla-type flowers have a long turkey-red tube, short turkey-red sepals and a deeper turkey-red corolla. Half hardy; Zones 9–10. Harris, UK, 1977.

'Torvill and Dean'

'Waltzing Matilda'

Named after the famous Australian folk song, this cultivar grows as a lax bush with light green, red-veined foliage. The flower buds are large and pointed, and the large double flowers have a pale pink tube, sepals that are light pink on top but darker underneath and a full, pale pink corolla with the outer petals streaked with rose. It is easy to train as a semi-weeping standard – the taller the better because of the flower size – and excellent for use in a container. Half hardy; Zones 9–10. Bromat, Australia, 1989.

'WALZ Kalebas'

This is an easily grown, bushy, multi-flowering cultivar with dull green foliage. The medium-sized single flowers have an unusual rose-red, rather pear-shaped tube, rose-red sepals with yellow-green tips curved upwards and a mid-red corolla. It is easy to grow as a quarter or half standard, and the unusual shape of the flowers makes it rather striking. Half hardy; Zones 9–10. Waldenmaier, Netherlands, 1990.

'Wigan Peer'

This is a relative newcomer, with small to medium-sized compact double flowers with a pink tube, white sepals flushed pale pink and a full white corolla. It is a strong

'WALZ Kalebas'

upright, self-branching fuchsia with mid-green foliage, and makes a good quarter or half standard. It is also an excellent pot plant because of the abundant, long-lasting flowers. Half hardy; Zones 9–10. Clark, UK, 1988.

'Winston Churchill'

This lovely free-flowering double-flowered cultivar has medium-sized compact blooms with a pink tube and sepals, and a lavender-blue corolla with reddish veins. It has upright and bushy self-branching

'Wigan Peer'

'Winston Churchill'

growth with wiry stems and rather narrow small mid- to dark green foliage. It makes a very nice quarter or half standard, and also makes a good pot plant. It is a good, reliable cultivar. Half hardy; Zones 9–10. Garson, USA, 1942.

'Yuletide'

This large double of American origin has similar flowers to 'Swingtime', but even larger in size. The flower has a red tube, broad red sepals, held slightly above the horizontal with reflexed tips and a full creamy white corolla with red veining. The growth is upright and self-branching and can be grown to a very good larger standard. Take care to support well when young, as the weight of the flowers can cause young branches to be torn off. Half hardy; Zones 9–10. Tiret, USA, 1948.

'Zaanlander'

This vigorous cultivar has strong upright growth and mid-green foliage, and is easy to train as a standard. The medium-sized single flowers have a longish pink tube flushed white, narrow orchid-pink sepals and a violet-purple corolla with white patches at the base of the petals. The abundant flowers mean it also looks good in a patio container but better in a shaded or part shaded location. Half hardy; Zones 9–10. Krom, Netherlands, 1989.

Trained structures

Fuchsia structures such as pyramids and fans are a challenge to grow but very satisfying when they are complete. It is best to overwinter them in green leaf with minimal heat to ensure that all parts of the structure will start to grow evenly again in the spring.

'Amy Lye'
This fuchsia is a cultivar bred by James Lye, who was one of the earliest producers to grow fuchsia pyramids. It is free- and early-flowering, with medium-sized single flowers that have a creamy white tube, white sepals tipped green and a coral-orange corolla. The growth is vigorous and spreading with medium-sized dark green leaves and is good for training as any tall structure such as a pillar or pyramid. Half hardy; Zones 9–10. Lye, UK, 1885.

'Beacon Rosa'
A sport from 'Beacon', this fuchsia inherits the same growth and similar darkish green leaves with wavy serrated edges, but with different flowers. They are medium-sized single flowers with a pink tube, pink sepals and a flared pink corolla with red veining on the petals. This cultivar is excellent for training as a fan, pyramid or standard,

'Beacon Rosa'

'Brutus'

and is a good garden hardy. Branches can occasionally partially revert to the darker flower colours of the parent; you need to cut these out at the point of origin or they will gradually take over the whole plant. Hardy; Zones 6–7. Growth 60cm (2ft). Bürgi and Ott, Switzerland, 1972.

'Berkeley'
Named after the city of Berkeley in California, this has large double flowers with a red-striped pale rose tube, large pale rose recurved sepals and a violet-pink corolla with salmon-pink at the base of the petals. The growth is vigorously upright but slightly lax, with mid- to dark green foliage. It is very floriferous for a large double, and is suitable to grow as a pyramid or similar trained shape. Half hardy; Zones 9–10. Reiter, USA, 1955.

'Brutus'
This is a vigorous hardy cultivar, which is very floriferous and bushy. It has wiry, arching growth with medium-sized mid-green foliage. The flowers are single but can often contain extra petaloids, making them into a semi-double; they have a rich cerise tube and sepals and a dark purple corolla. The manner of growth allows training to almost any shape, but this

'Ellen Morgan'

plant excels when trained as a pyramid, looking like a Christmas tree with lots of sparkling decorations. It is an adaptable cultivar, also trainable as a pillar, espalier or standard. Hardy; Zones 6–7. Growth 65cm (26in). Bull, UK, 1901.

'Crosby Soroptimist'
The medium-sized single flowers of this fuchsia have a short pink tube, long reflexed pink sepals and a short, white corolla with burgundy anthers and stigma. The pure colours of the flowers beautifully complement the medium-sized dark green foliage and the growth is upright, bushy and slightly wiry. It is excellent for growing upright, trained shapes and easy to grow as a bush or standard. Half hardy; Zones 9–10. Clark, UK, 1989.

'Ellen Morgan'
This seedling from 'Phyllis' has good upright self-branching growth that is excellent for growing trained shapes, standards and even to use as a bedding plant. The medium-sized double flowers have a short, thin white tube with green stripes, white sepals with green tips and a flaring mallow-purple corolla, with rose at the petal base and rose veining. Half hardy; Zones 9–10. Holmes, UK, 1976.

'Fuchsiade '88'

Named after a Dutch fuchsia festival, this has upright self-branching growth, small dark green leaves and an abundance of small single flowers with a reddish-purple tube, reddish-purple sepals that are lighter underneath and a dark purple quarter-flared corolla. It is very adaptable and easily trained into various smaller-scale shapes. Half hardy; Zones 9–10. de Graaff, Netherlands, 1989.

'Harlow Carr'

This is a very floriferous cultivar, suitable for growing smaller-scale trained shapes. It has slightly lax, upright, self-branching bushy growth with small, dark green leaves against which the flowers make a good contrast. The flowers are medium-sized singles with a pale pink tube, medium-length, recurving pink sepals and a white corolla with red anthers. It grows very easily to make an attractive small to medium-sized pyramid or pillar, and is also worth trying as a small fan. Half hardy; Zones 9–10. Johns, UK, 1991.

'James Lye'

This old British cultivar, named after the grower himself, has perfectly shaped medium-sized double flowers with a cerise tube, cerise sepals held horizontally and a bluish-mauve corolla that is pale mauve at

'Harlow Carr'

the base of the petals. The growth is strongly upright with medium-sized mid-green foliage, and it is easily trained into tall shapes such as pyramids, pillars and standards. It is sometimes confused with 'Constance', another of Lye's cultivars. Half hardy; Zones 9–10. Lye, UK, 1883.

'Lillian Annetts'

This fuchsia quickly became very popular after its introduction because of its beautiful flowers and tremendous versatility. The flower is a small to medium double with a white tube striped green,

white sepals and a lavender-blue corolla with patches of white and pink at the base of the petals. The upright lax growth is short-jointed and bushy, with small to medium mid-green foliage. This cultivar can be grown to most shapes, but it really excels as a fan. It is very floriferous and continues to flower over a long period. Half hardy; Zones 9–10. Clark, UK, 1993.

'Lindisfarne'

Named after the tidal island off the coast of Northumberland in the UK, this has small, semi-double flowers with a short, thick, pale pink tube, pale pink sepals held horizontally and a deep violet-blue corolla that holds its colour well. The growth is upright, short-jointed and self-branching, with small to medium-sized bright mid-green foliage. It is terrific for most types of trained shapes, excelling as a pyramid, pillar or standard. Half hardy; Zones 9–10. Ryle and Atkinson, UK, 1974.

'Little Beauty'

This is aptly named, with its small to medium-sized single flowers sparking among the small, dark green foliage. The flower has a pinkish-red tube and sepals and the corolla is lavender-blue. The wiry, slightly brittle growth makes a good pyramid or pillar. Half hardy; Zones 9–10. Raiser and date unknown.

'Lillian Annetts'

'Little Beauty'

'Marin Glow'

'Marin Glow'

This impressive fuchsia has medium-sized single flowers with a short white tube, white sepals with green tips and an imperial-purple corolla fading to magenta. The striking flowers seem to glow, standing out from the medium-sized mid-green serrated leaves. This cultivar is free-flowering, with upright and self-branching growth, and makes a very good pyramid or pillar, or a half or full standard. It is better to grow it in partial shade, as the sun will cause the corolla colour to fade. Half hardy; Zones 9–10. Reedstrom, USA, 1954.

'Melody'

This free-flowering US cultivar is an easy grower and has strong, upright bushy growth with attractive, bright green foliage. The medium-sized single flowers have a pale rose-pink tube, pale rose-pink reflexed sepals and a pale cyclamen-purple corolla. It excels when grown as a trained shape and makes a very good standard. Half hardy; Zones 9–10. Reiter, USA, 1942.

'Midwinter'

This is a smaller-growing cultivar which can be used for small pyramids, fans or standards. It has small to medium single flowers with a white tube veined with pink and white sepals, and a white corolla, inspiring its name. The growth is upright, slightly lax and self-branching, with dull, dark green foliage. Take care with the watering of this cultivar as it despises being overwatered. Half hardy; Zones 9–10. Flemming, UK, 1990.

'Mrs Marshall'

This very old cultivar is still widely grown today. It has medium-sized single flowers with a waxy cream-white tube and sepals, and a rose-cerise corolla. The growth is vigorous and upright with medium-sized mid-green foliage. It makes a very nice pyramid-trained plant, and is also good as a standard. When first introduced, it was named 'Grand Duchess Marie'. Half hardy; Zones 9–10. Jones, UK, probably introduced in 1862.

'Phyllis'

This strong-growing upright cultivar has an abundance of small semi-double flowers with a waxy rose tube and sepals, and a rosy cerise corolla. It has a tendency to produce flowers with more than four sepals. The growth is very vigorous with shiny mid-green foliage, and it is easily trained to excellent large pyramids and standards. It is a superb variety to use as a hedge up to 1–1.3m (3–4ft) high because of its hardy nature and growth habit. It was introduced by H.A. Brown, but according to Leo Boullemier the seedling's origin was from continental Europe. Hardy; Zone 6. Brown, UK, 1938.

'President George Bartlett'

Named after a former president of the British Fuchsia Society, this has small to medium-sized semi-double flowers with a burgundy-red tube and sepals, and a dark aubergine corolla, fading with age. The growth is upright and vigorous with a slightly lax habit, and the foliage is a glossy dark green. It is a very adaptable fuchsia – training to virtually any shape is possible, but it is particularly good as a fan, pyramid or standard. It is also very suitable for growing in hanging baskets or pots. Half hardy; Zones 9–10. Bielby and Oxtoby, UK, 1997.

'Midwinter'

'Phyllis'

'Sir Alfred Ramsey'

This fuchsia is named after England's World Cup winning football team manager, who was also a past president of the East Anglian Fuchsia Fellowship. It has large single flowers with a rose tube, neyron-rose sepals with recurved tips and a quarter-flared corolla that opens violet-purple and matures to violet-red. It has strong, upright self-branching growth with large, attractive light green leaves, and is good for all tall-trained forms, most especially pyramids and standards. Half hardy; Zones 9–10. Goulding, UK, 1984.

'Snowcap'

This is a very easy cultivar to grow, strongly recommended to anyone new to growing fuchsias, as well as those wanting to train an upright shape for the first time. The flowers are medium-sized semi-doubles with a bright red tube and sepals and a white-veined red fluffy corolla. The growth is vigorous, upright and self-branching, with small to medium dark green foliage, and it is very floriferous, with the flowers standing out well from a distance. It can be trained into most upright forms – pillar, pyramid, conical or espalier – and is also very good as a standard or a permanent planting. It works well as a quarter, half or full standard, but best as a half or full. Since it is not at all lax, it does not work well as a fan or in a hanging basket. Hardy; Zones 7–8. Growth 60cm (2ft). Henderson, UK, 1888.

'WALZ Bella'

'Suikerbossie' ('Sugarbush')

This cultivar has upright, self-branching growth. Left to its own devices it will form a natural conical shape, making it a good choice for training into small pyramids, conicals and pillars. It is extremely floriferous with small single flowers with a light green tube flushed pink, empire-rose sepals with green tips and a lilac-violet corolla. The large number of flowers sometimes hides the small, dark olive-green leaves, which are lighter underneath. Half hardy; Zones 9–10. Brouwer, Netherlands, 1985.

'Vivienne Thompson'

This attractive cultivar has medium, upright, self-branching growth with small light to mid-green foliage, and

'Waveney Gem'

is an excellent choice for training any of the upright shapes. The flowers are medium-sized semi-doubles with a pink tube, half-reflexed pink sepals with a neyron rose edge and green tips, and a white corolla veined with neyron-rose. It flowers over a long period and is best in partial shade. Half hardy; Zones 9–10. Reynolds, UK, 1983.

'WALZ Bella'

This strong-growing Dutch cultivar has large, ovate leaves in mid-green with serrated edges and magenta stems. The medium-sized single flowers have a long, thick orange tube, mandarin-orange sepals held downwards and a scarlet corolla, which matures to orange-rose. Its upright growth habit lends it to training into tall, upright shapes, especially standards and pillars. Half hardy; Zones 9–10. Waldenmaier, Netherlands, 1987.

'Waveney Gem'

This cultivar is strong-growing, self-branching and slightly lax with small mid-green leaves. It is very versatile and can be used in baskets or trained as pyramids, conicals, pillars, fans and standards. It excels when trained into a fan shape. The small to medium single flowers have a white tube and sepals, and a mauve corolla. This free-flowering fuchsia is quite quick to come into flower after a final pinch and is well worth a place in any collection. Half hardy; Zones 9–10. Burns, UK, 1985.

'Snowcap'

Hanging baskets and pots

Fuchsias commercially sold as basket cultivars have growth that is lax, trailing or cascading. Those with lax growth tend to have large double flowers, with the weight of the flowers bending down the branches; these types are particularly spectacular.

'Ada Perry'

This is one of many wonderful large, double-flowered trailing cultivars hybridized by the Americans – Annabelle Stubbs being one of the greatest exponents of this art. This cultivar has a rather stiff habit, with large dark green leaves that are distinctively red-veined. The large double flowers have a scarlet tube and sepals with a darker shade underneath and a full blue-purple corolla, streaked with rose. It is ideal for hanging baskets but also makes a splendid weeping half or full standard. It is rather tender and needs a heated greenhouse over the winter to stay at its best. Frost tender; Zone 11. Stubbs, USA, 1983.

'Allure'

This Dutch introduction has large double flowers with a very long, thin, ivory-white tube, white sepals flushed pink, which are semi-recurving, and a full pink corolla.

'Auntie Jinks'

'Allure'

The foliage is mid-green and the growth quite vigorous. This cultivar does not flourish in full sun, faring better when grown in semi-shade. Half hardy; Zones 9–10. Moerman, Netherlands, 1991.

'Annabelle Stubbs'

Named after the famous US hybridizer, this cultivar certainly should be special. The flowers are large full doubles with a light pink tube, coral-pink sepals and a reddish-purple corolla. The foliage is large and mid-green, and the fuchsia is excellent in hanging baskets where the large double flowers are an impressive sight. Half hardy; Zones 9–10. Riley, USA, 1991.

'Auntie Jinks'

This trailing fuchsia should be in every collection because it is so adaptable and can be used in a variety of garden sites. The medium-sized single flowers have a pink-red tube with stripes, white sepals and a cerise-purple corolla with paler patches at the base of the petals. The colour of the corolla fades as the flower matures. It is extremely floriferous, with the pointed buds looking very attractive against the small mid-green foliage. Use it in hanging baskets, hanging pots or to trail over the edge of a container. It also makes

a small weeping standard and can be used for other smaller trained shapes. Half hardy; Zones 9–10. Wilson, UK, 1970.

'Baby Pink'

This very pretty fuchsia from the USA has lovely trailing growth ideally suited to hanging baskets. The dark green leaves have a red central vein, green veins and red stems. It is surprisingly floriferous considering the size of the flowers, which are medium to large doubles, and are almost Triphylla-like, with a long white tube tinged green. The sepals are light pink with green tips that cup the corolla, first curving down and then up; the corolla is very full and tight, pale pink with dark pink veins. Half hardy; Zones 9–10. Soo Yun, USA, 1976.

'Blowick'

This cultivar is an adaptable plant that you can train to almost any shape, and makes an excellent basket. It has the growth habit of a lax bush with mid-green foliage and very pretty medium-sized single flowers. The flowers have a flesh pink tube and sepals and a mallow-purple corolla fading to an attractive shade of plum with age. This cultivar is also easy to train as a standard, with perhaps a half standard being the best. Half hardy; Zones 9–10. Porter, UK, 1984.

'Baby Pink'

'Blush of Dawn'

'Blue Butterfly'

This is excellent for hanging baskets because of its lax growth covered in dark green foliage. The medium to large semi-double flowers have a short white tube, broad white sepals and a deep violet-blue corolla splashed white that opens on maturity to reveal the lighter blue inner petals. Half hardy; Zones 9–10. Waltz, USA, 1960.

'Blush of Dawn'

This exceptional cultivar is not a true trailer but has the growth habit of a lax bush, with mid-green foliage and the weight of the large double flowers bending the branches down. The flowers appear quite late in the season but are worth waiting for. They have a waxy white tube, reflexed waxy white sepals tipped green and a full corolla in an unusual silver-grey and lavender-blue. It is excellent grown in hanging baskets, half baskets or as a half standard. Half hardy; Zones 9–10. Martin, USA, 1962.

'Caradella'

This cultivar has a striking flower that really catches the eye against the trailing mid- to dark green foliage. The medium single flowers have a pink tube and sepals and a violet-pink corolla. It is extremely free-flowering. While it is well worth growing in all sorts of hanging containers, it really excels in hanging pots. Half hardy; Zones 9–10. Delaney, UK, 1992.

'Cascade'

This cultivar is true to its name, with long cascading growths bearing many flowers at the ends. The flower is a medium single with a thin white tube flushed carmine, thin white sepals flushed carmine, which are

'Claudia'

held at the horizontal, and a deep carmine corolla. The foliage is medium to large mid-green and serrated. It is a very good cultivar for mixed baskets and can also be grown on its own, although it tends not to flower much on the top of the basket. Half hardy; Zones 9–10. Lagen, USA, 1937.

'Cecile'

This is a very large double-flowering cultivar which has plenty of flowers for its flower size. The flowers have a pink tube, broad deep pink-red sepals and a lavender-blue corolla that is very full and frilled. The foliage is light mid-green, and the flowers and fat pointed buds stand out from this beautifully. This is a deservedly popular cultivar and well worth growing on its own or in a mixed basket. Half hardy; Zones 9–10. Whitfield, USA, 1981.

'Claudia'

This newish trailing cultivar, with light to mid-green foliage and vigorous self-branching growth, is good for hanging baskets and mixed containers. It is very floriferous over a long period, with medium-sized double flowers with a light rose tube and sepals, and an orchid-pink corolla. Half hardy; Zones 9–10. Sinton, UK, 2000.

'Cecile'

'Dancing Flame'

This cultivar has a rather unusual and distinctive flower colouring. The flowers are often smaller and semi-double at first, but after a short period of flowering, they change to a medium-sized double. The tube is pale orange with darker stripes, the sepals are orange and darker underneath, and the corolla is orange-carmine, with the petal colour darker in the centre. It has stiff trailing growth with rather large mid- to dark green leaves, which set off the flower colour well. This fuchsia is ideal for use in mixed baskets. Half hardy; Zones 9–10. Stubbs, USA, 1981.

'Dee Star'

This Australian cultivar is a natural trailer with mid-green foliage and an added advantage of a long flowering season. The flower is a large double with a medium to long greenish-white tube that takes on a pink flush with more exposure to the sun, long rose-white sepals and a violet corolla maturing to reddish-violet-purple. It is an excellent cultivar to use in hanging baskets and mixed containers. Half hardy; Zones 9–10. Richardson, Australia, 1986.

'Deep Purple'

'Dancing Flame'

'Deep Purple'

This is a large-flowered basket cultivar from the USA with a spreading, trailing habit and medium-sized mid-green foliage. The large double flower has a medium-length white tube, white recurving sepals and a very full, dark purple corolla, which matures to purple on aging. It has a lovely colour contrast between the sepals, corolla and the leaf colour. It is excellent for use in a baskets or hanging containers, and with care can be grown to a weeping standard. Half hardy; Zones 9–10. Garrett, USA, 1989.

'Devonshire Dumpling'

This aptly named fuchsia freely produces large, fat double flowers that are superb in a hanging basket. Each flower emerges from a large, fat, slightly pointed bud and has a medium-length white tube and broad neyron-rose sepals that reflex strongly when the flower is fully open. The corolla is large and fluffy, with the outer white petals flushed pink and the inner petals white. The foliage is medium-sized and mid-green and although the growth is quite stiff, the huge quantities of large blooms cause the branches to bend down. The flowering period is surprisingly long for such a large flower. Half hardy; Zones 9–10. Hilton, UK, 1981.

'Ebbtide'

This unusual cultivar has vigorous, cascading growth, mid-green foliage and red wiry stems. It is an early-flowering cultivar, and the large white pointed buds open to reveal a large double flower, the tube changing from white to deep pink just before the flower opens. The sepals are white on top and pink beneath, and the light blue and pink corolla opens very wide and matures to lavender-pink. Half hardy; Zones 9–10. Erickson and Lewis, USA, 1959.

'Emma Louise'

This cultivar is superb in a hanging pot, producing abundant, flower-covered growth. The small to medium-sized double flowers have a pink tube and sepals and a powder blue and pale pink full corolla. The foliage is small and mid-green, and the growth is trailing and self-branching. It is also very good for mixed baskets and containers. Half hardy; Zones 9–10. Horsham, UK, 1990.

'Emma Louise'

'Eusebia'

'Falling Stars'

'Eureka Red'
This beautiful fuchsia is ideal for mixed hanging baskets and containers. It has large double flowers with a lovely two-tone colour. They have a greenish-white tube, deep rose sepals and a red or red-purple corolla that flares fully when mature. The medium to large foliage is dark green and the growth quite vigorous. Half hardy; Zones 9–10. Stubbs, USA, 1991.

'Eusebia'
This is a beautiful double-flowering cultivar from Annabelle Stubbs, named after one of her sisters. With rather stiff trailing or semi-trailing vigorous growth and plenty of medium to large double flowers, it is terrific in hanging baskets. The flowers have a greenish-white tube, white sepals with carmine splashes and a carmine-red corolla with white streaks on the petals. The foliage is an attractive mid-green. It makes an elegant weeping standard. Half hardy; Zones 9–10. Stubbs, USA, 1982.

'Falling Stars'
The classically shaped flowers of this fuchsia cascade off the trailing growth with its large mid-green leaves. The medium-sized single flowers have a pinkish-red tube, reddish-pink sepals and red corolla. It makes a superb half basket but also grows well in hanging baskets and pots. It can also be trained as a weeping half or full standard. Pinch it out well early on, because it is not a naturally self-branching cultivar. Half hardy; Zones 9–10. Reiter, USA, 1941.

'Fey'
This Australian cultivar has lax but stiff, trailing growth and light to mid-green foliage. It is excellent for hanging baskets, containers or as a weeping standard. The flowers are medium to large doubles with a white tube, slightly twisted white sepals and a full lilac corolla with the petals held tightly together, contrasting nicely with the foliage. Half hardy; Zones 9–10. Lockerbie, Australia, 1970.

'Frank Unsworth'
This is an excellent cultivar in hanging pots, small hanging baskets and mixed containers. It has short-jointed vigorous growth with a lax self-branching habit and small dark green leaves. The double flowers are small to medium-sized with a full white tube, white sepals with green tips and a white corolla with a hint of pink at the petal base. The flowers stay white even in sun, but gradually take on extra hints of pink. Half hardy; Zones 9–10. Clark, UK, 1982.

'Frosted Flame'
This cultivar is a natural trailer that makes a superb full or half basket. The medium-sized single flowers have a white tube and sepals, and a distinctive barrel-shaped flame-red corolla. The petals have a darker edge and are lighter towards the base. The medium-sized foliage is bright green and the growth strong. Pinch it well early on to get the best shape. Half hardy; Zones 9–10. Hanley, UK, 1975.

'Frosted Flame'

'Gerharda's Aubergine'

'Golden Marinka'

'Gerharda's Aubergine'

This stiff trailing cultivar introduced from the Netherlands has small to medium-sized single flowers. The tube and sepals are aubergine and the corolla is an aubergine colour that is very dark on opening, maturing to beetroot-red. It is a vigorous cultivar with mid- to dark green leaves that makes an excellent hanging basket or hanging pot. The colours are well set off by growing it with white or light pink fuchsias. Half hardy; Zones 9–10. de Graaff, Netherlands, 1989.

'Gloria Johnson'

This unusual trailing cultivar has very large flowers, 10cm (4in) long, which are extremely eye-catching. The single flowers have a long pink tube, long thin pale pink sepals held out below the horizontal and a bright rose corolla. The foliage is mid-green and the growth is strong with a vigorous trailing habit. If you want to try something different in a basket that looks a bit out of the ordinary look no further. This cultivar will turn heads. Half hardy; Zones 9–10. Bielby and Oxtoby, UK, 1994.

'Golden Anniversary'

This is a superb and very popular cultivar from Annabelle Stubbs that is good for hanging baskets, but you can also use it in other containers, both on its own and with other plants, and as a weeping standard. The flowers are medium to large full doubles with a greenish-white tube, broad white sepals and a dark violet corolla that fades to rich ruby. The medium to large foliage is light golden-green and provides a beautiful foil to the flowers. Half hardy; Zones 9–10. Stubbs, USA, 1980.

'Golden Marinka'

This is a sport from the famous basket cultivar 'Marinka', and probably one of the best trailing fuchsias with variegated foliage. The medium-sized single flowers are similar to the parent, with the tube, sepals and corolla being similar shades of red, contrasting well with the yellow, green and red foliage. Growth is not quite as vigorous as 'Marinka', but it is excellent for baskets and mixed containers. The best foliage colours develop with good exposure to the sun. Half hardy; Zones 9–10. Weber, USA, 1955.

'Greg Walker'

This Australian cultivar has lax spreading growth and is beautiful in a hanging basket, but you can also grow it as a pot plant supported by canes. The medium-sized double flowers have a white tube striped with carmine-rose, white-carmine sepals and a full violet corolla with red splashes. The new foliage is light green but matures to mid-green later in the season. Half hardy; Zones 9–10. Richardson, Australia, 1982.

'Harry Grey'

This fuchsia should be in everyone's collection, and is very adaptable in use. The small double flowers have a rose pink-streaked tube, white sepals and a fluffy white corolla, but the colours will become pale pink in the sun. The foliage is small, dark green and very dense on the vigorous self-branching wiry growth. It produces flowers as freely as a single-flowered cultivar, often starting to flower eight to nine weeks after the final pinching. It is suitable for all sorts of hanging containers, either planted in groups together or mixed with other plants. It will also make a good mini or quarter standard, or other smaller trained shapes. Half hardy; Zones 9–10. Dunnett, UK, 1980.

'Harry Grey'

'Haute Cuisine'

'Holly's Beauty'

'Haute Cuisine'

This wonderful Dutch cultivar is worth planting for its flowers and foliage, even though the growth is a bit untidy. The flowers are medium to large doubles with a dark red tube and sepals, and a wonderful dark aubergine corolla with red anthers and pistil. They make a striking contrast against the medium to large pale to mid-green foliage. The best description of the growth is strong, spreading and lax. It is good for mixed baskets and containers, and makes a lovely weeping standard. Half hardy; Zones 9–10. de Graaff, Netherlands, 1988.

'Hermiena'

This is an excellent, floriferous, self-branching cultivar that is ideal for hanging pots, small hanging baskets and mixed containers. The single flowers are small to medium-sized with both the tube and sepals in white with a hint of pink, and the corolla opening dark violet and maturing to dark plum, nicely contrasting with the small mid-green foliage. It does best with some shade and dislikes being over-watered. Half hardy; Zones 9–10. van Lavieren, Netherlands, 1987.

'Holly's Beauty'

This has large double flowers with a white tube, white sepals flushed pale rose and a pale lavender-lilac full corolla, an extremely pretty, unusual colour. The growth is trailing, with light to mid-green foliage, and it is very attractive in hanging baskets and containers. The colour looks superb blended with other blues and whites in a mixed basket. It resulted from a cross between 'Quasar' and 'Applause', and when first released it was subject to a trademark in California. Half hardy; Zones 9–10. Garrett, USA, 1989.

'Imperial Fantasy'

This is a very impressive and striking US cultivar, with trailing growth suitable for hanging baskets or containers. The large double flowers have a greenish-white tube, white sepals with a hint of red at the base and a full purple corolla with the outer petals splashed with white and pink patches. The leaves are large and dark green with distinctive red veins. Half hardy; Zones 9–10. Stubbs, USA, 1981.

'Intercity'

This trailing cultivar has medium-sized single flowers with a white tube, white sepals flushed pink with green tips and a lilac corolla with scalloped edges to the petals. The flowers are a nice contrast with the mid-green foliage, and this fuchsia is easy to grow in hanging baskets and does well in mixed containers. Half hardy; Zones 9–10. Strümper, Germany, 1986.

'Irene Sinton'

This cultivar, named after the hybridizer's sister-in-law, has large double flowers with a blush-pink tube and sepals, and a pale lilac corolla splashed pink with red veining on the petals. It has semi-lax growth with small to medium-sized mid-green leaves. It grows well in hanging baskets and hanging pots. It is prone to botrytis, so guard against stagnant, humid air around it, and do not overwater, especially in the early stages. Half hardy; Zones 9–10. Sinton, UK, 2004.

'Irene Sinton'

'Jack Shahan'

'Jess'

'Jack Shahan'

This rather stiff trailing fuchsia is one that has maintained its popularity over a number of years. It is very good for baskets, half baskets and even as a weeping standard. The flower is almost a self-coloured medium to large single with quite a long pale rose-bengal tube and rose-bengal sepals and corolla. The narrow leaves are mid-green and serrated. The growth can be a little wild, but it flowers continuously over a long period. Half hardy; Zones 9–10. Tiret, USA, 1949.

'Jane Humber'

The weight of the flowers of this cultivar causes the stems to bend down enough to overcome its stiff growth habit, making it effective in a hanging basket or container. The large double flowers have a pink tube, with broad pink sepals held slightly above the horizontal and a full rose-purple corolla with slightly darker petal edges. The foliage is mid-green while the very round fat buds are pink, adding to the attraction. Half hardy; Zones 9–10. Bielby, UK, 1983.

'Janice Ann'

This is a rather lax self-branching plant, which does well in hanging containers and makes a very nice hanging pot. The single flowers are small to medium with a turkey-red tube and sepals and a violet-blue corolla with bright pink anthers and pistil. The flowers stand out well on the dark green foliage and often appear to sparkle,

particularly if the container is in a shady position, catching the ambient light. It makes an excellent standard and is worth growing as trained shapes, especially as a fan or a small pyramid. Half hardy; Zones 9–10. Holmes, UK, 1994.

'Jess'

Vigorous and lax, this fuchsia is very floriferous and is ideal in hanging baskets or hanging pots. The flowers are medium-sized singles with a long, quite thin rose tube, broad deep rose sepals and a vivid cerise corolla. The medium-sized leaves

are mid-green and shiny, and the fat round flower buds add an extra attraction to the display. Half hardy; Zones 9–10. Meier, UK, 1987.

'Jimmy Carr'

This double cultivar has a good cascading habit, making it suitable for all kinds of hanging containers. The flowers are medium-sized doubles with a white-striped pink tube, horizontal white sepals with a hint of pink and a full purple corolla maturing to magenta, with light splashes at the base of the petals. It is quite free-flowering, and the flower colours contrast well with the medium-sized mid-green foliage. Half hardy; Zones 9–10. Rowell, UK, 1989.

'Joy Bielby'

This is an excellent lax, self-branching cultivar giving a good show in hanging baskets and hanging containers, inheriting its characteristics from its parents, 'Swingtime' and 'Blush o' Dawn'. The double flowers are medium to large with a white-streaked red tube, white sepals blushed with pink, tipped green and a white corolla flushed rose. The foliage is mid-green. Half hardy; Zones 9–10. Bielby, UK, 1982.

'Janice Ann'

'Julie Horton'

A large lax semi-double flowered trailing fuchsia which is excellent trained as a basket and still widely grown today. The large flowers have a medium-length pink tube, pink sepals held curled up against the tube with green tips. The corolla is a delightful shade of pale pink with large overlapping petals. The flowers contrast well against the dark green foliage which has a leathery appearance. Half hardy; Zones 9–10. Gagnon, USA, 1962.

'Kathy Louise'

This US cultivar is excellent in hanging containers. It has quite vigorous trailing growth with dark green glossy leaves. It is not especially self-branching and therefore needs plenty of early pinching. The flowers are large doubles with a longish carmine-red tube, carmine sepals with green tips and a soft rose corolla. It is quite heat-tolerant. Half hardy; Zones 9–10. Antonelli, USA, 1963.

'Kegworth Carnival'

This has the growth habit of a lax bush and is therefore ideal for hanging baskets and containers, or to grow as a pot plant with cane supports. The flowers are medium-sized doubles with a white tube,

'Kit Oxtoby'

long white sepals that are quite thin and a Tyrian-purple corolla changing to rose-purple as it ages. It has medium-sized mid-green foliage and is very floriferous. Half hardy; Zones 9–10. Smith, UK, 1990.

'Kit Oxtoby'

This has a good trailing habit, with medium to large double flowers. The tube is neyron-rose, as are the rather broad, horizontal

sepals, while the rose-coloured corolla has darker edges to the petals. It is a vigorous grower with medium-sized mid-green foliage, and is quite floriferous given the size of the flowers. Half hardy; Zones 9–10. Beilby and Oxtoby, UK, 1990.

'Kiwi'

This is a US cultivar with lax growth and an abundance of large double flowers. Each flower has a long greenish-white tube, white sepals with green tips and a rose-coloured corolla with pale pink splashes on the petals. The medium-sized mid-green serrated leaves provide a good foil for the flower colours and it is an excellent cultivar to use in mixed baskets. Half hardy; Zones 9–10. Tiret, USA, 1966.

'Kon Tiki'

This floriferous cultivar has rather wiry growth with small to medium dark green leaves and makes a nice hanging pot, but is also amenable to growing in baskets and containers. The medium double flowers have a white tube, white sepals flushed pink and a violet corolla with pink patches at the base of the petals. It is not the easiest cultivar to find, but is well worth the search. Half hardy; Zones 9–10. Tiret, USA, 1965.

'Kegworth Carnival'

'Kon Tiki'

'La Campanella'

This free-flowering cultivar is very versatile, with wiry trailing self-branching growth with small mid-green leaves. It is best to pinch it well early on. It is good in hanging baskets, hanging pots and containers, and will also make an attractive small standard. The flowers are small to medium semi-doubles, with a white tube, white sepals flushed pink and an imperial purple corolla that matures to magenta. It has been widely used for hybridization, especially in the Netherlands. Half hardy; Zones 9–10. Blackwell, UK, 1968.

'Lady in Grey'

This makes a lax, bushy shape with mid-green serrated leaves, and you can use it in hanging baskets or containers. It is tricky to grow, needs a cool area and is quite late to flower, but the unusual colour combination is well worth the effort. The flowers are large doubles with a greenish-white tube, white sepals flushed pink with green tips and a grey-blue to mauve corolla, maturing to lavender, with pink veins and splashes on the petals. Half hardy; Zones 9–10. Lockerbie, Australia, 1988.

'Lady Kathleen Spence'

This is a very pretty cultivar with wiry lax growth, making it easy to grow in hanging containers, and it is also useful

'Lady Kathleen Spence'

for weeping standards or trained shapes. The flowers are medium-sized singles with a white tube blushed with pale pink, long thin sepals that are rose-white on top and darker underneath, and a pale lavender corolla fading to light lilac. It is very free-flowering with medium-sized mid-green foliage. Half hardy; Zones 9–10. Ryle, UK, 1974.

'Land van Beveren'

This vigorous sun-loving trailing cultivar does well in all sorts of hanging containers, and grows extremely well in a half basket.

An easy plant for the beginner to grow, it is very floriferous and has medium single flowers with a long waxy white tube, waxy white sepals and a dark carmine corolla. The foliage is medium-sized and mid-green. It is vigorous enough to make a good half or full weeping standard. Half hardy; Zones 9–10. Saintenoy, Netherlands, 1988.

'Lovely Linda'

This cultivar has a lax self-branching habit. It is easy to grow and ideal for hanging pots and baskets. The flower is a medium-sized single with a waxy white tube and sepals and a rose pink corolla. The growth is vigorous and it is very free-flowering, the flowers standing out nicely on the mid-green foliage. Half hardy; Zones 9–10. Allsop, UK, 1998.

'Mancunian'

This is an excellent cultivar to use in hanging baskets, especially mixed baskets, because of its good trailing habit, strong vigorous growth and attractive light to mid-green foliage. The flowers are medium to large doubles with a white tube striped with red, white recurving sepals and a full white corolla with red veins and a red blush at the base of the petals. The large, white pointed buds add to the beauty of this plant. Half hardy; Zones 9–10. Goulding, UK, 1985.

'Land van Beveren'

'Mancunian'

'Marinka'

'Marinka'

This fuchsia, hybridized more than 100 years ago, is still a popular cultivar grown the world over. It was first thought to have originated in France in 1902, but now it seems it came from Germany some years earlier. It does not have many faults, but the main one is the tendency for the leaves to mark and turn red with sudden changes in temperature, for instance when moving it out of the greenhouse. The flowers are single, almost a self-red with a red tube, red sepals initially cupping the corolla and eventually held just below the horizontal, and a dull red corolla. The pretty flowers and buds look superb held in the mid-green foliage and the growth is naturally trailing, easily making an excellent hanging basket. This one is also worth growing as a weeping half standard. Half hardy; Zones 9–10. Stika, Germany, 1890.

'Mood Indigo'

This is an unusual cultivar, strong-growing and extremely floriferous, and is suitable for hanging baskets or containers. The medium-sized double flower has a light yellowish-green tube with red blush, yellowish-green recurving sepals, red at the base, and a deep mauve corolla with an indigo tinge, pink at the petal base and splashed with red. The foliage is mid-green on top, yellowish-green underneath, and it has a lax but rather untidy growth habit. Half hardy; Zones 9–10. de Graaff, Netherlands, 1987.

'Moonlight Sonata'

This fuchsia has rather lax and wiry growth and grows best when trained as a basket. It has a medium to large single flower with a rose tube, rose sepals and a light violet corolla, flushed pink at the petal base. Quite free flowering and can also be trained as an excellent weeping standard. Half hardy; Zones 9–10. Blackwell, UK, 1963.

'Multa'

This cultivar is a small-flowered single with a red tube, red sepals and a mauve-purple corolla. It is very easy to grow, and definitely a good one for a beginner to try,

'Mood Indigo'

with lax growth and medium-sized mid- to dark green foliage. It is very free-flowering over a long period. As well as being an excellent half basket plant covered with flowers, it also makes a good standard with a lax habit, and is effective in mixed planting in any kind of container. Half hardy; Zones 9–10. van Suchtelen, Netherlands, 1968.

'Normandy Bell'

This trailing cultivar makes a lax bush with rather long, light green leaves with serrated edges. The flowers are medium-sized singles with a short pale pink tube with darker stripes, long, broad, pinkish-white sepals tipped green and a light blue bell-shaped corolla with pink veining. It prefers some shade to full sun. Half hardy; Zones 9–10. Martin, USA, 1961.

'Novella'

This pretty fuchsia has medium-sized semi-double flowers with a long flesh-pink tube, long rosy-pink sepals and a salmon-orange corolla. The growth is rather lax, with medium-sized, mid-green serrated foliage. It grows very well in hanging baskets, hanging pots and containers, and makes an attractive weeping standard. Half hardy; Zone 10. Tiret, USA, 1967.

'Novella'

'Orange Drops'

'Orange King'

'Orange Drops'

This cultivar has one of the best orange colours and is suitable for basket or weeping standard training. It has the growth habit of a lax bush, with serrated mid-green leaves that can grow very large if overfed early in the season. The flowers are medium-sized singles with a long, light orange tube, light orange sepals and a dark orange corolla, which is slightly iridescent. The flowers tend to display and hang together in clusters. Half hardy; Zones 9–10. Martin, USA, 1963.

'Orange King'

One a group of orange-flowered cultivars, this makes an excellent fuchsia for hanging baskets because of its trailing habit. It has medium to large double flowers with a white tube blushed pale pink, pale pink arching sepals and a very full corolla that opens orange, maturing to smoky salmon-pink with orange splashes. The serrated foliage is mid-green, and the contrasting flower colour makes it quite striking. Half hardy; Zones 9–10. Wright, UK, 1975.

'Ovation'

This fuchsia is beautiful for hanging baskets and larger hanging pots. The medium-sized double flowers have a long ivory tube with faint pink stripes, broad horizontal ivory sepals with a pink flush and a full deep red corolla. The trailing growth has quite large mid-green leaves and it is reasonably free-flowering. Half hardy; Zones 9–10. Stubbs, USA, 1981.

'Panique'

This relatively new introduction is quite small-growing, but has a tremendous quantity of small single flowers. The tube is pink, the sepals are orchid-pink and the corolla is a deeper pink. The foliage is also small to medium in size and mid-green in colour. With its compact growth, this plant is excellent for a smaller hanging basket or for use in mixed containers. Half hardy; Zones 9–10. de Graaff, Netherlands, 2000.

'Patricia Ann'

This is a vigorous trailer, ideal for hanging baskets. It tolerates heat if shaded, and has rather large mid-green leaves. The large double flowers have a long neyron-rose tube with pink stripes, long white sepals with a pale pink stripe above and darker pink beneath and a full neyron-rose corolla, with a paler colour at the base of the petals, which are veined dark pink. Half hardy; Zones 9–10. Clements, UK, 1982.

'Pink Galore'

This is one of the best pinks in the group of trailing cultivars. The flowers are medium-sized doubles with a medium-length pale pink tube, long pale pink sepals tipped green swept upwards and a pale candy-pink corolla. The abundant flowers stand out well against the rather glossy, ovate, dark green leaves. It is not the most vigorous of cultivars, so use one or two extra plants when planting a hanging basket. Half hardy; Zones 9–10. Fuchsia-La, USA, 1951.

'Pink Galore'

'Pink Marshmallow'

'Postiljon'

'Pink Marshmallow'

This strong-growing trailing cultivar has very large double flowers with a long pale pink tube, broad pale pink reflexing sepals and a full white corolla with loose, pink-veined petals with some pink blushing, depending on the amount of sun. The medium to large foliage is light green. It makes a very impressive hanging basket or can be used in mixed containers for its stunning flowers. In common with many double whites, it is prone to botrytis, so water carefully early in the season. Half hardy; Zones 9–10. Stubbs, USA, 1977.

'Postiljon'

This vigorous self-branching and trailing cultivar is well worth growing, an easy choice for the beginner. It is early-flowering and makes a good basket quickly. Its small single flowers have a short white tube flushed pink, and broad cream-white sepals flushed rose, held out over the rosy-purple corolla. The flowers contrast well with the small mid-green foliage as it hangs down from containers. It is also good for hanging pots, mixed containers and small weeping standards. Half hardy; Zones 9–10. van der Post, Netherlands, 1975.

'President Margaret Slater'

A seedling from 'Cascade', this has a similar growth habit and is named after a former president of the British Fuchsia Society. The true cascading growth habit and medium-sized dark green serrated foliage make it ideal for hanging containers, especially the mixed ones. The flowers are medium-sized singles with a white tube, white sepals flushed with pink and tipped green and a mauve corolla with a salmon-pink blush. It is very floriferous, tolerates heat and develops the best flower colours in the sun. Half hardy; Zones 9–10. Taylor, UK, 1972.

'Princessita'

This older variety of fuchsia is still widely grown because it is very free-flowering over a long period. It has strong trailing growth with medium-sized mid- to dark green foliage and medium-sized single flowers with a white tube, long, narrow white upturned sepals flushed pink underneath, and a deep rose-pink corolla. It makes excellent full or half baskets, and is also a good cultivar for filling containers. Half hardy; Zones 9–10. Niederholzer, USA, 1940.

'Quasar'

This is a large-growing, spreading lax double, trailing owing to the size and weight of the flowers. The medium to large double flowers have a white tube, white sepals and a compact dauphin-violet corolla with white patches at the base of the petals. The medium to large foliage is light green and contrasts well with the unusual flower colours. This plant is very good for growing in mixed containers. Half hardy; Zones 9–10. Walker, USA, 1974.

'Queen of Hearts'

This cultivar is good in hanging baskets because of the large double flowers with a short carmine tube, flaring broad carmine sepals and a full corolla with violet-purple centre petals and carmine pink outer petals. Note that there is an upright bushy single cultivar with the same name raised by Tabraham in 1974 , so check which one it is before buying. Half hardy; Zones 9–10. Kennett, USA, 1961.

'Quasar'

'Red Shadows'

'Roesse Blacky'

'Red Shadows'

This is a lax cultivar from the US Waltz stable, with rather unusual flowers in a very nice colour combination. The large double flowers have a crimson tube and crimson sepals, which cup the dark burgundy-purple corolla, with crimson at the base of the petals. The flowers change colour as they mature, finally becoming a ruby-red. The foliage is mid-green with red veins. The growth is best classed as a lax bush, so it can be used in a hanging basket or as a pot plant with support. Half hardy; Zones 9–10. Waltz, USA, 1962.

'Red Spider'

This superbly floriferous fuchsia is very vigorous and makes quite long, stiff trailing growth with mid-green foliage, but it does not self-branch and needs a lot of pinching out early on. The medium-sized single flowers have a long crimson tube and sepals, and a rose corolla. It is an excellent cultivar, good for mixed baskets and containers. Note that it has nothing in common with, nor any special predilection towards the pest of the same name. Half hardy; Zones 9–10. Reiter, USA, 1946.

'Roesse Blacky' ('Blacky')

This relatively new introduction from the Roesse stable, commonly marketed with the name 'Blacky', has a quite startling colour. The medium semi-double flowers have a red tube and sepals and a deep purple corolla that is almost black when it first opens. The foliage is small to medium in size and mid-green in colour, and the growth is lax and arching. It is very good for use in containers and baskets, particularly when viewing the flowers at eye level. You could also try growing this fuchsia as a weeping standard, as its manner of growth is quite suitable for this shape. Half hardy; Zones 9–10. Roes, Netherlands, 2002.

'Ronald L. Lockerbie'

When first introduced, this was promoted as the first yellow fuchsia, although it is actually more of a creamy white. It had the honour of being named after Ronald Lockerbie, a prolific Australian hybridizer of fuchsias. The flower is a medium-sized double with a cream tube flushed carmine, white sepals and a cream to pale yellow corolla, fading to white. The foliage is medium-sized and light green, with quite

long joints between the leaf nodes. This plant grows well in baskets and containers. Half hardy; Zones 9–10. Richardson, Australia, 1986.

'Ruby Wedding'

This is a good choice if you want large double flowers with an unusual colour for a hanging basket. The medium-length tube is ruby, the ruby sepals are quite broad and semi-reflexed, and the full corolla is red with overtones of orange and mauve. It is quite floriferous for the size of the flowers and grows strongly with arching stems and large mid-green foliage. It is an ideal gift for those couples reaching that landmark. Half hardy; Zones 9–10. Forward, UK, 1990.

'Ruth King'

This is a stiff trailing fuchsia with medium-sized mid-green foliage. The medium to large double flowers have a pink tube and sepals and a lilac and white compact corolla. This cultivar is very suitable for growing in the centre of mixed baskets and containers and is well worth trying as a weeping standard. Half hardy; Zones 9–10. Tiret, USA, 1967.

'Ruby Wedding'

'Seventh Heaven'

'Southgate'

'Seventh Heaven'

This naturally trailing cultivar has medium to large double flowers, a white tube with green streaks, white sepals shading to pink and a full orange-red corolla. It is an eye-catching and very floriferous fuchsia, with mid-green foliage and arching growth. It makes a nice basket on its own, but is also excellent in mixed hanging containers. The flowers are at their best when viewed from eye level or slightly below, and for this reason it is another fuchsia that looks superb grown as a weeping standard. It should be in everyone's collection. Half hardy; Zones 9–10. Stubbs, USA, 1981.

'Sophisticated Lady'

The trailing growth habit of this fuchsia makes it very suitable for hanging baskets. The medium to large double flowers have a short pale pink tube, long and quite broad pale pink sepals, and a short, full white corolla. The small to medium-sized serrated foliage is mid-green with red veining. Half hardy; Zones 9–10. Martin, USA, 1964.

'Southgate'

This grows in the manner of a lax bush with mid-green foliage, and is ideal for hanging baskets or as a pot plant with supports. The striking flowers are medium-sized doubles with a pink tube, pink sepals that are paler above and darker underneath, and a powder-pink fluffy corolla with pink veining on the petals. Because of its slightly stiff habit of growth it can be trained in various ways, for example as a standard or even a fan. Half hardy; Zones 9–10. Walker and Jones, USA, 1951.

'Susan Green'

This is a very pretty trailing cultivar with strong, self-branching growth and medium-sized mid-green foliage. The flowers are medium-sized singles with a pale pink tube, pale pink sepals with green tips and a coral-pink corolla. It can be grown as an excellent hanging pot plant or in a hanging basket, and is equally at home in a hanging container with mixed plants. It also makes a superb weeping half standard. Half hardy; Zones 9–10. Caunt, UK, 1981.

'Swingtime'

This superb fuchsia is grown by many gardeners and has been consistently popular for many years. It is a classic basket fuchsia against which many other trailing cultivars are judged. The flowers are double and medium to large with a red tube, red sepals and a very full, fluffy white corolla with red veining on the petals. The foliage is on the small side, mid- to dark green with red veining, and the growth is vigorous, wiry and trailing. It does very well in any type of basket or container, and can also be grown as an excellent weeping full or half standard. Half hardy; Zones 9–10. Tiret, USA, 1950.

'Sylvia Barker'

This fuchsia has rather small flowers but they are numerous, with a long waxy white tube, waxy white sepals with green tips and a smoky-red corolla. The colours are quite distinctive and stand out well against the dark green leaves. It makes an arching, lax trailing plant that is excellent when grown in a half basket or hanging pot. This cultivar also grows very well in mixed containers and makes a superb weeping standard. Half hardy; Zones 9–10. Barker, UK, 1973.

'Susan Green'

'Taffeta Bow'

Excellent for hanging baskets, this cultivar has distinctive medium to large double flowers with a short pink tube, long carmine-rose sepals and a purple-violet corolla with serrated petal edges and pink splashes. As the fuchsias mature, the petals develop an unusual curved shape, which is what gives it its name. It has good vigorous growth with dark green foliage and an abundance of flowers. Half hardy; Zones 9–10. Stubbs, USA, 1974.

'Tom West'

This very old and adaptable cultivar has a number of different uses, including hanging baskets and pots. The flowers are small to medium-sized singles with a carmine tube and sepals, and a purple corolla. It has very attractive variegated foliage with patches of green, cream and cerise, becoming redder in the sun. The growth is rather wiry and spreading but it grows well in a basket, particularly a half basket, and is also good when trained as a standard or used in summer bedding schemes. Frost hardy; Zones 7–8. Meillez, France, 1853.

'Tom West'

'Trailing Queen'

This old German cultivar has vigorous, long trailing growth and is very floriferous, though it can suffer from premature flower drop when conditions are too hot and dry. The flowers are medium-sized singles with a thin red tube and red sepals, and the corolla opens a red-violet and matures to a dull red. The unusual foliage is bronze-green with red veining in the leaves, and the buds add to the attraction, changing colour as they grow. Half hardy; Zones 9–10. Kohene, Germany, 1896.

'Trudi Davro'

This is a relatively new trailing fuchsia, a good addition to the range of whites. The flowers are a medium double with a pale pink tube and sepals and a full white corolla that stands out within the small to medium-sized bright green foliage. The pink colouring of the flower becomes more intense when grown in the sun. It makes a superb hanging pot, but is also well worth using in baskets or other hanging containers mixed with fuchsias of other colours. Half hardy; Zones 9–10. Raiser unknown, UK, introduction date unknown.

'Veenlust'

'University of Liverpool'

'University of Liverpool'

This newer cultivar is excellent for hanging baskets with its vigorous lax growth, and it flowers well over a long period. The flowers are medium-sized singles with a white tube and sepals, and a red bell-shaped corolla, with up to three flowers growing from each leaf axil. The foliage is mid- to dark green, contrasting well with the flowers. It is well worth trying as a weeping standard. Half hardy; Zones 9–10. Clark, UK, 1998.

'Veenlust'

This lax cultivar is a good choice for hanging pots, hanging baskets and mixed containers. The medium to large double flowers have a medium-length white tube, white sepals with green tips and a full bright red corolla, some of the petals with pink splashes. The inner petals can sometimes grow in a lower ring, giving a very deep corolla with structural similarities to 'Two Tiers'. The foliage is mid-green and the growth vigorous and lax, though not very self-branching. Half hardy; Zones 9–10. Jansink, Netherlands, 1994.

'Walsingham'

This is a stunningly beautiful cultivar with pastel flowers and rather bright green foliage. It has the habit of a lax bush with semi-trailing growth, and it is very effective in all types of raised containers, especially half baskets and hanging pots. The flowers are medium-sized semi-doubles with a pale pink tube and sepals, and a pale lavender-lilac corolla. Some catalogues list it as a double but it is really a semi-double with some double flowers. Take care not to overwater, because it can be prone to botrytis early in the season. Half hardy; Zones 9–10. Clithero, UK, 1979.

'Wave of Life'

This is an old cultivar, probably grown more for its foliage than its flowers. It has small to medium-sized single flowers with a scarlet tube and sepals, and a magenta-purple corolla. It bears splendid greenish-yellow and gold leaves, while the growth is lax but not especially vigorous. Probably best used in hanging pots or mixed containers for its leaf colour. Half hardy; Zones 9–10. Henderson, UK, 1896.

'Wendy's Beauty'

This beautiful trailing cultivar has large double flowers with a white tube and long white sepals flushed with rose, and an unusually coloured violet to pale purple full

'Wilson's Pearls'

corolla. The flowers are produced very freely for such a large double and the lax growth has dark yellowish-green leaves, among which the flowers stand out well. Half hardy; Zones 9–10. Garrett, USA, 1989.

'Wilson's Pearls'

This is a floriferous trailing cultivar with pale to mid-green foliage, ideal in hanging baskets or pots and all kinds of raised containers. The flowers are medium-sized singles with a medium length red tube,

red sepals that curl back and twist, and a white corolla veined red. The petals often become blushed pink when grown in the sun. This one is easy to grow and is widely available. Half hardy; Zones 9–10. Wilson, UK, 1967.

'Windhapper'

This is a fine cascading Dutch cultivar, excellent for hanging baskets and elevated containers with its large, bright mid-green leaves with a distinctive red central vein. It has large single flowers with a short greenish-white tube, long white sepals with a pink blush and green tips, and a violet corolla with lighter colour at the petal base. The best flower colours develop in areas with more shade. Half hardy; Zones 9–10. Moerman, Netherlands, 1991.

'Zulu King'

This is a cultivar for those looking for a very dark coloured fuchsia to grow in a basket or hanging pot. The medium-sized single flowers have a deep carmine tube and sepals, and a dark black-purple corolla that holds its dark colour well through to maturity. It has good trailing growth and rather dark green foliage. Grow it where the flowers are easy to see. Half hardy; Zones 9–10. de Graaff, Netherlands, 1990.

'Wendy's Beauty'

'Zulu King'

Triphylla fuchsias

These hybrids all need winter protection in temperate areas. They need minimum temperatures of 10°C (50°F) to grow on in green leaf through the winter and 5°C (41°F) to overwinter in a dormant state. Cooler than this, the spring growth is delayed a few weeks.

'Adinda'
This fairly new cultivar is a slightly smaller variety than many older Triphylla hybrids, with beautiful small single flowers growing in terminal clusters, the flowers being a salmon-pink self. The foliage is an attractive shade of sage green, with upright growth. It makes an excellent pot plant and a great summer bedder. Tender; Zone 11. Dijkstra, Netherlands, 1995.

'Andenken an Heinrich Henkel' ('Heinrich Henkel')
This is a beautiful lax Triphylla, with medium rose-crimson flowers growing in terminal clusters. The flowers make a beautiful contrast to the large dark green foliage, and it tolerates full sun quite happily. It grows well as a lax pot plant, but be careful not to overwater it. Try it in a hanging basket or as a lax standard. Tender; Zone 11. Berger, Germany, 1896.

'Billy Green'
This popular cultivar is a Triphylla type rather than a true Triphylla, which means the flowers grow from the leaf axils rather than in terminal racemes. The flower is a Triphylla shape, albeit a little fatter. The flower is a salmon-pink self colour and the growth vigorous and upright, with lovely olive-sage-green foliage. It makes an excellent specimen plant in a single season of growth. This is one for a patio because it happily stands full sun. Try using it as a summer bedder as well. Frost tender; Zones 10–11. Raiser unknown, UK, 1962.

'Bornemann's Beste'
This strong-growing fuchsia is a Triphylla type suitable for use as a pot or bedding plant. The flowers are medium-sized orange-red singles with long tubes, growing mainly in terminal clusters. Current opinion states that this fuchsia is the same as the one named 'Georg Bornemann' in Germany. Tender; Zone 11. Bonstedt, Germany, 1904.

'Chantry Park'
Unlike most Triphyllas, this cultivar has short-jointed, bushy and slightly lax growth with medium mid- to olive green foliage. It is still truly terminal-flowering, with medium-sized flowers in terminal clusters. The flowers have a scarlet tube

'Billy Green'

and sepals and a bright scarlet corolla, the sepals and corolla being a little larger in proportion to the tube than the average Triphylla. It grows very well in a hanging pot or basket, and is very suitable for a wall pot. Tender; Zone 11. Stannard, UK, 1991.

'Coralle' ('Koralle')
This cultivar resulted from the work of the German hybridizer Carl Bonstedt, and is also known by the alternative German spelling 'Koralle'. It is a strong, upright grower with medium-sized flowers produced in terminal clusters. The flowers are orange-red self-coloured, with large, deep sage green, velvety foliage. Tender; Zones 10–11. Bonstedt, Germany, 1905.

'Adinda'

'Coralle'

'Edwin J. Goulding'

This is an upright and bushy fuchsia with medium-sized Triphylla flowers in terminal clusters, with a darkish red tube and sepals, and a brighter red corolla. It has medium to dark green foliage that contrasts well with the flower colour. Tender; Zone 11. Stannard, UK, 1992.

'Elfriede Ott'

This fuchsia is rather unusual because of its stiff, spreading upright growth that will make a tall plant. The distinctive flowers, which grow in terminal clusters, have a slightly bent salmon-pink tube and sepals, and a darker salmon-pink corolla. The four curled and folded petals give the appearance of a semi-double and the stamens almost hide in the flowers. The medium-sized dark green foliage is a perfect foil to the salmon-pink flowers. This fuchsia resulted from a hybridization cross between 'Coralle' and *F. splendens*. Frost tender; Zone 11. Nutzinger, Austria, 1976.

'Firecracker'

This Triphylla is a truly variegated sport from 'Thalia', which is now widely grown. It flowers in terminal clusters, as does 'Thalia', and the medium flowers are orange-scarlet self-coloured, but it has beautiful leaves with a startling olive green and cream variegation with traces of red. Use it in pots or as a summer bedder, but be aware that it needs growing on the dry side or you will lose it to botrytis. This cultivar is subject to breeder's rights protection. Tender; Zone 11. Fuchsiavale, UK, 1987.

'Fred Swales'

The stiff and lax growth habit of this fuchsia looks very effective in hanging baskets and containers. The flowers are borne in terminal clusters and have a reddish-orange tube and sepals with a corolla that opens orange with a purple edge to the petals that matures to orange. The foliage is mid-green above and lighter underneath, with red veining and stems, while the mature branches are brown. Tender; Zones 10–11. Bielby and Oxtoby, UK, 1988.

'Elfriede Ott'

'Gartenmeister Bonstedt'

This is one of Carl Bonstedt's superb Triphylla cultivars. The flowers appear in terminal clusters, being orange-red with a long tube. They are very similar to 'Thalia' but have a more pronounced bulge in the tube. The strong, upright bushy growth has a covering of bronze-green foliage. Heat and sun are not a problem, and this Triphylla makes an excellent summer bedding and specimen pot plant. In a greenhouse, it will continue flowering well into the winter. Frost tender; Zones 10–11. Bonstedt, Germany, 1905.

'Insulinde'

This is a newer Triphylla hybrid, with strong, upright growth and startling dark green shiny foliage. The medium-sized flowers are borne in terminal clusters, with a tomato-red tube, sepals that are tomato-red on the topside and vermilion-pink on the underside, and a tomato-red corolla. It is a strong growing plant, naturally quite self-branching, and the colour combination makes it a welcome addition to the range. It makes a very nice pot plant and grows well as a summer bedder. Frost tender; Zone 11. de Graaff, Netherlands, 1991.

'Gartenmeister Bonstedt'

'Insulinde'

'Jackqueline'

'Orient Express'

'Jackqueline'

This Triphylla cultivar has terminal clusters of medium flowers with a scarlet tube and sepals, and an orange corolla. It has good upright growth with dark green velvety leaves, and is happy in full sun. Use it as a pot plant or a striking specimen plant. Tender; Zone 11. Oxtoby, UK, 1987.

'Mantilla'

This fuchsia is a very interesting Triphylla type, excellent when used in hanging baskets and pots. It has strong, vigorous and pendant growth with lovely dark green

'Mantilla'

foliage. The flowers are borne in terminal clusters and have long rich carmine tubes, short light carmine sepals and a vermilion corolla. The corolla is unusually large and well exposed beneath the sepals. It grows best in a well-lit, warm position and makes an excellent half basket. Tender; Zone 11. Reiter, USA, 1948.

'Mary'

This is another of Carl Bonstedt's raisings, and arguably one of the best Triphyllas in cultivation. It bears its medium-sized vivid crimson self-coloured flowers in terminal clusters. The tube is distinctly slimmer at the top and widens close to the flower. The growth is upright, self-branching and slightly lax, with large velvety leaves that are a beautiful shade of sage green. It is quite happy in full sun and makes an excellent specimen plant. It will also make a nice, slightly lax quarter or half standard, though great care is needed when growing the stem, because of the terminal-flowering habit. If it starts to flower while you are growing the stem, it will not grow any higher. Frost tender; Zone 11. Bonstedt, Germany, 1897.

'Obergartner Koch'

This is a strong upright cultivar with large, red-veined olive-green leaves, suitable as a pot plant or for summer bedding. The

flowers are borne in terminal clusters with a long bright orange tube, which is very thin at the top, with a pronounced bulge before the sepals. The sepals and corolla are also bright orange. Tender; Zone 11. Sauer, Germany, 1912.

'Orient Express'

This has strong upright growth and needs hard pinching in the early stages to make a well-shaped plant. It has quite unusually coloured flowers, borne in terminal clusters, with a long pink tube striped with darker pink, red-tipped pale pink-white sepals and a rose-pink corolla. It has large mid-green leaves which, when combined with the flowers and buds, makes it an interesting addition to the range of Triphyllas. Frost tender; Zone 11. Goulding, UK, 1985.

'Our Ted'

The first-ever white-flowered Triphylla cultivar, this was named after Ted Stiff, a great fuchsia personality in the east of England. The growth is upright, with terminal clusters of medium white self-coloured flowers, though the corolla petals can have a touch of pink. The foliage is dark green and quite glossy. This cultivar is one for the experienced gardener because it is not easy to grow. Tender; Zone 11. Goulding, UK, 1987.

'Roos Breytenbach'

This is a strong-growing, slightly lax upright with terminal clusters of long scarlet flowers. The sepals are long for a Triphylla, and the corolla rather different with the petals pleated together to form an unusual shape. The foliage is mid- to dark green and slightly more of an ovate shape than other Triphylla hybrids. This cultivar is excellent in hanging baskets and containers. Tender; Zone 11. Stannard, UK, 1993.

'Sparky'

This new Triphylla cultivar is unusual in that the small flowers are thrown outwards and upwards in terminal clusters. The tube and sepals are dark blood-red, as is the corolla. It has upright growth and is short-jointed and very bushy, with small to medium (for a Triphylla) dark green leaves. It grows well as a pot plant and makes a good quarter standard. It does well growing in a conservatory. Tender; Zone 11. Webb, UK, 1994.

'Stella Ann'

This is a vigorous upright and self-branching cultivar that is extremely floriferous, with dark olive green leaves with purple ribs and veins. The flowers, held in huge terminal clusters, have a thick poppy-red tube, poppy-red sepals with green tips and an Indian orange corolla.

'Sparky'

This is an excellent choice for growing as a smaller specimen pot plant or in a summer bedding scheme. Tender; Zone 11. Dunnet, UK, 1974.

'Thalia'

This is probably the best-known Triphylla hybrid. It has strong upright growth with medium-sized, orange-scarlet self-coloured flowers borne in terminal clusters. The dark olive-green foliage shows the flowers off very well. Often used in public bedding schemes, where it makes a good show, it can also form an excellent specimen

plant and a good quarter or half standard. Once it starts flowering it does not stop until you have to cut it back in autumn. Frost tender; Zones 10–11. Bonstedt, Germany, 1905.

'Traudchen Bonstedt'

This beautiful Triphylla is one that should be more widely grown. It has single flowers in terminal clusters with a long, light salmon-pink tube and short sepals of the same colour. The corolla is light orange with white anthers and a pale salmon pistil that almost hides in the flower. The light sage-green leaves have a velvety texture with a reddish tint underneath. To ensure the plant's survival over winter, it should be kept in green leaf rather than allowed to go dormant. Tender; Zone 11. Bonstedt, Germany, 1905.

'Whiteknights Cheeky'

This smaller Triphylla is very suitable for pots, with its small flowers held horizontally in terminal clusters. The flowers are a single main colour, described as either Tyrian-purple or red-aubergine. The colour varies depending on the conditions in which the plant is grown, and is best when grown in full sun. The attractive foliage is small and dark green with a velvety texture. The plant originated from an interspecies cross between *F. triphylla* and *F. procumbens*. Frost tender; Zone 11. Wright, UK, 1980.

'Thalia'

'Whiteknights Cheeky'

Fuchsias in pots

Excellent plants for growing in pots, fuchsias can be used for brightening up dark corners around the garden, for displays or for exhibition. Free-flowering varieties, which possess an upright and self-branching habit of growth, are the best types to use.

'Abigail Reine'

The first part of the name of this cultivar is variously spelt as 'Abigale', 'Abigayle', 'Abigayles' and 'Abbigayle' in different catalogues. It is the best variegated sport from 'Rose Fantasia', with mid-green leaves with bright yellow variegation. The flower is identical to that of 'Rose Fantasia', a medium-sized single, upward-facing with a deep pink tube and sepals, and a pale pink corolla with a hint of mauve. It makes an attractive pot plant, but you should keep it in as much light as possible to enhance the foliage colours. Half hardy; Zones 9–10. Hunton, UK, 1998.

'Alaska'

This is a good upright that grows with strong stems and striking, large white double flowers with a white tube, white sepals tipped green and a very full, fluffy

'Abigail Reine'

'Alberttina'

white corolla. The foliage is dark green, and when in full flower there is some arching of the stems caused by the weight of the flowers. It is well worth growing as a half or full standard, and ideal for placing in dull corners where the white flowers stand out. It is an excellent addition to any collection. Half hardy; Zones 9–10. Schnabel, USA, 1963.

'Alberttina' ('Albertina')

This strong-growing, self-branching plant will form a good bush or shrub with minimal shaping. The small to medium-sized single flowers have a white tube flushed rose, rose-flushed white reflexed sepals and a flared lavender-rose corolla. There is medium-sized mid- to dark green foliage. This fuchsia is free-flowering and makes a good pot plant or smaller standard. Try using it for summer bedding as well. Half hardy; Zones 9–10. Netjes, Netherlands, 1988.

'Atlantic Star'

The upright, self-branching, short-jointed growth of this fuchsia creates an excellent compact pot plant. The flowers are medium-sized singles with a cream-striped pink tube, white sepals blushed pink and a bell-shaped white corolla with faint pink veins. The medium-sized

mid-green leaves have a serrated edge and red stems, providing a perfect foil for the flowers. The plant is also excellent grown as a quarter standard. Half hardy; Zones 9–10. Redfern, UK, 1986.

'Bealings'

This is a good choice for growing as a medium-sized pot plant or small standard. The flowers are small to medium-sized doubles with a white tube and sepals, and the corolla is very full and dark violet, fading with age. The upright, short-jointed self-branching growth carries small mid-green leaves and plenty of flowers for a double cultivar. Half hardy; Zones 9–10. Goulding, UK, 1983.

'Ben Jammin'

This is a very pretty cultivar with compact, short-jointed growth, excellent when grown as a smaller pot plant or small standard. The distinctive, small to medium-sized single flowers have a pale pink tube, pink-flushed aubergine sepals, and a dark aubergine corolla that caused a stir when first released. The foliage is small to medium in size and mid- to dark green in colour. Many nurseries list this cultivar as hardy in their catalogues, but this has not been proven by any definitive trials. Half hardy; Zones 9–10. Carless, UK, 1998.

'Ben Jammin'

'Border Raider'

'Border Raider'

This fuchsia has made a big impression in the exhibition world since its introduction. The prolific flowers are small to medium-sized semi-erect singles with a deep rose tube and sepals, and a white corolla with slightly scalloped edges to the petals. The growth is naturally shrub-like, with small to medium-sized light green leaves. It makes a very nice quarter standard or pot plant. It does not overwinter well in a dormant state, and is better to keep in green leaf if possible. Half hardy; Zones 9–10. Gordon, UK, 2001.

'Brookwood Belle'

This strong, upright bushy cultivar is excellent for pot plants and is popular as an exhibition plant, having been in the top-ten list for some years. The flowers are medium-sized doubles with a deep cerise tube and sepals, and a pink-flushed white corolla veined red. The medium-sized foliage is bright mid-green. It is very floriferous and has a long period of flowering. Half hardy; Zones 9–10. Gilbert, UK, 1988.

'Cambridge Louie'

This cultivar should be in everyone's collection as it is a vigorous grower and will easily form a large pot plant covered in flowers. It is best to grow it in direct sun, as long as you can keep the roots cool;

'Caspar Hauser'

the sun encourages it to produce harder wood that is not so likely to collapse under the weight of flowers. The medium single flowers have a pink-orange tube and sepals and a rosy-pink corolla, and they stand out well on the small, light green foliage. Half hardy; Zones 9–10. Napthen, UK, 1977.

'Caspar Hauser'

This cultivar is worth growing for its unusual flower colours. The growth is spreading, upright and self-branching, with light to mid-green foliage. It is a vigorous plant and quickly makes an impressive shrub. The flowers are small to medium-sized doubles with a cardinal red tube and sepals, and a rather tight ruby-red corolla with lighter red patches at the base of the petals. Try it in baskets or containers as a centre plant as they will benefit from its lax but stiff upright growth. Half hardy; Zones 9–10. Springer, Germany, 1987.

'Cloverdale Pearl'

This fuchsia is very easy to grow as a pot plant, with its upright, self-branching growth and small mid- to dark green leaves. The flower is a medium-sized single with a white tube, pale pink sepals with green tips and a white corolla with red veining on the petals. You can grow this cultivar as a summer bedder or train it as a standard and various other shapes. Half hardy; Zones 9–10. Gadsby, UK, 1974.

'Cotton Candy'

This good strong upright-growing cultivar will make a nice shrub with medium-sized double flowers with a white tube, white sepals flushed pink and a fluffy pale pink corolla with cerise veins. The medium to large mid- to dark green leaves make a good foil for the flowers, which are freely produced for a double. It will make a large plant quite quickly, so it is also possible to grow it as a half standard. Half hardy; Zones 9–10. Tiret, USA, 1994.

'Cotton Candy'

'Delta's Sara'

'Doris Joan'

'Delta's KO'

This vigorous upright will quickly make a large bush or shrub. The flowers are large doubles with a cream-coloured tube, cream sepals flushed rosy-purple, much darker beneath, and a deep purple corolla. The combination of the medium-sized and mid- to dark green foliage with the flowers gives a striking overall effect. Half hardy; Zones 9–10. Vreeke and van't Westeinde, Netherlands, 1994.

'Delta's Sara'

This is a strong-growing, upright, floriferous Dutch cultivar with medium-sized semi-double flowers. They have a white tube and sepals, and a bluish-purple flared corolla with pink patches on the petals set against medium-sized mid-green leaves. It needs early pinching out to improve the bushiness, and easily makes a bush, medium-sized standard or bedding plant. Some nurseries claim it is hardy, but this has not been proven by any definitive trials. Half hardy; Zones 9–10. van't Westeinde, Netherlands, 2002.

'Doris Joan'

This is a strong-growing upright with mid- to dark green, slightly glossy leaves and rather unusual flowers. They are small to medium-sized singles with a cream and carmine tube, cream and carmine reflexed sepals with green tips and a pale pink and lavender corolla with pronounced scalloped edges to the petals, giving the flower its distinctive shape. Half hardy; Zones 9–10. Sheppard, UK, 1997.

'Dulcie Elizabeth'

This is an excellent cultivar for growing in pots, with upright, bushy, self-branching growth and medium-sized mid-green foliage. The flowers are medium-sized doubles with a rose tube and sepals, and a full blue corolla with pink splashes, the outer petals being lighter than the inner ones. This variety tends to be a slightly late flowerer, but the attractive flowers are well worth the wait. Half hardy; Zones 9–10. Clyne and Aimes, UK, 1974.

'Eden Lady'

A sister seedling to 'Border Queen', this has similar growth, being upright, self-branching, bushy and short-jointed. It easily makes a superb bush or shrub. The flowers are medium-sized singles with a rose tube and sepals, and a hyacinth-blue corolla, and they stand out beautifully among the mid-green leaves. It is excellent as a half or quarter standard, and in summer bedding. Either 'Eden Lady' or 'Border Queen' should be in every beginner's collection. Half hardy; Zones 9–10. Ryle, UK, 1975.

'Eden Princess'

The medium to large single flowers of this fuchsia have a reddish-pink tube and sepals, and a mallow-purple corolla that contrasts beautifully with the golden foliage. New leaves at the growing tips have distinct red veining. The strong upright growth makes it ideal as a pot plant or standard. Half hardy; Zones 9–10. Mitcheson, UK, 1984.

'Eden Princess'

'Eleanor Leytham'

This cultivar has stiff upright and bushy growth with small glossy mid-green leaves. The profuse small semi-erect single flowers have a white flushed pink tube and sepals and a pink corolla with deeper coloured edges to the petals. This is an excellent plant for growing in smaller pot sizes or as smaller standards. Half hardy; Zones 9–10. Roe, UK, 1973.

'Estelle Marie'

This cultivar is one of the upward-flowering types. The flowers are small singles with a greenish-white tube, white sepals with green tips and a violet-blue corolla maturing to violet. It is extremely floriferous and has strong, stiff, short-jointed upright growth with light to mid-green foliage. Use it as a single specimen plant in an attractive pot or in mixed containers on the patio with other fuchsias or companion plants. It is also very effective when used as part of a summer bedding scheme, either individually or in blocks; the flowers look rather similar to little pansies, nodding in the breeze. Half hardy; Zones 9–10. Newton, UK, 1973.

'Finn'

This is a strong upright with a good bushy habit that responds well to pinching. The flowers are medium-sized singles with a longish ivory-white tube, ivory-white

recurving sepals blushed pink and a long tubular corolla in an unusual shade of orange-red. The medium-sized, mid- to dark green foliage adds to the healthy look. This cultivar is excellent used as a pot plant, standard or summer bedder. Half hardy; Zones 9–10. Goulding, UK, 1988.

'Flying Cloud'

The large double flowers of this cultivar are very freely produced for their large size. Each flower has a white tube, white recurved sepals blushed rose underneath and a full white corolla that is pink at the base. The whole flower takes on a pinker tinge grown in full sun. 'Flying Cloud' makes a lax bush and may need some support when grown as a pot plant to help support the weight of the large blooms. It also makes a nice semi-weeping standard and can be used in containers. Half hardy; Zones 9–10. Reiter, USA, 1949.

'Forward Look'

This cultivar has upright and bushy growth with medium-sized mid-green foliage. The attractive medium-sized single flowers, held semi-erect, have a short china-rose tube, china-rose sepals tipped green and a wisteria-blue corolla fading to mauve. It is well suited to growing as a pot plant or medium-sized standard. Half hardy; Zones 9–10. Gadsby, UK, 1972.

'Flying Cloud'

'Frank Saunders'

This fuchsia has very pretty small single flowers with a white tube and sepals, and a small lilac-pink corolla. The flowers are semi-erect, tending to stand out from the foliage. The growth habit is upright, bushy and self-branching, with small dark green leaves. It forms a dense shrub very easily and is excellent as a pot plant, or try growing it as a beautiful miniature or quarter standard. Half hardy; Zones 9–10. Dyos, UK, 1984.

'Estelle Marie'

'Frank Saunders'

'Gay Fandango'

'Gay Fandango'
With its lax bushy habit, this fuchsia responds well to different ways of training. The flowers are medium to large doubles with a rosy-carmine tube, large rosy-carmine sepals and a long rosy-magenta corolla with the petals in two tiers. The mid-green foliage is medium to large in size and a lovely foil for the flowers. The large flower size may necessitate some support when training it as a pot plant. This cultivar is recommended for growing half or full standards. Half hardy; Zones 9–10. Nelson, USA, 1951.

'Gay Spinner'
The strong, vigorous and upright growth of this fuchsia creates a good pot plant if given plenty of early pinching to encourage branching. It is easy to train as a half or full standard as the stem will quickly grow to the necessary length. The flowers are medium to large semi-doubles with a pink tube, large pink sepals and an imperial purple corolla, with pink at the base at of the petals and extra petaloids inside. Raised by John Lockyer and released by his father Stuart. Half hardy; Zones 9–10. Lockyer, UK, 1978.

'Gordon Thorley'
This is a strong, upright and self-branching fuchsia with medium-sized single flowers with a pale rose-pink tube, pale rose-pink sepals held horizontally and a white corolla with petals edged and veined with rose. The plant is very floriferous, with mid- to dark green foliage contrasting beautifully with the flowers. It makes an excellent pot plant, and is very good for use in the border. This cultivar was hybridized from 'Cloverdale Pearl' and 'Santa Barbara'. Half hardy; Zones 9–10. Roe, UK, 1987.

'Happy Wedding Day'
This Australian cultivar has large double flowers featuring a white tube, white sepals with rose-bengal colouring near the tube and on the sepal edges and a tight white corolla. The foliage is mid-green with serrated edges and the growth is strong and pright, but made lax by the number and weight of the flowers, so it is best to add some canes as supports when growing it in a pot. It will rapidly make a spectacular plant. Half hardy; Zones 9–10. Richardson, Australia, 1985.

'Heidi Ann'
This cultivar is a bushy upright-growing plant, which will make a very good specimen pot plant or quarter standard

'Gay Spinner'

'Happy Wedding Day'

for the patio or garden. It has medium-sized double flowers with a carmine-red tube and sepals, and a lilac-veined cerise corolla with a double skirt of petals and petaloids, which are paler at the base. The growth is self-branching, with small dark green leaves with a red central vein. Both of this plant's parents, 'Tennessee Waltz' and 'General Monk', are hardy, and this cultivar inherits those characteristics, so it is a good choice for a permanent planting in the garden. Hardy; Zone 7. Growth 40cm (16in). Smith, UK, 1969.

'Herzilein'
This German cultivar is a bushy upright plant, whose name translates as 'Little Heart'. It has small single flowers with a long light orange-red tube and short light orange-red sepals that hang downwards, partially covering the dark red corolla. It is very free-flowering with medium-sized light to mid-green foliage. The plant is quite tolerant of full sun and looks good on its own in a pot or a patio container. Equally, it is very suitable for mixing with other plants in larger containers where it fills the gaps excellently. Half hardy; Zones 9–10. Strümper, Germany, 1989.

'Igloo Maid'

'Hessett Festival'

This is an upright and self-branching cultivar with very large double flowers, and grows to an impressive pot plant. The flowers have a short white tube, long white recurving sepals and a full lavender-blue corolla with white streaks. The medium-sized mid-green leaves have a fine serration around the edges. The plant makes a good half or full standard. Half hardy; Zones 9–10. Goulding, UK, 1985.

'Hidcote Beauty'

This cultivar, found by a British Fuchsia Society member growing at Hidcote Manor in Gloucestershire, England, has an abundance of medium-sized single flowers with a long waxy cream tube, waxy cream sepals tipped green and a pale salmon-orange corolla with pink shading. The foliage is medium to large and light green, and the growth upright and slightly lax. It makes an excellent specimen plant, a nice half standard and is also well worth using as a summer bedder. It is on the American Fuchsia Society's list of gall mite-resistant plants. Half hardy; Zones 9–10. Introducer Webb, UK, 1949.

'Hot Coals'

When first introduced, this fuchsia caused a stir because of its unusual flower colouring, aptly described by its name. The medium-sized single flowers have a dark red tube, dark scarlet-red semi-reflexed sepals and a dark aubergine corolla. The growth is upright, short-jointed and self-branching with mid- to dark green foliage. It forms a lovely pot plant with a minimum of effort. Half hardy; Zones 9–10. Carless, UK, 1993.

'Igloo Maid'

This is an upright-growing cultivar with medium to large double flowers with a white tube, white sepals tipped green and a full white corolla with a hint of pink. The medium-sized leaves are yellowish-green.

'Hidcote Beauty'

It makes a very impressive pot plant, and is often described as one of the best white doubles. Half hardy; Zones 9–10. Holmes, UK, 1972.

'Impudence'

This US cultivar is a naturally upright bush and makes a superb pot plant. The medium-sized single flowers have a light red tube, long light red sepals that are fully reflexed around the tube and a white corolla veined with rose in which the four petals are almost flat when fully open. The mid-green leaves complement the flower shape and colour. The upright habit makes the plant a good one to train as an espalier or fan. Half hardy; Zones 9–10. Schnabel, USA, 1957.

'Ivana van Amsterdam'

This is a cultivar with parentage from 'Pink Fantasia', in this case crossed with 'Lambada'. It shows some of the 'Pink Fantasia' characteristics, with its medium-sized single flower held erect with a greenish-white tube, pale rose sepals with green tips and a blue corolla which opens tight, then flares, maturing to pale mauve. It has a very bushy natural growth habit and is very free-flowering, so it will make a nice pot plant or smaller standard. Half hardy; Zones 9–10. van der Putten, Netherlands, 2002.

'Impudence'

'Jenny May'

'Jomam'

'Jenny May'

This is a very vigorous, strong-growing, self-branching upright with a slightly lax habit. It has medium to large single flowers with a creamy-pink tube, long creamy-pink sepals and a violet corolla with pink splashes. The foliage is medium to large in size and mid-green in colour, and the growth is especially suited to bush-training as a pot plant. Half hardy; Zones 9–10. Bush, UK, 1998.

'Jessica Reynolds'

This is a more recent cultivar with a very good upright, short-jointed and self-branching habit. The plentiful medium-sized single flowers have a white tube, white sepals flushed aubergine and a compact aubergine corolla. The medium-sized mid-green leaves perfectly complement the flower colours. It is quite strong-growing, so it makes an excellent pot plant and quarter or half standard. Half hardy; Zones 9–10. Reynolds, UK, 2000.

'Joan Goy'

The erect flowers of this fuchsia create a very fetching pot plant, but it needs hard pinching early on. The flowers are medium-sized singles with a white-pink tube and sepals, and a lilac-pink flared corolla with pale patches at the petal base. The buds grow in clusters at the end of the stems

and the flowers appear to grow as they mature, but the gradual flaring of the corolla probably causes this effect. The small to medium-sized foliage is dark green. It is a delightful cultivar that is well worth growing. Half hardy; Zones 9–10. Webb, UK, 1989.

'Joel'

This is an upright cultivar that is quite self-branching, but benefits from extra pinching early on. The flowers are pretty, medium-sized singles held semi-erect, and have a white tube, white reflexed sepals with a faint pink blush and an exquisite pale violet-blue corolla that flares beautifully.

It is not the strongest growing cultivar but is well worth trying for the flowers and their contrast with the small to medium-sized mid- to dark green leaves. It is excellent when grown as a smallish pot plant or small standard. Half hardy; Zones 9–10. Humphries, UK, 1993.

'Jomam'

This upright, short-jointed bushy fuchsia makes a superb, really eye-catching pot plant. The flowers are medium-sized singles with a rose-pink tube, quite large rose-pink sepals that tend to twist slightly and a quarter-flared pale blue-violet corolla that matures to light violet-pink. The strong stems produce vigorous growth with dark yellowish-green leaves, and it quickly becomes a large plant. Take care to keep the roots cool because it dislikes being overheated. Half hardy; Zones 9–10. Hall, UK, 1984.

'Kath van Hanegem'

This small-growing cultivar is very pretty and suitable for growing as a smaller pot plant or miniature standard. It is named after an enthusiastic fuchsia grower living in the east of England and married to a Dutchman. The small but exquisite single flowers have a dark red tube, red sepals and an aubergine corolla. The mid-green leaves contrast well with the flowers. It is also suitable for a rockery in warm areas. Frost hardy; Zones 7–8. Carless, UK, 1998.

'Kath van Hanegem'

'Karen Louise Tinkler'

'London 2000'

'Karen Louise Tinkler'

This is a compact growing, very floriferous fuchsia well into the exhibition category. It has upright and self-branching growth. It is very floriferous, with small single flowers with a short pink tube. Pale pink sepals are held half up with recurved tips and darker pink underneath. The corolla is half flared with petals of bright mauve which fade to reddish mauve on maturity. Half hardy; Zones 9–10. Wilkinson, UK, 2021.

'Kobold'

This bushy fuchsia has small to medium-sized semi-erect single flowers with a red tube and sepals, and a bell-shaped violet-blue corolla. When grown as a pot plant or standard, the flower colour is really eye-catching, and it continues flowering over a long period. The upright, short-jointed growth carries small to medium-sized mid-green leaves. Half hardy; Zones 9–10. Götz, Germany, 1990.

'Lady Isobel Barnett'

This is one of the most floriferous cultivars, with as many as four flowers from each leaf node. The single flowers are small to medium-sized with a rosy-red tube and sepals, and a rose-purple corolla with darker edges on the petals. The growth is upright, self-branching and bushy with medium-sized mid-green foliage. It is easy to grow as a specimen pot plant or for summer bedding. Half hardy; Zones 9–10. Gadsby, UK, 1968.

'Lambada'

This is a compact, pretty cultivar which is very useful for small pots. It has small single flowers with a pale pink tube and sepals and a mallow-purple flared corolla with white patches at the petal base. The growth is upright and compact with small

'Lady Isobel Barnett'

mid-green foliage. It has a tremendous number of flowers, making it a great pot plant or small standard. It is also excellent for use in mixed plantings. Half hardy; Zones 9–10. Götz, Germany, 1989.

'Lilac Lustre'

This is an attractive cultivar that has beautifully shaped flowers and fat, round buds that hang in the bright mid-green foliage. The freely produced medium-sized double flowers have a rose-red tube and sepals, and a powder-blue corolla with ruffled petals. It makes an excellent pot plant, but prefers to grow in a shady position. Half hardy; Zones 9–10. Munkner, USA, 1961.

'London 2000'

This is a good, strong and vigorous upright cultivar, excellent as a pot plant or a small to medium standard. The flowers are medium-sized singles with a white tube blushed pink, white sepals flushed pink and a cyclamen-purple corolla with cerise areas at the base of the petals. The corolla fades to cerise as the flower matures. The medium-sized mid-green leaves provide an excellent backdrop for the abundant flowers, and it can also be trained into other shapes, such as a fan. Half hardy; Zones 9–10. Weston, UK, 2000.

'Marcus Graham'

'Marcus Graham'

An introduction from Annabelle Stubbs, this spectaculrar cultivar never fails to make an impact. The growth is upright, quite vigorous and self-branching, and needs to be well hardened to support the large double flowers, which have a thin white to flesh-pink tube, long broad dusky pink sepals and a fully flared salmon-pink full corolla with orange streaks on the petals. The foliage is quite large and mid-green. This fuchsia can be grown as a specimen bush or standard as well as a pot plant. Half hardy; Zones 9–10. Stubbs, USA, 1985.

'Margaret Roe'

This is a free-flowering cultivar that has vigorous and upright growth. The medium-sized single flowers are held upright and have a short rosy-red tube and sepals, and a violet-purple corolla. The medium-sized foliage is dull mid-green and the strong growth benefits from early pinching. It is excellent as a pot plant, in a patio container or planted permanently in the garden. Hardy; Zone 7. Growth 75cm (30in). Gadsby, UK, 1968.

'Maria Landy'

With its vigorous, upright, self-branching growth, this makes an excellent compact specimen plant. The prolific flowers are semi-erect small singles with a pale pink tube, recurving pink sepals and a pale violet corolla. The foliage is small and dark green, a perfect foil for the beautiful flowers. It can be trained as a small standard, or used in mixed planting or for summer bedding. Half hardy; Zones 9–10. Wilkinson, UK, 1991.

'Micky Goult'

Upright and free-flowering, this has clusters of small, single, semi-erect flowers with a short pale pink tube, horizontal pale pink sepals tipped green and a short mallow-purple corolla. The foliage is light to mid-green, and quite large for the flower size. Its upright growth needs heavy early pinching to create a bushy shape, but if left to grow naturally it flowers early and over a long period. Half hardy; Zones 9–10. Roe, UK, 1986.

'Mrs Susan Brookfield'

'Maria Landy'

'Mrs Susan Brookfield'

This is an attractive upright with medium-sized double flowers with a dark rose tube, reflexed dark rose sepals and a full mauve corolla with attractive pink and rose splashes. The medium-sized bright pale to mid-green foliage provides an excellent foil to the flowers. The growth is strongly upright with reasonable self-branching, but it is helped by early pinching. The best colours with the brightest petal splashes are obtained when grown outside in part direct sun, part shade, where it makes an excellent pot plant or half to full standard. Half hardy; Zones 9–10. Rimmer, UK, 1991.

'Negrita'

This fuchsia has short jointed and self-branching upright growth with dark green leaves. It has plentiful single flowers with a rose tube, red sepals and a violet-blue half flared corolla fading to violet on maturity. Half hardy; Zones 9–10. Demonceau, Belgium, 1987.

'Nico van Suchtelen'

This Dutch cultivar has strong upright self-branching growth with large mid-green leaves. The flowers are long medium-sized singles, almost Triphylla-like with a long carmine pink tube, streaked with a darker shade, light carmine pink sepals held downwards and a short carmine corolla, which is deep carmine pink at the base. It makes an unusual large pot plant and thrives in full sun. Half hardy; Zones 9–10. Benders, Netherlands, 1986.

'Northway'

This produces small single flowers held semi-erect with a pale pink tube, pale pink sepals held just below the horizontal and a bright cherry-red corolla. It flowers from early summer to early autumn. The foliage is light to mid-green and contrasts well with the flower colours. With upright self-branching growth, it makes a striking pot plant. It can also be trained up a tree, espalier, pillar or trellis. Prune back dead or broken branches in spring. Half hardy; Zones 9–10. Golics, UK, 1976.

'Northumbrian Pipes'

This cultivar is something different, with unusual flower colours and buds. It has Triphylla-type flowers held on part terminal and part axial flowering growth. They are medium-sized singles with a long china-rose tube, short china-rose sepals tipped green and a light lavender-pink corolla. The growing buds are also an attractive, unusual colour, with the ovary and half of the tube almost aubergine, and the remainder green. The lax bushy upright growth has long mid- to dark green leaves, which are lighter underneath. It does well in a pot or small patio container. Half hardy; Zones 9–10. de Graaff, Netherlands, 1983.

'Onna'

Very floriferous, this fuchsia is upright and self-branching with Triphylla-shaped flowers, but they emerge from the leaf axils and not the end of the stems. The medium-sized single flowers have a long orange tube, short orange sepals held down over the corolla with recurving tips, and a crimson corolla. The largish leaves are mid-green and lighter underneath with green stems. It makes a nice pot or patio container plant. Half hardy; Zones 9–10. Bögemann, Germany, 1987.

'Onna'

'Orange Flare'

'Orange Flare'

This cultivar is perhaps one of the best orange-flowered fuchsias, apart from those in the Triphylla Group. It has an early-flowering habit, and is a plant that will be quite happy in full sun, although the colours do benefit from slight shading. The flowers are medium-sized singles with a short thick orange-salmon tube, orange-salmon sepals and an orange corolla, lighter at the petal base and darker on the petal edges. The growth is upright and bushy with medium-sized mid-green foliage. It makes a good pot plant or standard. Half hardy; Zones 9–10. Handley, UK, 1986.

'Our Darling'

This is a strong upright-growing cultivar that self-branches very well and is suitable for training as a bush, a shrub or a standard. The medium-sized single flowers have a short deep rose tube, reflexed deep rose sepals and a flared violet-blue corolla veined with rose and with lighter patches at the petal base. It is very floriferous with medium to large mid-green leaves, and makes a beautiful specimen plant in a pot. Half hardy; Zones 9–10. Hall, UK, 1984.

'Pabbe's Kirrevaalk'

'Phenomenal'

'Pabbe's Kirrevaalk'

This Dutch cultivar has bushy upright growth with small single flowers, held semi-erect, with a short dark reddish-purple tube, reddish-purple sepals held horizontally and a flared saucer-shaped corolla opening dark purple, maturing to reddish-purple. The small mid-green foliage provides a good foil to the copious amounts of flowers. It is easy to grow as a pot plant or smaller standard. Half hardy; Zones 9–10. Koerts, Netherlands, 2004.

'Patio Princess'

This is a vigorous and spreading self-branching bush which is easy to grow and, as its name suggests, will make an excellent specimen plant for the patio. It flowers early in the season with small to medium double flowers with a neyron-rose tube, neyron-rose three-quarters recurving sepals, and a flared white corolla veined with red. The foliage is small to medium, mid-green with a red vein in the leaf. It does tend to throw a number of semi-double flowers as well, but the sheer quantity of flowers produced will compensate for this. Half hardy; Zones 9–10. Sinton, UK, 1988.

'Phenomenal'

This fuchsia is certainly a striking sight today, but it must have been really spectacular when it was first released in the middle of the 19th century. It has large double flowers with a thin scarlet tube, broad scarlet sepals and a lovely indigo-blue corolla with cerise veining on the petals, which are paler at the base. The mid-green foliage is largish and serrated, and the flowers are freely produced for their size. The branches may need some staking to support the weight of the flowers. Half hardy; Zones 9–10. Lemoine, France, 1869.

'Plumb Bob'

The flowers of this fuchsia are large doubles with an ivory tube flushed pink, ivory sepals with a pink flush and a red corolla with mauve tones, and they are quite numerous for their size. The medium-sized foliage is mid- to dark green and a perfect backdrop to the flowers. Use this vigorous sturdy upright as a specimen pot plant, a standard or in summer bedding. Half hardy; Zones 9–10. Goulding, UK, 1974.

'President Leo Boullemier'

This is a vigorous upright cultivar that will make a good specimen pot plant or a standard, and also grows well as a summer bedding plant. The flowers are medium-sized singles with a square white tube streaked magenta, white recurving sepals and a bell-shaped magenta corolla. The foliage is medium-sized and dark green in colour. The plant is a cross between 'Joy Patmore' and 'Cloverdale Pearl'. Half hardy; Zones 9–10. Burns, UK, 1983.

'Queen Mary'

This old cultivar, one of a pair of seedlings named after the then reigning British monarchs, is a vigorous upright bush. It has large single flowers, which are quite abundant for their size, with a pale pink tube, long pink sepals tipped greenish-white and a rose corolla that matures to mauve-purple. The largish mid-green leaves help create an impressive pot plant that can easily be trained into a medium to large standard. Half hardy; Zones 9–10. Howlett, UK, 1911.

'President Leo Boullemier'

'Query'

'Ratatouille'

'Query'

This very old cultivar, still popular, has a small single flower with a pale pink tube, pale pink sepals with green tips and a purple corolla veined pink that matures to magenta. The growth is upright and self-branching with rather small light to mid-green leaves, and it makes a nice pot plant. This cultivar is very similar to 'Chillerton Beauty', introduced by the same hybridizer in the same year, and some believe it may be the same plant. Hardy; Zones 6–7. Growth 60cm (24in). Bass, UK, 1848.

'Ratatouille'

This Dutch cultivar has an unusual parentage, a result from crossing a fuchsia species with a showy US double. This created the small to medium-sized double flowers with an ivory-white tube, ivory-white sepals blushed lilac underneath and a pale aubergine corolla with white stripes. The growth is upright and slightly lax with medium-sized, bright mid-green foliage, and it makes an excellent pot plant. Half hardy; Zones 9–10. de Graaff, Netherlands, 1988.

'Robert Lutters'

This is a vigorous upright bush that is excellent as a pot plant or trained as a standard. The plentiful flowers are medium-sized singles with a white tube blushed rose, rose sepals held horizontally and slightly twisted, and a quarter flared bengal-red corolla with a classic bell shape. The medium-sized light to mid-green leaves complement the flowers very well. Half hardy; Zones 9–10. Beije, Netherlands, 1989.

'Rocket Fire'

This is a vigorous upright bush cultivar with unusual double flowers that are medium in size with a magenta tube, dark rose sepals and a corolla with purple pleated outer petals and dark pink inner petals. The foliage is medium to large and mid-green, and provides a nice background to the flowers. This fuchsia makes a good pot plant. Half hardy; Zones 9–10. Garrett, USA, 1989.

'Rolla'

This old French cultivar grows excellently as a bush, vigorous and upright. It was one of the 50 cultivars sent to the USA in 1930 and is probably in the parentage of many of the large US double fuchsias. The flowers are large doubles with a short pale pink tube, pale pink sepals fully reflexed over the tube and a full pure white corolla with pink tinges at the petal base. The medium-sized mid-green foliage helps make it an attractive pot plant, and it can be trained into large structures. Half hardy; Zones 9–10. Lemoine, France, 1913.

'Roy Walker'

This cultivar is one of the better white doubles, staying white even in the sun. The growth is upright and self-branching with medium-sized mid-green foliage; it needs to be grown hard (outdoors as much as possible) to make the wood strong enough to support the flowers. The flower is a medium to large double with a white tube flushed pink, white-veined red sepals and a flared white corolla. This fuchsia takes a long time from final pinching to flowering, typically 12 to 14 weeks. It will make a striking specimen plant or half standard. Half hardy; Zones 9–10. Fuchsia-La, USA, 1975.

'Roy Walker'

'Sarah Eliza'

'Sarah Eliza'

There is some confusion over the growth habit of this cultivar. It is often listed as a trailing fuchsia, but it has growth that is more bush-like, and it is just the weight of the flowers that makes the branches hang downward. The flower is a medium to large double with a white tube, white sepals flushed pale pink and a full white corolla flushed pink. Like most white fuchsias, the flower becomes pinker in the sun, especially the sepals. The growth is upright and spreading with light green leaves, and it is quite floriferous, making it ideal as a pot plant or in the centre of a mixed basket or container. Half hardy; Zones 9–10. Clements, UK, 1992.

'Satellite'

This has rather unusual medium to large double flowers with a greenish-white tube, white sepals with green tips and a dark red corolla streaked white. The strongly upright growth has medium-sized mid-green foliage and the flowers look superb together with it, standing out in the sunshine. It makes a very striking pot plant for the terrace or patio. Take care not to overwater it as it is prone to botrytis. Half hardy; Zones 9–10. Kennett, USA, 1965.

'Silver Dawn'

This is a strong upright bushy cultivar with medium-sized mid-green foliage, and is excellent for growing as a pot plant or a half standard. The medium-sized double flowers have a long white tube, broad white sepals tipped green and a beautiful aster-violet corolla. Half hardy; Zones 9–10. Bellamy, UK, 1983.

'Snowfire'

This is an introduction from Annabelle Stubbs. A very striking fuchsia, it will make an excellent pot plant, or is useful for growing in mixed containers. The flower is a large double with a pink tube, wide white sepals and a bright coral corolla with white patches, which are larger on the outer petals. The foliage is medium to large in size and dark green in colour. This fuchsia always attracts people's attention. Half hardy; Zones 9–10. Stubbs, USA, 1978.

'Sunray'

This is one of the best of the variegated-leaf cultivars. It forms a slow-growing bush, with the best leaf colours developed in the sun or bright conditions. Although grown more for its foliage than the flowers, they are not unattractive, being small to medium-sized singles with a cerise tube, cerise sepals and a rosy-purple corolla. The foliage is medium-sized and has yellow, green and red colours in the leaf. This fuchsia will form an attractive smaller pot plant or blend well in a mixed container. An alternative plant to consider is 'Tom West', which is a little faster growing, but the leaf colours are not quite as good. Half hardy; Zones 9–10. Rudd, UK, 1872.

'Symphony'

This beautiful cultivar is very tall and graceful, with medium-sized single flowers with a pale phlox-pink tube, slightly reflexed pale phlox-pink sepals and a cobalt-violet corolla. The mid-green foliage with slightly lighter yellow-green new growth helps make an attractive, striking pot plant. Quite fast growing, it will make a shrub quickly. It prefers a shady position. This is a plant that deserves to be more widely grown than it is. Half hardy; Zones 9–10. Neiderholzer, USA, 1944.

'Snowfire'

'Symphony'

'Thamar'

'Taddle'

A vigorous free-flowering upright self-branching cultivar with medium-sized light green foliage, this fuchsia can be trained as a bush with the minimum of effort. The flowers are medium-sized singles with a short deep rose-pink tube, fully reflexed rose-pink sepals and a waxy white-veined pink corolla. Half hardy; Zones 9–10. Gubler, UK, 1974.

'Tamar Isobel'

This fuchsia has vigorous upright and bushy growth with small to medium-sized mid-green leaves. The medium-sized single flowers have a white tube striped with pink, fully recurved white sepals with a slight pink blush and a reddish-purple corolla with pink streaks. It makes an excellent pot plant with minimal effort, and is easy to grow as a standard, best as a half standard. This was one of the last introductions from the hybridizer before his death that same year. Half hardy; Zones 9–10. Mitchinson, UK, 1988.

'Tangerine'

This US cultivar is a *F. cordifolia* seedling with medium-sized single flowers with a long, flesh-pink tube, flesh-pink sepals tipped green and a flared orange corolla with overlapping petals maturing to rose. The growth habit is upright and bushy with

mid-green leaves, and it makes an attractive spreading pot plant. Half hardy; Zones 9–10. Tiret, USA, 1949.

'Thamar'

This eye-catching cultivar is rather unusual, with its upright growth and many flowers held erect like little pansies. The flowers are small singles with a white tube, white cupped sepals with a faint pink blush and a pale blue corolla with white patches at the base. The foliage is medium-sized and dark green. It is a very floriferous plant, but the growth is not self-branching, so it benefits from early pinching. It stays in flower for a long time and makes a good specimen pot plant, container plant or summer bedder. This cultivar is well worth growing for its impact. Half hardy; Zones 9–10. Springer, Germany, 1986.

'Ting a Ling'

This is an upright bushy cultivar, which is excellent grown as a shrub pot plant or as a quarter or half standard. It has medium-sized single flowers with a white tube, three-quarters recurved white sepals and a white bell-shaped, flared corolla. The medium-sized foliage is mid-green and it grows well but, like many whites, can be prone to botrytis. Half hardy; Zones 9–10. Schnabel and Paskesen, USA, 1959.

'Ting a Ling'

'Twinny'

This relative newcomer is already very popular, making an impressive pot plant or a smaller standard up to half standard size. The flowers are small to medium-sized singles with a red tube, pink-red sepals and white corolla with red veining. The growth is upright, self-branching, very bushy and floriferous, with small mid- to dark green leaves. It dislikes heat, so when grown in a pot, terracotta is best, and the pot should be shaded. Half hardy; Zones 9–10. Gordon, UK, 1999.

'Twinny'

'Upward Look'

'Vobeglo'

'Upward Look'

This vigorous upright bushy cultivar has medium-sized erect single flowers with a carmine tube, carmine sepals with green tips and a pale purple corolla. This was the first notable fuchsia with erect flowers released since 'Bon Accord' in 1861. It has dull mid-green foliage and grows well in full sun, and makes an excellent specimen pot plant, standard and summer bedder. Half hardy; Zones 9–10. Gadsby, UK, 1968.

'Uranus'

This German cultivar has medium-sized single flowers with a short fat red tube, long reflexed red sepals and a dark purple corolla. Upright growing and bushy with mid- to dark green foliage, it is easy to train to a bush or shrub pot plant or even as a standard. Half hardy; Zones 9–10. Strümper, Germany, 1986.

'Vincent van Gogh'

This Dutch cultivar, named after the famous artist, has strong upright bushy growth covered by bright mid-green foliage. The flowers are small to medium-sized singles with a long pink tube, pale pink sepals with green tips that hang down and a pale lilac-pink corolla that is slightly flared. It is a good plant for training as a bush or shrub in a pot. Half hardy; Zones 9–10. van der Post, Netherlands, 1984.

'Violet Bassett-Burr'

The flowers of this fuchsia are beautiful and highly unusual, sure to create a striking impression. They are large doubles with a greenish-white and pink tube, almost fully recurved white sepals with green tips and pink at the base, and a very full pale lilac corolla. The growth is upright

'Voodoo'

and bushy, and the foliage dark green. It is at its best grown as a specimen pot plant or a full or half standard. This fuchsia is one that will turn heads, and is well worth growing. Half hardy; Zones 9–10. Holmes, UK, 1972.

'Vobeglo'

This compact, low-growing fuchsia has small erect single flowers with a pink tube, rose-red sepals and a lilac-purple corolla. The growth is bushy but not very vigorous, with small to medium-sized mid-green foliage. It will happily make a small pot plant, a small standard, or can be used in a rockery. Half hardy; Zones 9–10. de Groot, Netherlands, 1974.

'Voodoo'

This has spectacular large double flowers with a dark red tube, long dark red sepals and a very full dark purple-violet corolla with some red splashes at the base of the petals. The growth is vigorous, bushy and upright, with medium to large mid-green foliage. Grow outside as much as possible to harden the wood so that it can support the large flowers, or use stakes. It is an excellent cultivar to grow as a specimen plant for a large pot. Half hardy; Zones 9–10. Tiret, USA, 1953.

'White Joy'

'White Joy'

This strong-growing cultivar with an upright, bushy habit is very easy to grow as a pot plant or a quarter or half standard. The flowers are medium-sized singles with a short white tube with a pink blush, white recurving sepals with a pink blush and a flared bell-shaped white corolla. The foliage is medium-sized and light to mid-green. Half hardy; Zones 9–10. Burns, UK, 1980.

'Wilson's Sugar Pink'

This vigorous cultivar is bush-like but can tend to become a little lax. Growing it in full sun strengthens the wood and helps keep it upright. The flowers are produced in great abundance. They are small singles with a white tube shading to pink, pale pink sepals and a silver-pink corolla. The small to medium-sized leaves are an attractive shade of light green. Half hardy; Zones 9–10. Wilson, UK, 1979.

'Wingrove's Mammoth'

This has very large double flowers with a short turkey-red tube, long turkey-red sepals and a very full white corolla veined and splashed with carmine. It is upright and bushy but the heavy flowers drag the branches down, so some support and staking may be necessary. The medium-sized foliage is mid-green. Half hardy; Zones 9–10. Wingrove, UK, 1986.

'Woodnook'

This upright and bushy cultivar has attractive medium-sized double flowers with a white tube striped with carmine, white sepals flushed carmine and tipped with green and a pale violet-purple full corolla with rose-bengal splashes. The

medium-sized foliage is mid-green in colour and the profuse flowers stand out beautifully. This vigorous growing fuchsia makes a superb pot plant and is excellent grown as a half standard. Half hardy; Zones 9–10. Pacey, UK, 1987.

'Yolanda Franck'

This Dutch cultivar has medium-sized single flowers with a thick light rose tube, light rose sepals tipped green hanging down and a pale orange-red corolla. The strong upright growth is self-branching with medium-sized mid-green leaves. Fairly free-flowering, it makes a nice pot plant and is happy in full sun. Half hardy; Zones 9–10. Franck, Netherlands, 1988.

'Zwarte Snor'

This attractive Dutch cultivar has medium-sized single to semi-double flowers with a slightly barrel-shaped cardinal-red tube, cardinal-red sepals hanging down and a purple-aubergine corolla with red at the base of the petals. The growth is upright, self-branching and slightly lax, with medium-sized mid-green foliage, which contrasts well with the abundantly produced flowers. It does best in a shady position, and is easy to grow to a good-sized pot plant, trained as a shrub. Half hardy; Zones 9–10. Weeda, Netherlands, 1990.

'Wilson's Sugar Pink'

'Wingrove's Mammoth'

Hardy fuchsias

When planted correctly outside, hardy fuchsias should survive winter temperatures down to –23°C (–10°F). The heights stated are typically achieved with winter temperatures between –18 and –12°C (0 to 10°F), when the fuchsias are planted in a sunny position.

'Abbé Farges'

This pretty cultivar has small semi-double flowers with a light cerise tube, light cerise reflexed sepals and a lilac-blue corolla with slightly scalloped petal edges. The growth is rather wiry and slightly brittle, but it is surprisingly vigorous and free-flowering. Try growing it as a quarter standard, which will be completely covered in flowers. It is a good garden hardy that is ideal for the middle or front of the hardy border. Hardy; Zone 6. Growth 45–60cm (18–24in). Lemoine, France, 1901.

'Achievement'

This vigorous old cultivar is easy to grow, making it a good choice for beginners. It has large single flowers with a short red tube, long red sepals and a corolla that opens purple and fades to reddish-purple on maturity. The foliage is yellowish-green with a distinct red midrib. It is sometimes confused with 'Charming' but has longer, narrower, less reflexed sepals. It is good in the middle of the hardy border or can be grown as a pot plant. Hardy; Zone 6. Growth 55cm (22in). Melville, UK, 1866.

'Alice Hoffman'

One of the smaller-growing hardy fuchsias, this cultivar has small semi-double flowers with tube and sepals both coloured rose, and a white, veined rose corolla. The growth is wiry, spreading and upright, and the foliage is small and bronze-green. A compact growing bush, it does well at the front of the hardy border and is useful in the rockery. It will also make an effective small standard. This cultivar has an RHS Award of Garden Merit, awarded in 2002. Hardy; Zones 7–8. Growth 45cm (18in). Kiese, Germany, 1911.

'Army Nurse'

This is a strong upright bush with medium-sized semi-double flared flowers with a short red tube, red sepals and a mauve-blue corolla, pink blushed at the petal base. It has vigorous growth with light to mid-green foliage, making a fair-sized plant in one season. Grow it as a pot plant, or plant it out as a summer bedder. It received an RHS Award of Garden Merit in 1993. Hardy; Zone 7. Growth 1m (3ft). Hodges, USA, 1947.

'Baby Blue Eyes'

'Baby Blue Eyes'

This cultivar has upright and strong bushy growth with small single flowers. The flowers have red sepals and tube and a dark lavender corolla, and the foliage is medium-sized and dark green in colour. It is very floriferous, and grows well in the middle of a hardy bed where it forms a compact bushy shrub. This cultivar has an RHS Award of Garden Merit, awarded in 2005. Hardy; Zones 6–7. Growth 1m (3ft). Plummer, USA, 1952.

'Bashful'

This small upright, self-branching bushy cultivar has small double flowers with a deep pink tube and sepals and a white corolla with red veining. Raised and bred in the Scilly Isles, it is one of the Seven Dwarfs series of cultivars and has compact growth with small dark green foliage, making it ideal for a rockery or to the front of the hardy border. Although listed as a hardy, it is probably better classified as a marginal hardy. Hardy; Zones 7–8. Growth 30cm (12in). Tabraham, UK, 1974.

'Alice Hoffman'

'Army Nurse'

'Beacon'

This old hardy cultivar has quite stiff upright growth and medium-sized single flowers with a deep pink tube and sepals, and a mauvish-pink flared corolla. The foliage is a darkish green with wavy serrated edges. It is a very reliable plant, which you can also train as a standard. Older specimens have very unusual bark on the wood, which becomes flaky and peels off. There is a sport from 'Beacon' called 'Beacon Rosa', where the flowers are the same shape but self-pink in colour. Hardy; Zone 7. Growth 60cm (2ft). Bull, UK, 1871.

'Brilliant'

This reliable old hardy has strong upright, vigorous open growth and mid- to dark green foliage. The medium-sized single or semi-double flowers have a long scarlet tube, slightly reflexed scarlet sepals and a violet-magenta corolla with red veining on the petals. It is a good hardy for the middle to rear of any hardy scheme, but is also suitable as a summer bedder or trained as a standard. Hardy; Zone 7. Growth 70cm (28in). Bull, UK, 1865.

'Caledonia'

This has quite vigorous, spreading upright growth and medium-green foliage. The single flowers are rather unusual for a

'Brilliant'

hardy fuchsia, having long cerise tubes, cerise sepals that hang down and a crimson corolla. It is a good candidate to grow in the mid-position in the hardy border and also makes an attractive low hedge. Hardy; Zones 6–7. Growth 65cm (26in). Lemoine, France, 1899.

'Charming'

This is an easily grown hardy cultivar, upright and vigorous with medium-sized single flowers with a carmine tube, nicely reflexed reddish-cerise sepals and a rose-purple corolla. The flower is the classic

fuchsia shape and sits well against the medium-sized yellowish-green foliage. It makes a successful standard. It is sometimes confused with 'Drame', but has longer flowers and more upright growth. It received an RHS Award of Merit in 1929. Hardy; Zones 6–7. Growth 70cm (27in). Lye, UK, 1895.

'Chillerton Beauty'

Strong and reliable, this fuchsia has upright bushy growth and a profusion of small single flowers. The white tube is blushed pink and the horizontal sepals are the same colour, becoming pinker with more sun. The red-veined mauvish-violet corolla fades as the flower ages. It makes a good medium-sized hedge. Some believe it to be identical to 'Query'. Hardy; Zones 6–7. Growth 65cm (26in). Bass, UK, 1847.

'Cliff's Hardy'

This upright bushy cultivar has single medium-sized semi-erect flowers with a light crimson tube, light crimson sepals tipped green and a violet corolla. The flowers sit nicely held off the small mid- to dark green leaves. It is a vigorous grower, ideal for a fuchsia hedge. Do not overfeed, because it will make growth at the expense of flowers. Hardy; Zones 6–7. Growth 55cm (22in). Gadsby, UK, 1966.

'Caledonia'

'Charming'

'David'

'David'

A seedling from 'Pumila' and 'Venus Victrix', this has small leaves and flowers. It inherits many of the former's characteristics, carrying profuse single flowers with a cerise tube and sepals, and a rich purple corolla. The growth is compact and upright with small dark green leaves, making it very useful in the rockery, at the front of the hardy border and as an edging plant. Hardy; Zones 6–7. Growth 45cm (18in). Wood, UK, 1937.

'Display'

This excellent old exhibition-class cultivar is a strong upright and bushy grower with serrated mid- to dark green foliage. It has medium single flowers with rose-pink tube and sepals, and a darker pink flared corolla. It is very easy to train and can be used for most forms of trained growth, including pyramids and standards. It is popular in Germany and the Netherlands. This is an ideal candidate for everyone's collection. Hardy; Zones 6–7. Growth 60cm (2ft). Smith, UK, 1881.

'Dollar Prinzessin' ('Dollar Princess'/'Princess Dollar')

Although still sold widely as 'Dollar Princess', research has shown that the original name of this fuchsia was 'Dollarprinzessin'. Attributed to Victor Lemoine and introduced in 1912, a year after his death, it now seems it was first introduced in Germany by Kroger in 1910. It is a cultivar which, when grown in the border, will make a mound covered in flowers. It has medium-sized double flowers with cerise tube and sepals and a rich purple full corolla, splashed red, with mid- to dark green foliage. It is one of the few double cultivars that can be treated as a hardy in cold areas, and will be in flower shortly after midsummer. It is at its best in the second or third year when grown as a pot plant, and also makes a good standard. Hardy; Zones 6–7. Growth 40cm (16in). Kroger, Germany, 1910.

'Empress of Prussia'

This old cultivar was thought to have been lost from cultivation, but a plant was discovered in an English garden in 1956, where it had been growing for more than 60 years. After propagation, Bernard Rawlings reintroduced it. It has medium to large single flowers with a scarlet tube and sepals, and a corolla of reddish-magenta petals with a paler patch near the base. It is very floriferous, throwing up to four flowers from each leaf axil, with strong upright growth. Hardy; Zones 6–7. Growth 90cm (3ft). Hoppe, UK, 1868.

'Display'

'Dollar Prinzessin'

'Enfant Prodigue' ('Prodigue'/'Prodigy')

This old cultivar has strong, vigorous upright growth, inherited from one of its parents, 'Riccartonii'. It has medium-sized semi-double – sometimes double – flowers with a deep red tube and sepals, and a deep blue corolla with red at the base of the petals. With its medium-sized, mid-green foliage, it is best towards the back of the hardy border where it will form a large plant. Hardy; Zones 6–7. Growth 90cm (3ft). Lemoine, France, 1887.

'Eva Boerg'

This cultivar is an unusual hardy, being quite lax and growing into a spreading bush. It is a good cultivar for use in hanging baskets, beds held back by a retaining wall and permanent planting in planters built into walls. The growth will soon spread over the wall and trail down it. The flesh-pink buds are very fat and round before opening into a medium-sized semi-double flower with a greenish-white tube, pinkish-white sepals and pinkish-purple corolla splashed pink at the base. The foliage is a light green, and the cultivar is often confused with the very similar 'Lena'. This fuchsia is easy to grow into a weeping standard because of its strong growth. Hardy; Zone 7. Growth 45cm (18in). Yorke, UK, 1943.

'Flash'

This hardy US cultivar is vigorous, bushy and upright in growth habit, with small, finely serrated light green foliage. It is quite floriferous, carrying small single flowers with a light-magenta tube and sepals, and a light-magenta corolla fading to red. It is quite a strong grower, well suited for use in the centre of the hardy border. Hardy; Zone 7. Growth 75cm (30in). Hazard and Hazard, USA, 1930.

'Foxgrove Wood'

This fairly recent cultivar has upright bushy growth and mid-green foliage. The pretty, small single flowers have a pink tube and sepals and blue corolla. This fuchsia can be grown in a hardy border, but in colder areas is best used as a summer bedder. Hardy; Zones 7–8. Growth 60cm (2ft). Stiff, UK, 1993.

'Frau Hilde Rademacher'

This is a beautiful fuchsia with rather lax, spreading growth. It is very floriferous for the size of the flowers, and has some resemblance to 'Dark Eyes'. The fat red buds open into medium to large double flowers with a short red tube, horizontal red sepals and a full, frilled, deep blue corolla. The foliage is dark green with red veining. It can be trained as a weeping half standard. Hardy; Zones 7–8. Growth 90cm (3ft). Rademacher, Germany, 1925.

'Garden News'

This is a good hardy double cultivar for the garden, with strong upright growth and mid-green foliage. The double flowers are medium to large with a pink tube and sepals and a full magenta corolla with ruffled petals. It is reliable and quite free-flowering for a double. Hardy; Zones 6–7. Growth 60cm (2ft). Handley, UK, 1978.

'Genii' ('Jeanne')

This is an excellent cultivar in all ways, and should be in everyone's garden. It is one of the few hardies originating from the USA. It was originally named 'Jeanne', but is now much more widely known as 'Genii'. It has beautiful small pale green foliage, which becomes lighter in the sun. It has single small to medium flowers with a cerise tube and sepals and a violet corolla. Because of its leaf colour, it seems to sparkle and stand out in the hardy border. You can also train it as a standard or grow it as a specimen plant in a large pot. Hardy; Zones 6–7. Growth 70cm (28in). Reiter, USA, 1951.

'Garden News'

'Gustave Doré'

This old French cultivar is upright, bushy and self-branching with mid-green foliage. The flowers are medium-sized doubles with a deep pink tube, deep pink sepals and a creamy-white corolla, very full and fluffy, with attractive scalloped petal edges. This fuchsia is a good choice for the front of the border. Hardy; Zone 7. Growth 40cm (16in). Lemoine, France, 1880.

'Frau Hilde Rademacher'

'Genii'

'Happy'

This is one of the Seven Dwarfs series, a very attractive bush with compact, self-branching growth. It has small semi-erect single flowers with a red tube and sepals, and a deep purple-blue corolla turning magenta. The flowers resemble small stars twinkling on a small green mound of foliage. It is excellent as an edging plant or for use in the rockery, or the front of the hardy border and grown as a small pot. Hardy; Zone 8. Growth 40cm (16in). Tabraham, UK, 1974.

'Hawkshead'

This is a superb vigorous cultivar with small mid- to dark green foliage. It has small white self-coloured single flowers. It is that rare fuchsia: a white variety that stays white even in the full sun, with the flowers sparkling against the foliage. It is best placed at the back of the border because of its strong upright growth. In milder areas it will make a very large plant. Its parentage was *F. magellanica* var. *molinae* crossed with 'Venus Victrix'. Hardy; Zones 6–7. Growth 1.2m (4ft). Travis, UK, 1973.

'Hawkshead'

'Howlett's Hardy'

'Herald'

This is a strong upright-growing cultivar with attractive pale green foliage. It makes a very reliable garden plant for the middle of the hardy border and can also be used as a specimen plant in a large tub or container. The flowers are medium-sized singles with a medium-length bulbous red tube, recurved red sepals and a bluish-purple corolla with pink patches on the petals. The corolla fades to red as it ages. Hardy; Zones 6–7. Growth 60cm (2ft). Sankey, UK, 1895.

'Hobo'

This hardy cultivar is also reputed to show fuchsia gall mite resistance according to American northwest sources. It is an upright mid-sized cultivar with mid- to dark green foliage. The flower is classified as semi-double but will also produce double flowers. It has a medium red tube, red upswept petals held close to the tube when fully open and a deep red-purple corolla with red at the base of the petals Hardy; Zones 7–8. Growth 60cm (2ft). Carless, UK, 1997.

'Howlett's Hardy'

This upright and quite vigorous cultivar has medium-sized single flowers with a red tube and sepals, and a blue-violet corolla with paler pink patches at the base. The foliage is medium to large, mid-green and serrated. The flowers are of a good size for a hardy, and quite freely produced. It can be used in the centre of a border, is a good pot plant and is easy to grow to a half standard. It received an RHS Award of Garden Merit in 2005. Hardy; Zone 7. Growth 55cm (22in). Howlett, UK, 1952.

'Isis'

One of three different cultivars named 'Isis', this entry refers to the one raised by de Groot, one of a series hybridized from *F. regia typica*, this one from a cross with 'Alice Hoffman'. It has upright growth and medium-sized single flowers with a red tube and sepals, and a purple corolla fading to reddish-purple with age. The leaf is an attractive dark green with a red midrib, and this fuchsia works well placed toward the front of a hardy border. Hardy; Zone 7. Growth 50cm (21in). de Groot, Netherlands, 1973.

'Isis'

'Jack Wilson'

This smaller growing floriferous cultivar makes a slightly lax bush with mid-green foliage, and is excellent at the front of the hardy border. The medium-sized single flowers have a medium to long white tube, white sepals that are pale pink underneath and a violet-cerise corolla with blue shading. Hardy; Zone 7. Growth 40cm (16in). Wilson, UK, 1979.

'Janna Roddenhof'

This hardy fuchsia is a cross between *F. regia typica* and 'Mood Indigo', and has quite an unusual colour. It has mid-green leaves, and the medium-sized single flowers have a red tube and sepals, and a beetroot-red corolla. A strong upright cultivar, it is useful in the middle of the border, but is not very widely available. Hardy; Zone 7. Growth 70cm (28in). de Groot, Netherlands, 1993.

'Joan Cooper'

The unusual colour combination of this fuchsia resulted from extensive work on hardy fuchsias by Mr W.P. Wood. It is a compact grower with attractive light green

'Janna Roddenhof'

foliage, and has small single flowers with a pale rose-opal tube, fully reflexed pale rose-opal sepals and a cherry-red corolla. It is a valuable addition to the range of hardy fuchsias, and is excellent for the front of a border with its spreading growth. Hardy; Zone 7. Growth 53cm (21in). Wood, UK, 1954.

'Joep Hendrik Jan'

A good upright growing fuchsia demonstrated to be hardy in the Netherlands. It has single flowers with a medium-length red tube, red sepals

hanging half down and a slightly paler rose corolla. Hardy; Zones 6–7. Growth 75cm (2½ft). de Groot, Netherlands, 2011.

'Kerry Ann'

This cultivar is an upright self-branching bush with mid-green foliage. The single flowers are medium-sized with a neyron-rose tube, neyron-rose sepals that curve upwards and an aster-violet corolla that is paler at the base of the petals. Although it is not listed as hardy in the UK, it has a hardy rating in the Netherlands, parts of which are Zones 7–8. Hardy; Zones 7–8. Growth 60cm (2ft). Pacey, UK, 1971.

'Komeet'

This cultivar resulted from a cross between *F. regia typica* and 'Beacon', giving an upright plant with mid- to dark green foliage. The medium-sized single flowers have a short red tube, long narrow red sepals that droop down and a purple corolla maturing to lilac-red as the flower ages. It is a good strong growing plant that is suitable for the centre of the hardy border. Hardy; Zone 7. Growth 70cm (28in). de Groot, Netherlands, 1970.

'Joan Cooper'

'Komeet'

'Lady Thumb'

F. magellanica var. gracilis

'Lady Thumb'

This cultivar is a sport from 'Tom Thumb', inheriting many of its parent's characteristics but with very different flowers – small to medium semi-doubles, sometimes doubles, with reddish-light carmine tube and sepals and a fluffy white corolla. The foliage is mid-green and small in size and the growth bushy and compact. It is excellent for use in the rockery or as an edging plant, and can be grown to a superb miniature or quarter standard. Hardy; Zone 7. Growth 40cm (16in). Roe, UK, 1966.

'Liebriez'

This is a very old German cultivar. It has compact, somewhat lax upright growth forming a small dome with mid-green foliage. The plentiful small to medium-sized semi-double flowers have a pale red tube, reflexed pale red sepals and a pale pink corolla with red veining. It is good at the front of the border, as an edging plant and in the rockery. Hardy; Zone 7. Growth 26cm (10in). Kohne, Germany, 1874.

'Madame Cornelissen'

This strong upright shrub has small semi-double flowers with a red tube and sepals, and a milky-white corolla with red veining on the petals. It is very free-flowering with the small, dark green serrated foliage providing a nice contrast to the flowers. It is also very suitable for growing as a low dividing hedge in the garden. It received an RHS Award of Garden Merit in 1993. Hardy; Zones 7–8. Growth 60cm (2ft). Cornelissen, Belgium, 1860.

F. magellanica var. gracilis

This is one of the natural species variants of F. magellanica, also known in the USA as 'Senorita'. It has a vigorous, almost rampant, arching, slender growth with small, mid- to dark green leaves and single flowers that are slightly longer than

F. magellanica var. pumila

those of F. magellanica itself. The flowers are small with a red tube and sepals, and a deep purple corolla. This plant makes a very attractive specimen hardy shrub because of its arching growth, and is also suitable for growing as a hedge. This cultivar has an RHS Award of Garden Merit, awarded in 1993. Hardy; Zone 6. Growth 1m (3ft). Lindley, South America, 1824.

F. magellanica var. molinae

This is another of the natural species variants of F. magellanica, often sold as F. magellanica alba. In the USA it is known as 'Maiden's Blush'. Extremely hardy, this upright, strong and vigorous shrub with small light to mid-green bright foliage has small flowers with a white tube and sepals and a pale lilac corolla (nearer white in the shade). Hardy; Zone 6. Growth 1.2m
(4ft). Espinosa, location not known, 1929.

F. magellanica var. pumila

This natural variant of F. magellanica is the smallest of the group. It has very small flowers with a scarlet tube and sepals and a purple corolla, and it grows into a small mound with small dark leaves, covered with tiny flowers. This fuchsia is best used at the front of the border or in a rockery. Hardy; Zone 6. Growth 45cm (18in).

F. magellanica var. *riccartonii*

F. magellanica var. *riccartonii* ('Riccartonii')

There is some disagreement in the published literature about this fuchsia, and nurseries grow different fuchsias under this name. Often described as a *F. magellanica* variant, it was raised by James Young at the Riccarton estate in Scotland from a seed from 'Globosa' crossed with an unknown fuchsia, so more correctly it should be a cultivar. It is extremely hardy and vigorous, with small to medium single flowers with a red tube and narrow sepals held almost horizontally, and a dark purple corolla. This photograph is from the RHS garden at Wisley, England. Hardy; Zone 6. Growth 1.2m (4ft). Young, UK, 1830.

'Monsieur Thibaut'

This old French cultivar has medium-sized single flowers with a bulbous waxy red tube, broad waxy red sepals held horizontally and a mauve-purple corolla with paler patches at the base of the petals, which hardly fade. The growth is strong, vigorous and upright with dark green leaves, and it flowers early, profusely and fairly continuously. It will also make a

'Monsieur Thibaut'

nice standard that will grow quickly to the desired height because of its strong and vigorous habit. Hardy; Zones 6–7. Growth 85cm (33in). Lemoine, France, 1898.

'Mr A. Huggett'

This is a compact bushy cultivar that is very floriferous, usually covered in small, pretty single flowers. They have a short red tube, horizontal red sepals and a mauve corolla with a pronounced purple edge, being paler pink at the base of the petals. It is a good plant for the middle to front of the hardy border, and has upright, self-branching growth and mid-green foliage. It also works well as a pot plant or small standard. Hardy; Zone 7. Growth 68cm (27in). Raiser unknown, UK, 1930.

'Mrs Popple'

This excellent old hardy cultivar is one of the first fuchsias to flower each year, and one of the last to stop. It has vigorous upright growth with dark green serrated foliage and medium-sized single flowers with a short, thin scarlet tube, scarlet sepals and a violet-purple corolla with cerise veining. It is one of the most popular fuchsias, ideal for the hardy border, and

an exceptional cultivar for a fuchsia hedge. It received an RHS Award of Garden Merit in 1993. Hardy; Zone 6. Growth 1.2m (4ft). Elliot, UK, 1899.

'Nicola Jane'

This free-flowering bush cultivar has attractive medium-sized double flowers with a deep pink tube and sepals and a mauve-pink corolla, veined with cerise. The growth is upright and bushy, with mid-green foliage. It is a prettily coloured double-flowered cultivar that is very useful for growing toward the front of the hardy bed, and also makes an excellent shape when grown as a shrub in a pot. It is a useful addition to the range of hardy doubles. Hardy; Zone 7. Growth 40cm (16in). Dawson, UK, 1959.

'Nunthorpe Gem'

This newer hardy cultivar has an upright bushy shape with mid- to dark green foliage. The flowers are medium-sized doubles with a red tube, red sepals held horizontally and a deep purple corolla with red patches at the petal base. This hardy double is excellent for the centre of the hardy bed or used as summer bedding. Hardy; Zones 7–8. Growth 75cm (30in). Birch, UK, 1970.

'Mrs Popple'

'Papoose'

This is one of the few hardy fuchsias hybridized in the USA. It has a spreading habit, growing twice as wide as it is high, producing small but profuse semi-double flowers with a red tube and sepals, and a dark purple corolla. The small serrated leaves are mid-green. It is an excellent plant to grow in a rockery, and also suitable for a hanging pot. Hardy; Zone 7. Growth 40cm (16in). Reedstrom, USA, 1963.

'Pee Wee Rose'

This vigorous US cultivar grows with a rather lax, willowy habit. The flowers are small singles, sometimes semi-doubles, with a medium-length rose-red tube, short rose-red sepals drooping downwards and a rosy-mauve corolla. The rather small foliage is mid-green. Use in the centre of the hardy bed. This fuchsia is also very suitable to train as an espalier. Hardy; Zone 7. Growth 70cm (28in). Niederholzer, USA, 1939.

'Peggy King'

This hardy cultivar is a bushy self-branching upright with mid- to dark green foliage. The small single flowers are freely produced with a rose-red tube, rose-red sepals held slightly above the horizontal and a reddish-purple corolla, which fades

'Prosperity'

as the flower ages. A reliable fuchsia to position between the middle and back of the hardy border. Hardy; Zone 7. Growth 81cm (32in). Wood, UK, 1954.

'Prosperity'

This is a newer, vigorous, free-flowering hardy cultivar with medium-sized double flowers with a crimson tube and sepals, and a pale neyron-rose corolla with red veining on the petals. It has strong upright growth with medium to large dark green leaves. It will make a striking impression in the hardy bed, its double flowers being larger than those of most hardy fuchsias. It received an RHS Award of Garden Merit in 1993. Hardy; Zone 7. Growth 70cm (28in). Gadsby, UK, 1974.

'Reading Show'

This floriferous hardy cultivar has lovely medium-sized double flowers with a short red tube, long thick red sepals and a deep blue corolla, which is almost purple. It is an upright grower with mid- to dark green foliage very suitable for the front part of the hardy border. Hardy; Zones 7–8. Growth 45cm (18in). Wilson, UK, 1967.

'Red Ace'

This strong upright cultivar has yellowish-green foliage with distinct veining. With its vigorous growth, it makes an excellent specimen plant or one for the centre of a hardy border. The flowers are medium doubles and almost self-coloured with a dusky-red tube, dusky-red recurving sepals and a slightly darker dusky-red corolla that is very open. Its parentage is 'Rufus' x 'Herald', and it seems to have inherited the hardy characteristics of both parents. Hardy; Zone 7. Growth 65cm (26in). Roe, UK, 1983.

'Peggy King'

'Reading Show'

'Rufus'

'Rose of Castile'

One of the oldest hardy cultivars, this is still widely grown and well worth trying. The flowers are medium-sized singles with a white tube tinged with green, white sepals with green tips and a reddish-purple corolla with white patches at the base of the petals. The growth is vigorous, upright and bushy with mid-green foliage, and it is perfect for the middle of the hardy border. It can also be trained as a quarter or half standard. Hardy; Zone 7. Growth 46cm (18in). Banks, UK, 1855.

'Rufus'

This is a strong-growing hardy cultivar which develops naturally into an upright bush and is an early flowerer. The flower is a medium-sized single, almost a red self, with a red tube and turkey-red sepals and corolla. The foliage is mid-green with quite large leaves that are slightly serrated. It is suitable for the middle of the hardy border, or for training as a half standard. This cultivar is sometimes incorrectly named as 'Rufus the Red'. It is an easy one for the beginner to grow, and highly recommended. Hardy; Zones 6–7. Growth 50cm (21in). Nelson, USA, 1952.

'Saturnus'

This is a very hardy, good strong upright resulting from hybridization with *F. regia typica*, which forms a mound of dull green foliage covered in flowers. The latter are small singles with a red tube, long red sepals and a light purple corolla fading to mauve on maturity and veined with red. It received an Award of Garden Merit from the RHS in 2005 and the Dutch 'Ned-H3 goed winterhard' classification. Hardy; Zones 6–7. Growth 60cm (2ft). de Groot, Netherlands, 1970.

'Sealand Prince'

This hardy fuchsia is a strong grower that naturally forms an upright bushy shrub. It has medium-sized single flowers with a pink tube, long pink sepals and a violet-blue corolla with paler patches at the base of the petals. The medium-sized foliage is light green and contrasts nicely with the well-shaped flowers. This is a good plant for use between the middle and back of the hardy border. Hardy; Zones 6–7. Growth 75cm (30in). Walker, UK, 1967.

'Sleepy'

This low-growing plant is one of the Seven Dwarfs series raised by Tabraham in the Scilly Isles. Although listed as hardy, there is a debate over just how hardy it is. The flowers are small singles with a pale pink tube and sepals and a lavender-blue corolla. The growth is compact and low with small pale green leaves, so it works best at the front of the hardy border, in the rockery or as an edging plant. Hardy; Zone 8. Growth 26cm (10in). Tabraham, UK, 1954.

'Sealand Prince'

'Son of Thumb'

This cultivar is a dwarf-growing compact plant, one of the sports from the cultivar 'Tom Thumb'. It is ideal for growing at the front of the hardy border or in the rockery. The flowers are small singles with a cerise tube and sepals, and a lilac corolla. The foliage is small and mid-green, and the growth is bushy, self-branching and compact. As with the other cultivars in the Thumbs series, it is an excellent plant for growing a pretty miniature or quarter standard and as a pot plant. This cultivar has an RHS Award of Garden Merit, awarded in 1993. Hardy; Zone 7. Growth 30cm (12in). Gubler, UK, 1978.

'Son of Thumb'

'Tausendschön'

This is a rather small, self-branching upright bush with small to medium well-shaped double flowers with a shiny red tube and sepals that almost look as if they have been lacquered, and a light rose corolla veined red. The growth is compact with small mid- to dark green foliage. It is an ideal fuchsia for growing toward the front of the hardy border and the rockery, or as a miniature or quarter standard. It will also make a very pretty double-flowered compact pot plant. Hardy; Zone 7. Growth 40cm (16in). Nagel, Germany, 1919.

'Tennessee Waltz'

This is a very attractive hardy fuchsia. Although some references express doubts about its hardiness, testing in the Netherlands in an exposed Zone 7 site labelled it 'Ned-H3 goed winterhard' (truly winter hardy). Another factor, such as waterlogging could have affected its hardiness in other trials. The flower is a medium to large semi-double, but often has enough petals to be a double, with a red tube, rose-madder sepals and a lilac-lavender corolla splashed with rose. The

'Tennessee Waltz'

'The Tarns'

growth is upright, self-branching and bushy, with medium-sized light to mid-green leaves. It is an easy one for beginners to grow and will make a nice bush or larger standard. Hardy; Zones 7–8. Growth 60cm (2ft). Walker and Jones, USA, 1950.

'The Tarns'

This hardy cultivar has medium-sized single flowers with a short pink tube, long pink sepals and a violet-blue corolla with paler rose patches at the base of the petals. The growth is upright and bushy with medium-sized dark green foliage. Hardy; Zones 7–8. Growth 55cm (22in). Travis, UK, 1962.

'Thornley's Hardy'

This fuchsia is, unusually for a hardy cultivar, a trailing plant. This makes it difficult to use in the hardy border, but it can be grown instead on the edge of walls or similar places where it can trail downwards, and can also be used in baskets or hanging pots. The flowers are small singles with a waxy white tube, waxy white sepals and a red corolla. The growth is lax, with small mid-green leaves. It is

very floriferous and early-flowering. Hardy; Zones 7–8. Growth 30cm (12in). Thornley, UK, 1970.

'Variegated Pixie'

This variegated sport from 'Pixie', though less vigorous than its parent, does have interesting yellow and green leaves. The flowers are the same as the parent, being small singles with a cerise tube and sepals, and a rosy-mauve corolla with carmine veins. It makes an attractive variegated plant for the front of the border. Hardy; Zones 7–8. Growth 30cm (12in). Russell, UK, 1960.

'Vielliebchen'

This old German cultivar, the result of a cross between 'Charming' and *F. magellanica* var. *macrostemma*, is a strong upright with small mid-green foliage. The flowers are small singles with a red tube, shining red sepals and a dark purple corolla fading to red-purple. Because its height tends to exceed its spread, it is better used toward the back of the hardy border where its flowers will be seen. Hardy; Zones 6–7. Growth 81cm (32in). Wolf, Germany, 1911.

'Thornley's Hardy'

'Voltaire'

This old French hardy cultivar is a bushy upright that is still grown for its vivid and well-shaped flowers shining among the mid-green foliage. The flowers are medium-sized singles with a thick scarlet tube, slightly reflexed broad scarlet sepals and a beautifully contrasting pale magenta corolla with red veins. This is an excellent vigorous growing plant for the middle of the hardy border or simply to use as a summer bedder. Hardy; Zones 7–8. Growth 65cm (26in). Lemoine, France, 1897.

'Wharfedale'

This relatively new cultivar is listed as hardy in the UK, and resulted from a cross between 'Border Queen' and 'Celia Smedley'. It has very vigorous growth and forms a large bushy shrub that is quickly covered by mid-green foliage and flowers. The latter are medium-sized singles with a white tube, white sepals blushed with pink and a magenta corolla. Use it at the back of the border or as a specimen plant, and it probably also makes an excellent standard. Hardy; Zones 7–8. Growth 1m (3ft). Hanson, UK, 1993.

'Voltaire'

'White Pixie'

'White Pixie'

This reliable hardy cultivar was a sport from 'Pixie', which, in turn, was itself a sport from 'Graf Witte'. The upright, bushy self-branching growth is covered with attractive yellowish-green foliage with red veins. The flowers stand out well and are small singles with a short red tube, red sepals held horizontally and a white corolla veined with pink. It works well in the centre of the hardy border or as a small standard. Hardy; Zone 7. Growth 60cm (2ft). Merrist Wood, UK, 1968.

'Whiteknights Blush'

This hardy cultivar emerged from the work of J.O. Wright at Reading University and was the result from a hybridization cross between *F. magellanica* var. *molinae* and *F. fulgens*. It has compact upright bushy growth with small dark green foliage with paler green veins. The plentiful small single flowers have a pale pink tube, pale pink sepals with green tips and a clear pink corolla. It is happy in full sun and is excellent for the hardy border and summer bedding. Hardy; Zone 7. Growth 55cm (22in). Wright, UK, 1980.

'Whiteknights Pearl'

This is another cultivar from the work of John Wright, also originating from *F. magellanica* var. *molinae*. The flowers are rather similar to its parent, but somewhat larger, being small to medium-sized singles with a white tube, pale pink sepals with green tips and a pink corolla. The growth is vigorous, upright and bushy, with small dark green leaves and light green stems, excellent for the back of the hardy border. This fuchsia is very suitable for training as pyramids and pillars. Hardy; Zones 7–8. Growth 1m (3ft). Wright, UK, 1980.

'Wicked Queen'

This upright hardy cultivar is bushy and floriferous with dark green foliage. It has medium to large double flowers, quite large for a hardy, which start as a pointed bud and open to a flower with a red tube, red recurving sepals and a deep blue corolla splashed with pink. It is a good choice for the centre of the hardy border, growing as a half standard or a pot plant. Marketing of this cultivar is often in a group along with the Seven Dwarfs series and 'Snow White'. Hardy; Zones 7–8. Growth 70cm (28in). Tabraham, UK, 1985.

'Wicked Queen'

Summer bedding

Many fuchsias can be used in summer as temporary residents in a border, standing out with their strong shapes and beautiful flowers. Desirable characteristics include strong bushy growth and distinctive flowers. The following cultivars are among the best.

'Alde'

This is a strong-growing cultivar which does very well as a temporary resident in the summer border. It has small single flowers with a pale orange tube, pale orange sepals and an apricot corolla with attractive pleated petals. The medium-sized foliage is mid- to dark green and the growth is upright and slightly lax. This cultivar also grows well and looks very good in a half basket. Half hardy; Zones 9–10. Goulding, UK, 1989.

'Anita'

This is a vigorous bush cultivar with small to medium single flowers with a clear white tube, clear white sepals and an orange-red corolla. The growth is upright and self-branching with medium-sized mid-green foliage, and it is very floriferous. It is an excellent plant for summer bedding or patio containers, being happy in full sun. There is another cultivar with the same name by Niederholzer, but this is a red and purple double. Half hardy; Zones 9–10. Götz, Germany, 1989.

'Becky'

This compact upright and self-branching cultivar is lovely as a bedding fuchsia. The plentiful single flowers have a short glossy red tube, glossy red upswept sepals and a bell-shaped aubergine corolla which matures to red. Half-hardy; Zones 9–10. Goulding, UK, 1994.

'Border Queen'

This is a striking fuchsia that should be included in any enthusiast's collection. With its good upright bushy and self-branching growth, with small to medium-sized mid-green leaves and red stems, it is excellent as a summer bedding plant, but will also make a lovely pot plant and is suitable for training into most shapes. The flowers are medium-sized singles with a short, pale pink tube, narrow pale pink sepals tipped green and an amethyst-

'Canny Bob'

violet corolla with pink veins on the petals. Half hardy; Zones 9–10. Ryle and Atkinson, UK, 1974.

'C.J. Howlett'

Small and hardy, this fuchsia makes a fine summer bedding plant, with its compact self-branching growth. Very floriferous, it has small single flowers with a reddish-pink tube, reddish-pink sepals tipped green and a bluish-carmine corolla with pink patches at the petal base. It tends to be early-flowering and sometimes throws additional semi-double flowers. Hardy; Zone 7. Growth 50cm (20in). Howlett, UK, 1911.

'Canny Bob'

This stiff and vigorous upright has small semi-erect single flowers with a white tube, white sepals and a glowing pink corolla. It grows long upright stems with small to medium-sized mid-green leaves with heavy clusters of flowers at the growing tips. It makes an excellent summer bedding, container or pot plant. Half hardy; Zones 9–11. Hewitson, UK, 1997.

'Anita'

'Border Queen'

'Chang'

'Chang'

This US cultivar, hybridized from
F. cordifolia, has profuse small single
flowers with an orange-red tube, orange
sepals tipped green and a brilliant
orange corolla. The growth is quite upright
with small to medium-sized mid-green
foliage. It thrives in the sun and does well
when planted out for the summer, with
continuous production of the orange-red
flowers. It is not easy to overwinter this
cultivar, so it is worth taking autumn
cuttings, which can be kept in growth over
the winter in a greenhouse as a precaution
against losing it during the winter
dormancy. Half hardy; Zones 9–10.
Hazard and Hazard, USA, 1946.

'Cloth of Gold'

This old cultivar was a sport from
'Souvenir de Chaswick', and is grown
more for its foliage than its flowers. It
grows quite vigorously as an upright bush,
and has beautiful golden-yellow and green
new foliage, which turns to a lovely bronze
colour with red on the underside on
ageing. The flowers are small singles with
a red tube and sepals, and a purple corolla
that is quite late to appear and rather
insignificant. This fuchsia is ideal for
creating a backdrop for other plants. Half
hardy; Zones 9–10. Stafford, UK, 1863.

'Dark Eyes'

This US cultivar grows as a slightly lax
self-branching bush with small to medium-
sized dark green foliage, and makes an
excellent border plant in summer. The
flowers are medium-sized doubles with a
short red tube, red upswept sepals and
a tight violet-blue corolla with rolled petals.
Try combining it with white-flowering
fuchsias or border bedding plants for
a bright contrast. It also works well as a
weeping standard. Half hardy; Zones 9–
10. Erickson, USA, 1958.

'Dawn Fantasia'

This plant is one of a number of fuchsias
originally derived from the cultivar 'Pink
Fantasia'. It is a free-flowering variegated
sport from 'Rose Fantasia', itself a sport
from 'Pink Fantasia'. It is self-branching,
bushy and upright with cream margined
light to mid-green leaves. The small, erect
single flowers have a pale rose tube and
sepals, and a white corolla flushed with
pink. It is excellent for summer bedding
and pot plants. Half hardy; Zones 9–10.
Thornton, UK, 1999.

'Emily Austen'

This self-branching upright, bushy cultivar
has an abundance of small single flowers.
Each has a pale pink tube and sepals, and
a pink-orange corolla. It is an excellent
choice for summer bedding and pot
plants. Half hardy; Zones 9–10. Bielby
and Oxtoby, UK, 1990.

'Dark Eyes'

'Eternal Flame'

This US cultivar flowers profusely,
normally well into autumn, and even into
winter with the heat in a greenhouse or
conservatory. The attractive flowers are
medium-sized semi-doubles with a
salmon-pink tube, dark salmon-pink
sepals tipped green and a rose corolla
streaked orange. The growth is strong,
bushy and upright with medium-sized
dark green leaves, which are a perfect
foil to the flowers. It does extremely well
as a summer bedder, and is also good in
containers or as a standard. Half hardy;
Zones 9–10. Paskesen, USA, 1941.

'Dawn Fantasia'

'First Kiss'

'Golden Eden Lady'

'First Kiss'

This compact, upright bushy Dutch cultivar has rather square-shaped buds, and makes a nice pot plant or summer bedder. The flowers are medium to large semi-doubles with a cream tube, pale neyron-rose sepals tipped green and a half-flared rose corolla with a long, pale yellow style. The foliage is rather small and dark green, making a nice backdrop for the pale-coloured flowers. Half hardy; Zones 9–10. de Graff, Netherlands, 1985.

'Galadriel'

This strong upright bushy fuchsia makes an excellent bedding plant with the many flowers concentrated at the ends of the branches. The small single flowers have an ivory-white tube, horizontal ivory-white sepals and a cup-shaped orange-red corolla. The foliage is medium-sized and mid- to dark green. It has been tested and accepted in the Netherlands as a hardy cultivar. Hardy; Zones 7–8. de Graff, Netherlands, 1982.

'Golden Eden Lady'

This is a golden-leaf sport from the cultivar 'Eden Lady', sister seedling to 'Border Queen', with bright yellow leaves with green patches, but retaining almost the same flower. The flowers are medium-sized singles with a rose tube and sepals and a hyacinth-blue corolla. It makes a very good summer bedding plant, especially where a change in foliage colour helps the planting scheme. Half hardy; Zones 9–10. Cater, UK, 1982.

'Golden Treasure'

This fuchsia has the habit of a low-growing bush, with very attractive green and gold foliage highlighted with red veins. Both the

'Galadriel'

growth and the colour make it ideal for edging. The small single flowers are rather sparse, with a scarlet tube and sepals, and a purple corolla. Hardy; Zone 7. Carter, UK, 1860.

'Gwen Dodge'

This fuchsia has stiff upright growth and pretty single flowers, making it ideal for summer bedding. The semi-erect medium-sized flowers have a white tube and sepals, both of which flush with pink in the sun, and a lilac-blue to purple flared corolla that is white at the petal base. The medium-sized foliage is mid-green, and this cultivar is very floriferous. Half hardy; Zones 9–10. Dyos, UK, 1988.

'Hiawatha'

This Dutch cultivar has compact, upright and bushy free-flowering growth, and makes an excellent small pot plant or summer bedder. The small single flowers have a short white tube and sepals, both flushed with rose, and a dark red corolla. The foliage is small and mid-green, and it happily takes the full sun and starts flowering very early in the season. This cultivar was a seedling from 'La Campanella' parentage. Half hardy; Zones 9–10. van Wijk, Netherlands, 1984.

'Honnepon'

This semi-lax upright thrives in sunny areas, producing an abundance of flowers. The small single blooms are held outwards with a white corolla tinged pink, white sepals shaded with mauve and tipped green, and a purple-mauve corolla with pink patches at the petal base. The medium-sized foliage is olive green and has red stems. Half hardy; Zones 9–10. Brouwer, Netherlands, 1988.

'Ingram Maid'

This is an almost white-flowered cultivar which tolerates the sun very well, maintaining its colours. It has strong upright growth with medium-sized mid-green leaves, and benefits from some early pinching. The medium-sized single flower has a white tube, white sepals flushed with rose and held outwards, and a creamy white corolla. Half hardy; Zones 9–10. Ryle, UK, 1976.

'Isle of Mull'

A strong upright fuchsia with arching growth that requires early stopping for the best results. The medium-sized single flowers have a medium-length white tube, striped with deep pink, horizontally held white sepals, pink at the base with

reflexed green tips and a rose-magenta corolla. Half-hardy; Zones 9–10. Tolley, UK, 1978.

'Jack King'

A sport from the old French hardy cultivar 'General Monk', this is more vigorous and with slightly larger flowers. It tolerates the sun very well and therefore makes an excellent bedding plant. Although not recognized as a hardy, it might be worth trying in milder areas because sports tend to inherit many characteristics of the parent. The flowers are medium-sized doubles with a crimson tube and sepals, and a flared lilac corolla, the petals having rose veins with pink at the base. Growth is upright with medium-sized mid-green leaves. Half hardy; Zones 9–10. Holmes, UK, 1978.

'Jack Siverns'

This is a superb cultivar from a hybridizer normally famed for his compact small-flowered introductions. It is a very strong upright, being self-branching and extremely floriferous, and makes a terrific pot plant or standard, also being ideal for bedding outdoors in the summer. The medium-sized, classically shaped single flowers have a pink tube, pale pink

'Ken Jennings'

upswept sepals flushed with aubergine and a beautiful, tight bell-shaped aubergine corolla. The small to medium-sized foliage is mid- to dark green. This cultivar is likely to become very popular as its fame spreads. Half hardy; Zones 9–10. Reynolds, UK, 2001.

'John Bartlett'

This newish cultivar is very floriferous and frequently throws three flowers in succession from each leaf joint. The plant is also quite self-cleaning of seedpods, which means that the residual ovaries from the old flowers fall off before growing into berries. The flowers are medium-sized semi-erect singles with a red tube and sepals, and a white corolla with red veining on the petals. The foliage is medium-sized and dark green. It is worth growing this cultivar as a standard, or as a temporary summer resident in the border where it will flower all summer. Half hardy; Zones 9–10. Humphries, UK, 2003.

'Ken Jennings'

Upright, bushy and strong, this fuchsia makes a good pot or bedding plant in summer. The medium-sized single flowers have a pink tube, rhodamine-pink sepals held horizontally and a deep purple corolla. The medium-sized leaves are mid-green. Half hardy; Zones 9–10. Roe, UK, 1982.

'Jack Siverns'

'John Bartlett'

'Kleine Gärtnerin'

This is an upright self-branching cultivar with mid- to dark green foliage, which is quite happy in full sun. It has medium-sized semi-double to double flowers with a white tube striped green, white sepals tinged with pink at the base and a white corolla tinged with pink at the base. is suitable for summer bedding or as a pot plant. Half hardy; Zones 9–10. Strümper, Germany, 1985.

'Leo Goetelen'

This strong-growing upright fuchsia with some similarities to 'Celia Smedley' thrives in full sun. It has medium to large single flowers with a cream tube tinged pink, pink sepals tipped green and a smoky-red corolla. The flowers stand out well against the medium-sized light to mid-green leaves with their serrated edges. It is very good as a summer bedding plant and grows well as a standard. Half hardy; Zones 9–10. Tamerus, Netherlands, 1987.

'Lydia Götz'

This German cultivar is popular as a summer bedder in many parts of Europe. It is upright and bushy with medium-sized mid- to dark green foliage. The flowers are medium-sized singles with a red tube,

'Lydia Götz'

red sepals held out horizontally and a very pretty lilac-blue corolla. Half hardy; Zones 8–9. Götz, Germany, 1958.

'Mieke Meursing'

Strong growing, upright and self-branching fuchsia with medium-green foliage. The flowering is prolific, and it is repeat flowering. The single/semi-double flowers have a short red tube, red sepals, and a very pale pink corolla with red veining on the petals. For a while the same variety was sold under the name Pink Spangles in the late 1970s. Half-hardy; Zones 9–10. Hopgood, UK, 1968.

'Minirose'

This plant is small and compact but also quite vigorous. It is early-flowering, and continues to flower well over a long period. The flowers are small singles that are held outwards and have a white tube blushed with rose, white sepals blushed with rose and a dark cyclamen-purple corolla. The foliage is small to medium in size and light to mid-green in colour. It grows well in pots, makes effective smaller standards and will grow quite happily in the border over the summer. Half hardy; Zones 9–10. de Graaff, Netherlands, 1985.

'Mieke Meursing'

'Minirose'

'Nice 'n' Easy'

'Nicis Findling'

'Mrs W. Castle'

This is a strong and upright cultivar which is very floriferous and tolerates full sun. The flowers are medium singles, sometimes semi-doubles, with a red tube and sepals, and a pinkish-mauve corolla. The flowers contrast well with the dark green foliage, making this a good summer bedder and pot plant. Some catalogues claim it is hardy. Hardy; Zone 8. Growth 60cm (24in). Porter, UK, 1984.

'Nice 'n' Easy'

This is an upright, self-branching, compact fuchsia that is very floriferous and, as its name suggests, easy to grow. The flowers are medium-sized doubles with a carmine tube, carmine sepals held out horizontally and a white corolla veined carmine. The foliage is medium-sized, mid-green and quite narrow. It is excellent as a bedding plant in summer, and also makes a good standard or pot plant. Half hardy; Zones 9–10. Sinton, UK, 1988.

'Nicis Findling'

The spelling of this cultivar's name varies in many catalogues and references. It is frequently listed as 'Nicki's Findling', 'Nickis Findling' or 'Nici's Findling', but according to German references the spelling above is correct. It is an excellent summer bedding cultivar with strong upright growth, tolerating hot, dry conditions well. The small single flowers are held semi-erect and are produced towards the ends of the branches. They have an orange-rose tube and sepals, and a deeper orange corolla. The flowers contrast nicely with the medium to large mid-green foliage. Half hardy; Zones 9–10. Ermel, Germany, 1985.

'Other Fellow'

This cultivar flowers extremely well and makes an excellent plant for the border over the summer, with its long, continuous flowering period. The flowers are small singles with a long waxy white tube, waxy white sepals tipped with green and a coral-pink corolla. The growth is upright and quite vigorous, with medium-sized mid-green serrated leaves. This fuchsia is also worth growing as a pot plant, a quarter or half standard or in mixed containers. Half hardy; Zones 9–10. Hazard and Hazard, USA, 1946.

'Peter Bielby'

A very vigorous upright fuchsia, this needs plenty of pinching out at an early stage, and will then make a good bush relatively quickly. It also makes an excellent bedding plant with its medium to large double flowers with a long thin red tube, long recurving red sepals and a full purple-red corolla with salmon splashes on the petals. The flowers contrast against the quite large light to mid-green foliage. Half hardy; Zones 9–10. Bielby, UK, 1987.

'Pink Fantasia'

This cultivar made a tremendous impact on its first release, and it is now quite widely grown both as an exhibition plant and for garden displays. The medium-sized erect single flowers have a pinkish-red tube and sepals, and a violet to mauve corolla. The growth is upright and bushy with medium-sized mid- to dark green foliage, and it produces many flowers over a long period. Because of its erect-flowering habit, it makes an excellent plant for the summer border, but it will also make a striking standard or pot plant, which at its peak of flowering almost makes the leaves invisible. Half hardy; Zones 9–10. Webb, UK, 1989.

'Pink Fantasia'

'Queen's Park'

This is quite a free-flowering older cultivar with an upright bushy habit and mid-green foliage. It is happy in full sun and therefore excellent for summer bedding. The medium to large double flowers have a waxy red tube and sepals, and a full violet corolla. It is not that easy to find, but is still listed in some larger nursery catalogues and well worth searching for. Half hardy; Zones 9–10. Thorne, UK, 1959.

'Ravensbarrow'

This cultivar flowers very early in the year, and stays in flower for the whole summer. Although the single flowers are small they have a very good form, with a short scarlet tube, slightly reflexed scarlet sepals and a purple corolla with scarlet patches at the base of the petals. It is an upright-growing shrub with small mid- to dark green leaves and although not listed as a hardy, one of its parents is 'Hawkshead' so it may be worth trying as a hardy plant in milder areas. Note that in some catalogues it is erroneously referred to as 'Raven's Barrow'. Half hardy; Zones 9–10. Thornley, UK, 1972.

'Rose Fantasia'

This cultivar is a sport of 'Pink Fantasia', and perhaps actually more suited to its parent's name. It has almost the same

'Shanley'

growth habit as its parent, but the flower is a much softer colour. It has a medium erect single flower with a deep pink tube and sepals, and a pale pink corolla with a hint of mauve. The foliage is still a mid-green, a shade or two lighter than 'Pink Fantasia', and it is still very free-flowering. Like its parent, it is excellent for use in summer bedding schemes, as a pot plant or trained as a standard. Half hardy; Zones 9–10. Wilkinson, UK, 1991.

'Shanley'

This cultivar has attractive medium to large single flowers with a long, pale salmon-orange tube, pale salmon-orange sepals

with green tips, held horizontally, and an orange corolla. With its strong upright growth it makes a good bedding plant, with the flowers standing out against the large ovate mid-green leaves. It is happy growing in a sunny position. Half hardy; Zones 9–10. Mrs Shutt (Jnr), USA, 1968.

'Sharon Allsop'

This is a very floriferous compact cultivar that is ideal as a smaller pot plant and garden bedder, when combined with low-growing plants. The flowers are medium-sized doubles with a short carmine tube and downward-curving carmine sepals that cup the fluffy white corolla. The flowers stand out well against the small mid- to dark green leaves, making a neat mound of colour. Half hardy; Zones 9–10. Pacey, UK, 1983.

'Superstar'

This is a superb upright, bushy short-jointed cultivar with attractive light green foliage. It is very floriferous, with small to medium-sized semi-erect single flowers with a pink tube, pink sepals tipped green and an attractive rose-purple corolla. It is an excellent cultivar, suitable for pot plants and small standards, and the sun tolerance inherited from one of its parents, 'Cambridge Louie', makes it a good bedding plant for summer use. Half hardy; Zones 9–10. Sinton, UK, 1988.

'Rose Fantasia'

'Superstar'

'WALZ Jubelteen'

'Welsh Dragon'

'Tom Knights'

This is a tall upright and self-branching variety with light green foliage very suitable for bedding out in the summer border. The pretty single flowers are medium-sized with a short pale pink tube, pale pink sepals with slightly deeper pink underneath and a pale violet corolla with white patches at the petal base. This variety is also very amenable to standard training. Half-hardy; Zones 9–10. Goulding, UK, 1983.

'WALZ Jubelteen'

This is an erect-flowering fuchsia, a strong upright bushy grower that is quite happy in full sun and is extremely floriferous. The small single flowers have a pale pink tube, pale pink sepals with green tips and a pinkish-orange corolla that is flared almost flat when fully open. The foliage is medium-sized light to mid-green. It is excellent as a specimen pot plant, most standard sizes except miniature, andis particularly suitable as part of a summer bedding scheme. Half hardy; Zones 9–10. Waldenmaier, Netherlands, 1990.

'Waveney Waltz'

This bushy upright and self-branching cultivar with light green foliage makes a good pot plant and an attractive summer bedding plant. The flowers are medium-sized singles with a short pink tube, pink sepals held out horizontally and a white corolla. It will occasionally produce extra petals, giving semi-double flowers. It is also well worth trying growing it as a standard, especially a quarter standard. Half hardy; Zones 9–10. Burns, UK, 1982.

'Welsh Dragon'

With its strong upright bushy growth, this fuchsia tolerates full sun, so is excellent for summer bedding. The flowers are large doubles with a long rose-red tube, rose-red sepals held horizontally and a full magenta-rose corolla with the petals in layers. It is very free-flowering for a large double, and the medium-sized mid-green leaves contrast well with the flowers. It is good for pot plants and larger standards. This is one of those cultivars where the flowers drag the branches down, so it can be used in the centre of baskets. Half hardy; Zones 9–10. Baker, UK, 1970.

'White Ann'

This cultivar is a sport from 'Heidi Ann' – it shows the same growth characteristics but with different flower colours. Note that an almost identical sport named 'Heidi Weiss' is separately registered. The growth is upright and bushy, with mid- to dark green foliage, and the flowers are medium-sized doubles with a crimson tube and sepals, and a white, crimson-veined corolla. It is well worth growing in the border or in pots. Half hardy; Zones 8–9. Wills and Atkinson, UK, 1972.

'Zets Alpha'

This is an unusual cultivar for use as a bedding plant. It resulted from a hybridization cross between *F. vulcanica* and 'Citation', and has an upright vigorous habit with medium to large light to mid-green leaves, and produces a mass of flowers. The latter are medium-sized singles with a very long red tube, short rose-red sepals and an orange-red corolla. This fuchsia is very tolerant of a sunny position, making it highly suitable for summer bedding. Half hardy; Zones 9–10. Stoel, Netherlands, 1993.

'White Ann'

Species fuchsias

The species fuchsias grow in the wild in South and Central America, Mexico and New Zealand, and will grow true from seed. Many are tender, but some are quite hardy, and there is a tremendous variety of colour and form. Species are still being discovered in South America.

F. andrei
Found from southern Ecuador to northern Peru at altitudes of 1,800–3,000m (5,900–9,800ft), this is a shrub up to 4m (13ft) tall. The medium-sized single flowers are held in terminal racemes with a medium-length orange to red tube, horizontal red sepals and an orange-red corolla. The leaves are mid-green with a waxy texture, and are normally arranged in opposite pairs. Section Fuchsia; Tender; Zone 11. Johnston, Ecuador, 1925.

F. arborescens
This is found in Mexico and southern Peru at altitudes of 1,700–2,500m (5,570–8,200ft), where it grows as a large shrub or small tree up to 8m (26ft) tall. The tiny single flowers are held upright in panicles and have a rose-purple tube and sepals, and a lavender corolla eventually maturing to clusters of purple globular berries. The large glossy foliage

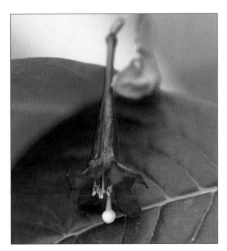

F. andrei

F. arborescens

is mid- to dark green. Often known as the lilac fuchsia, it is easy to grow but must not be allowed to dry out. Section Schufia; Tender; Zone 11. Sims, Mexico, 1825.

F. boliviana var. boliviana
The habitat of this fuchsia is spread from northern Argentina to southern Peru at altitudes of 1,000–3,000m (3,300–9,800ft), where it grows as a large shrub or small tree up to 4.5m (15ft) tall. The single flowers are held in large pendulous groups at the growing tips, with a 7.5cm (3in) long red tube, short reflexed red sepals and a red corolla. The large mid-green leaves have a hairy texture and red veining. Section Fuchsia; Frost tender; Zone 11. Carrière, Brazil, 1876.

F. coccinea
Naturally occurring in Brazil at altitudes of 1,400–2,000m (4,600–6,600ft), this grows as a dense shrub up to 1.5m (5ft) tall. The small single flowers have a pale red tube and sepals, and a violet corolla. The oval foliage is dark green on the top side, paler green beneath and the young branches are thin, red and covered with fine hair. Section Quelusia; Hardy; Zones 6–7. Drylander, Brazil, 1789.

F. denticulata

F. decussata
This fuchsia is found in Peru at altitudes of 2,900–3,400m (9,600–11,200ft), where it grows up to 3m (10ft) tall as a shrub with a lot of self-branching. The flowers are small to medium-sized singles with a dark red tube and sepals, and an orange-red corolla produced somewhat sparsely in the leaf axils, with small dark green foliage. Section Fuchsia; Frost tender; Zone 11. Ruiz and Pavon, Peru, 1802.

F. denticulata
This fuchsia comes from Peru and Bolivia at altitudes of 2,800–3,500m (8,200–11,500ft), where it grows up to 4m (13ft) tall. The dark green spear-shaped leaves usually grow in groups of three, with very attractive medium-sized single flowers appearing in the leaf axils. The flowers have a long, light pink-red tube with green at the tips and an orange to scarlet corolla. Most of the flowers appear in spring and autumn, sparser in the summer. This is an easy species for the beginner to try as a pot plant that is a little more frost-tolerant than many species. It was formerly known as *F. serratifolia*. Section Fuchsia; Half hardy; Zones 9–10. Ruiz and Pavon, Peru, 1802.

F. encliandra subsp. encliandra

This is found from Mexico to Panama at altitudes of 1,370–3,200m (4,500–10,500ft), where it grows up to 2.5m (8ft) tall. The profuse tiny single flowers are normally red with both staminate (male) and pistillate (female) flowers. The fern-like foliage is small and mid- to dark green. Section Encliandra; Hardy; Zones 8–9. Steudel, Mexico, 1840.

F. excorticata

This is found in both islands of New Zealand growing at altitudes of 1,000m (3,300ft), where it is a deciduous tree up to 15m (50ft) tall. A common tree in New Zealand, it is easily recognized by its distinctive cinnamon-brown bark, which peels in long strips, and the glossy leaves which are medium to dark green on top and light green, or sometimes white, beneath. The small single flowers have a tube and sepals that turn from green to purple-red and a dark purple corolla with distinctive blue pollen on the anthers. Section Skinnera; Half hardy; Zone 9. Forster, New Zealand, 1781.

F. fulgens

This fuchsia from Mexico occurs in humid areas beside flowing water at elevations of 1,450–2,300m (4,450–7,550ft), growing as a shrub 0.6–6.1m (2–20ft) tall. It has tuberous roots, often growing epiphytically in damp crevices and trees, and sheds its large light green foliage in

F. excorticata

dry seasons. The long single flowers are held in terminal clusters with a long dark pink to dull red tube, short pale red sepals with yellow-green tips and a bright red corolla. Section Ellobium; Tender; Zone 11. De Candolle, Mexico, 1828.

F. glazioviana

This fuchsia is from the highlands of eastern Brazil at altitudes of 1,500–2,000m (4,900–6,600ft), where it grows up to 4m (13ft) high with long spreading branches. The mid-green ternate leaves are quite shiny and appear in opposite pairs or in threes. The ends of the branches carry the small to medium-sized single flowers, which have a deep pink tube, deep pink sepals and a violet corolla.

It is a useful hybridization parent because of its natural resistance to many of the pests and diseases that afflict modern cultivars. Section Quelusia; Half hardy; Zones 9–10. Taubert, Brazil, 1888.

F. hatschbachii

This is found in the forests of eastern Brazil at altitudes of 900–1,200m (3,000–3,900ft), where it grows up to 5m (16ft) high as a climbing shrub. The flowers are small to medium-sized singles with a red tube, drooping red sepals and a violet corolla. The foliage is light to mid-yellow-green. Section Quelusia; Tender; Zone 11. Berry, Brazil, 1989.

F. jimenezii

A fairly recent discovery and the only current member of the Jimenezia section, this fuchsia comes from Panama and Costa Rica on the fringes of evergreen cloud forests at altitudes of 1,500–1,900m (4,900–6,200ft), where it grows up to 1.5m (5ft) high as a climbing shrub. It is named after its discoverer, Alfonso Jiménez Muñoz, and was first described by Breedlove, Berry and Raven in 1976. It has tiny single flowers held mainly in terminal racemes, with a red tube and sepals and a pink corolla. The foliage is quite large and dark green, being flushed purple underneath. Section Jimenezia; Tender; Zone 11. Muñoz, Panama/Costa Rica, 1967.

F. fulgens

F. hatschbachii

F. magellanica

F. paniculata subsp. paniculata

F. magellanica

From the central and southern Andes, this fuchsia grows between sea level and altitudes of 1,750m (5,700ft). This species, from which many modern cultivars originate, grows as an erect or semi-scandent shrub up to 3m (9ft) tall. The profuse small single flowers have a red tube and drooping sepals, and a purple corolla on wiry branches with small, thin, dark green leaves. Widely grown in cultivation and very hardy, it makes an excellent hedge. Section Quelusia; Hardy; Zone 6. Lamarck, Chile, 1768.

F. obconica

From the lower mountains of the trans-Mexican volcanic belt at altitudes of 1,675–2,450m (5,500–8,000ft), this fuchsia is a tall, spreading shrub that grows 1–3m (3–10ft) high. One of the more recently discovered species, it has tiny single flowers, both staminate (male) and pistillate (female), with a greenish-white tube and sepals, and a white corolla. It has small, ovate mid-green leaves that are slightly larger than typical Encliandras. The plant is easy to grow and readily available from specialist nurseries. Section Encliandra; Half hardy; Zones 9–10. Bredlove, Mexico, 1969.

F. paniculata subsp. paniculata

From southern Mexico to Panama, this fuchsia varies from a shrub growing to 2.5m (8ft) to a tree growing to 7.5m (25ft) in evergreen cloud forests at altitudes of 1,220–3,000m (4,000–10,000ft). The tiny single flowers are both perfect (male and female parts) and pistillate (female), held in terminal racemes with a rose-purple tube and sepals, and a lavender corolla. The large deep green shiny leaves are serrated on the edges, while the flowering racemes form globular purple berries with a waxy-blue bloom. It needs a warm position to grow well, and tends to lose berries and flowers with large temperature variations. Section Schufia; Tender; Zone 11. Lindley, Costa Rica, 1856.

F. petiolaris

This is found in Colombia and Venezuela, where it grows at altitudes of 2,900–3,900m (9,500–12,800ft) varying from a low shrubby bush 0.6–2m (2–6ft) tall to a climbing tree up to 5m (16ft). The single flowers have a long bright pink tube, bright pink sepals tipped green and a bright rose-pink corolla. The ternate leaves are dull mid-green on top and lighter beneath, held on dark pink stems. It likes warm conditions and takes longer to establish

than other species, but it will flower all summer. Section Fuchsia; Frost tender; Zone 11. Humbolt and Bonpland, Colombia, 1823.

F. procumbens

From the northern part of the north island of New Zealand, this fuchsia spreads and trails up to 6m (20ft) wide but grows just 23cm (9in) high. The tiny erect flowers have a greenish-yellow tube and green sepals tipped purple. There is no corolla but the upright stamens carry blue pollen. Many of the fertilized flowers grow to become very attractive large pink-red fruits. The small, light green heart-shaped leaves are borne on slender stalks attached to thin trailing stems growing a few metres (yards) long. It is quite hardy and a good ingredient in rockeries. Section Procumbentes; Hardy; Zone 7. Cunningham, New Zealand, 1834.

F. sessifolia

Found in Ecuador and Colombia at altitudes of 2,300–3,200m (7,500–10,500ft), this grows as a shrub or small tree to a height of 3m (10ft). The large dark green leaves are sessile (without stalks), hence the name, and the young branches are dark red. The single flowers are held in terminal clusters and have a long light red or pink tube, greenish-red sepals and a scarlet corolla. Section Fuchsia; Tender; Zone 11. Bentham, Ecuador, 1845.

F. petiolaris

F. simplicicaulis

From central Peru, this fuchsia grows in cloud forests at altitudes of 2,400m (8,000ft) where it is a vigorous climbing species, sending its scandent 5m (16ft) long growth through adjacent shrubs and trees. The single flowers, held in pendent racemes, have a long reddish-pink tube, short reddish-pink sepals and a bright red corolla. The leaves are darkish green with a satin texture, while the mature wood is light red with peeling bark. Section Fuchsia; Tender; Zone 11. Ruiz and Pavon, Peru, 1802.

F. splendens

This is from Mexico and Costa Rica at altitudes of 2,400–3,400m (7,900–11,100ft), where it grows in moist forests as a lax shrub up to 2.4m (8ft) tall and, occasionally, as an epiphytic plant on trees. The single flowers have a distinctive flat tube varying from rose to vivid scarlet, short green sepals with a reddish base and an olive-green corolla. The leaves are dull mid-green with marbled veining. It flowers all year in its natural habitat, but in northern Europe and the northern USA it tends to flower in the darker months. Section Ellobium; Frost tender; Zone 11. Zuccarini, Costa Rica, 1832.

F. thymifolia subsp. thymifolia

This fuchsia is found in Mexico at altitudes of 2,130–3,350m (7,000–11,000ft). It is a shrub with tiny single flowers with a greenish-white tube and sepals turning pink, and a white to pink corolla turning purple after fertilization. Section Encliandra; Hardy; Zone 7. Humbolt, Bonpland and Kunth, Mexico, 1823.

F. triphylla

This species exists in Haiti and grows as a shrub up to 2m (6ft) tall. It is one of the most difficult fuchsias to cultivate. It has Triphylla-type orange-red flowers held in terminal racemes with dull dark green foliage, and can flower when barely 30cm (12in) tall. It is a interesting one to try growing. Section Fuchsia; Tender; Zone 11. Plumier, Haiti, 1703.

F. splendens

F. thymifolia subsp. thymifolia

F. venusta

Growing naturally in Colombia and Venezuela at altitudes of 1,800–2,700m (5,900–8,850ft), this is one of the most beautiful species fuchsias. It grows as an upright spreading shrub to 3m (10ft) tall or climbs through trees up to a height of 10m (33ft). The single flowers have a long orange-red trumpet-shaped tube, orange-red sepals tipped green and an orange corolla. Glossy elliptical dark green leaves, lighter beneath, appear ternately (in groups of three) on red to bluish stems, and the mature wood has attractive peeling bark. The flowers appear axially singly and terminally in sub-racemes (small groups).

The plant enjoys even, warm conditions without large extremes in temperature, and does not like overwatering when it is young. Section Fuchsia; Tender; Zone 11. Humbolt, Bonpland and Kunth, Colombia, 1823.

F. vulcanica

Occurring in southern Columbia and Ecuador at altitudes of 3,340–4,000m (11,000–13,000ft), this fuchsia grows up to 4m (13ft) high. The long single flowers have a long thin orange tube, orange-red sepals tipped green and a red corolla. The foliage is dark matt green and the bark peels on older branches. Section Fuchsia; Tender; Zone 11. André, Ecuador, 1876.

F. triphylla

Unusual cultivars

If you are looking for something different, try growing some of these unusual cultivars. Many are produced by crossing fuchsia species and are quite tender, so in temperate climates they will need the protection of a heated greenhouse over the winter.

'Cotta Christmas Tree'
Produced by hybridizing two fuchsia species, *F. decussata* and *F. crassistipula*, this has upright spreading growth and almost naturally grows to a pyramid shape with flowers resembling hanging candles. The medium-sized single flowers are similar to those of *F. decussata* and have a long, tapered red tube, red sepals with green tips and an orange corolla. The foliage is medium-sized and mid- to dark green. Frost tender; Zone 11. Bielby and Oxtoby, UK, 1999.

'Daryn John Woods'
This Triphylla-type fuchsia has a most unusual flower colour and was produced by hybridizing 'Thalia' and *F. juntasensis*. The medium-sized Triphylla-type flowers are borne in terminal clusters and have a long aubergine-purple tube, short

'Fulpila'

'Lechlade Gorgon'

aubergine-purple sepals and a purple corolla. The foliage is quite large and dark green and, with its bushy growth habit, it makes a nice pot plant. Be patient, because it is rather late to flower. Frost tender; Zone 11. Goulding, UK, 2000.

'Delta's Drop'
This Dutch cultivar is an upright bushy grower that benefits from early pinching, with mid- to dark green foliage. The unusual eye-catching flowers are small to medium-sized singles with a red tube and sepals, and a purple corolla with a red base to the petals, which become petaloids growing as part of the outer anthers as the flower matures. Grow it in a shady position to get the best colours, because it can be bleached by too much sun. Half hardy; Zones 9–10. Vreeke and van't Westeinde, Netherlands, 1994.

'Fulpila'
This vigorous fuchsia, produced by hybridization between *F. fulgens* and *F. pilaloensis*, has spreading upright growth, and is ideal for a patio container. The long single flowers are held in terminal clusters with a long pale pink-orange tube, short pale pink-orange sepals tipped green and an orange corolla. The velvety foliage is light to mid-green. Tender; Zone 11. Beije, Netherlands, 1997.

'Lechlade Gorgon'
This large upright with 9–15cm (3½–5in) dark green glossy leaves makes a good patio pot plant. Hybridized by crossing *F. arborescens* with *F. paniculata*, it has the same type of paniculate flower clusters as its parents. The individual tiny single flowers have a rosy purple tube and sepals, and a pale mauve corolla with erect petals. With plenty of feeding and a large root run, it will put on a lot of growth in a season. Tender; Zones 10–11. Wright, UK, 1984.

'Martin's Yellow Surprise'
This unusual tender cultivar is an interspecies cross of *F. pilaloensis* x *F. fulgens* and forms a large-growing bush. The flowers are a good-sized Triphylla type – while not growing as true terminal clusters, they are concentrated at the ends of the branches. The tube and sepals are green-yellow, though they can take on a pink blush in full sun, and the corolla is green-yellow, though always partially hidden by the sepals. Its growth is upright and quite vigorous with large felt-like mid-green leaves. As the plant is quite tender, it needs a well-heated greenhouse over the winter. It is an unusual plant which can be grown as a specimen on the patio in the summer. Tender; Zone 11. Beije, Netherlands, 1995.

'Martin's Yellow Surprise'

'Nettala'

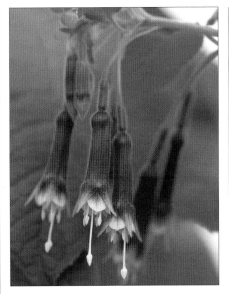
'Space Shuttle'

'Nettala'

This fuchsia was a sport from the cultivar 'Chang' and shares similar characteristics, being upright and strong-growing with mid-green foliage. It is distinguished by the flowers, which are small to medium-sized singles with a short dark red tube, dark red sepals and a violet-red corolla with the petals being petaloids growing as part of the outer anthers. Half hardy; Zones 9–10. Francesca, USA, 1973.

'Rose Quartet'

With its unusual flowers, this new cultivar created quite a stir when it was released in the USA, and it is now available in other countries. The breeder assigned the rights to Planthaven Inc. in the USA, where it is subject to a patent. The flowers are small to medium-sized erect singles with a pink tube and sepals, and a rose corolla; the petals are petaloids growing as part of the outer anthers, which rapidly extend when the buds open. The growth is upright, self-branching and bushy, with a young plant growing 60cm (2ft) a season. In the patent it is claimed to survive outdoors in Zone 9 areas, but it should be treated as half hardy until more details are known. Half hardy; Zones 9–10. Spanton, UK, 2006.

'Space Shuttle'

This Dutch cultivar is the result of crossing 'Speciosa' and *F. splendens*, and has the growth habit of a lax bush. It starts to flower early and has a long flowering period, with small to medium-sized single flowers with a medium to long red tube, short downward-pointing red sepals tipped green and a yellow-red corolla. The quite large foliage is light to mid-green, with a slightly furry matt surface that is heavily veined. Half hardy; Zones 9–10. de Graaff, Netherlands, 1981.

'Tarra Valley'

This unusual cultivar is an interspecies cross between *F.* x *colensoi* and *F. splendens*, and one for the collector. The buds are yellow-green and the flowers small singles with a long light greenish-yellow tube, short greenish-white sepals and a striking dark red-purple corolla. The growth is upright and bushy with light green foliage, but the plant is quite slow-growing. It is reported to flower quite well in winter. Half hardy; Zones 9–10. Felix, Netherlands, 1987.

'Two Tiers'

The flowers of this cultivar develop in two stages, and are quite unlike those of other fuchsias. They are large doubles with a long thin pink tube, broad reflexed pink sepals and a pale beetroot-purple corolla. When the flowers are about 4–5 days old, four of the petaloids drop to a lower level, forming two tiers, hence the name. It has a lax bush growth habit with large mid-green foliage that is very suitable for hanging containers. Half hardy; Zones 9–10. Porter, UK, 1985.

'WALZ Tuba'

This is an unusual Dutch cultivar with strong upright growth, becoming quite tall, and therefore ideal as a standard. It has medium-sized to large dark green foliage and strikingly beautiful long flowers. The flowers are singles with a thin red tube 6cm (2½in) long, small red sepals tipped green and a small Tyrian-purple corolla. Grow it in a shady but light position for the best flower colours. Half hardy; Zones 9–10. Waldenmaier, Netherlands, 1987.

'Tarra Valley'

Encliandras

Encliandra hybrids have very small leaves and flowers, quite vigorous growth and are often among the last fuchsias to lose their leaves in winter. The name, from the Greek for 'enclosed male', refers to the fact that just four stamens protrude from the flower.

'Ariel'

This has slightly lax and self-branching growth, with tiny glossy dark green leaves. The tiny single flowers that freely appear in the leaf axils have a short cylindrical magenta tube, horizontal magenta sepals and a deep pink corolla. Eventually the fertilized flowers produce attractive round black berries 12mm (½in) in diameter. This fuchsia tolerates full sun when planted in the garden and is ideal trained as topiary, bonsai or other smaller shapes. Frost hardy; Zones 8–9. Travis, UK, 1973.

'Chapel Rossan'

This slightly lax-growing cultivar is a very pretty Encliandra with tiny distinctive flowers. They have a mid-pink tube and sepals, and a bright orange-red corolla. The small dark green leaves and wiry branches make it ideal for trained shapes, especially when grown as a ring. Frost hardy; Zones 8–9. Morris, UK, 1996.

'Cinnabarina'

This old cultivated form of *F.* x *bacillaris* is quite a vigorous grower, becoming untidy when grown in a greenhouse but making a compact bush in the border. The flowers are tiny singles with an orange tube, orange-red sepals and an orange corolla. The small leaves are mid-green. This is a good small hardy plant for rockeries and listed as being gall mite resistant. Hardy; Zones 7–8. Growth 45cm (18in). Raiser unknown, introduced *c.*1829.

'Ariel'

'Jiddles'

This is a vigorous hybrid with strong upright growth and small light green foliage. The tiny single flowers are self-coloured with a white tube, sepals and corolla that slowly age to a pale pink. Although the flowers are small, they stand out against the light green fern-like foliage. Half hardy; Zones 9–10. Iddles, UK, 1996.

'Lottie Hobby'

This old Encliandra hybrid with vigorous growth has wiry stems and mid-green leaves, and is slightly larger than most Encliandra cultivars. The small flowers have a tiny single light crimson tube, light crimson sepals and a light purple corolla. This

'Lottie Hobby'

fuchsia is ideal for growing topiary shapes because of its wiry self-branching growth, and is useful as a permanent outdoor planting in milder regions. Frost hardy; Zones 8–9. Edwards, UK, 1839.

'Marlies de Keijzer'

This cultivar is a cross between *F. encliandra* and *F. thymifolia* subsp. *thymifolia*. It has tiny single flowers with a red tube, sepals and corolla, which sit among the attractive tiny grey-green shiny foliage. The growth is slightly more compact than most Encliandra hybrids, probably due to the influence of *F. thymifolia* in its parentage. Half hardy; Zones 9–10. de Keijzer, Netherlands, 1999.

'Marlies de Keijzer'

'Miniature Jewels'

'Miniature Jewels'

This has trailing, self-branching growth with tiny serrated green leaves and can be trained in several ways. The flowers are tiny singles with a rose tube, rose-white sepals and a whitish-pink corolla. As the flower matures, the sepals and corolla turn dark pink, then red, creating a mixture of flower colours. Half hardy; Zones 9–10. Francesca, USA, 1976.

'Neopolitan'

This is a rather unusual Encliandra hybrid because the flowers can be red, pink or white, all growing at the same time, which creates a striking multicoloured effect. The typical flower is a tiny single, but is slightly larger than other Encliandra cultivars, with a red tube and sepals, and a pinkish-white corolla. The growth is very thin and wiry, with tiny mid- to dark green fern-like foliage. It is excellent as a topiary plant. Half hardy; Zones 9–10. Clark, UK, 1984.

'Oosje'

Hybridized from *F. parviflora* and *F. microphylla*, this is a vigorous grower and makes quite a large bush in a short time. It is very floriferous, with many tiny single flowers with a red tube maturing to crimson, red sepals held outwards also maturing to crimson and a red corolla turning dark red. The foliage is small and mid-green with the typical fern-like Encliandra appearance. It is an excellent choice for topiary work. Half hardy; Zones 9–10. van der Grijp, Netherlands, 1973.

'Radings Inge'

The fairly vigorous spreading growth of this fuchsia makes it useful in any kind of container, including hanging ones. It is very floriferous, with tiny single flowers with a red tube and sepals, and a pink-orange corolla. The small leaves are mid-green. Frost hardy; Zones 8–9. Reiman, Netherlands, 1980.

'Variegated Lottie Hobby'

A sport from 'Lottie Hobby', this fuchsia is reasonably vigorous and self-branching, with attractive tiny silver-cream and green foliage. It has a profusion of eye-catching flowers, which are tiny singles with a crimson tube, crimson sepals tipped pink and a crimson corolla. This plant is hardy in more sheltered areas. Frost hardy; Zones 8–9. Raiser and introduction date unknown.

'Waldfee'

This is a strong grower with rather matt mid-green foliage, large for an Encliandra. The flowers are tiny singles with a lilac-pink tube, lilac-pink sepals and a pale lilac-pink corolla. It forms a lax upright bush or, with persuasion, trails effectively when grown in a basket, and is also ideal for topiary. This plant is hardy in more sheltered areas. Frost hardy; Zones 8–9. Travis, UK, 1973.

'Oosje'

'Variegated Lottie Hobby'

Recent introductions

This section lists some of the newer cultivars that have been introduced by hybridizers and nurseries since 2005. They all have interesting characteristics and are well worth trying, but only time will tell if they become popular classics or fade into obscurity.

'Alan Swaby'

A lovely introduction, one of the last from the late Sid Garcia. Named in honour of a former UK hybridizer and nurseryman, this fuchsia has medium-sized single flowers with a short white tube with a pale pink blush, broad white sepals, blushed pink and held just above horizontal with reflexed tips and a Bishop Violet corolla with the petals slightly interlaced. It is quite a strong growing shrub, with slightly lax growth and mid-green foliage. Half hardy; Zones 9–10. Garcia, UK, 2019.

'Anne Reid'

Since its first introduction, this has become a very popular cultivar both for show

'Boogie Woogie'

purposes and for general cultivation. It is very floriferous with small to medium single flowers. The medium-length tube is white, and the narrow white sepals are held horizontally with reflexed tips. The quarter flared corolla is a vivid violet-purple and very striking. The foliage is a light- to mid-green with upright bushy growth. The first year's growth can be a little soft and it is

better as a second-year plant. It will also make an excellent standard. Half hardy; Zones 9–10. Reid, UK, 2016.

'Big White'

This new trailing Flemish cultivar has large double flowers with a white tube flushed mauve-rose, and long white sepals with a mauve-rose flush that are held downwards over a full white corolla. The medium-sized foliage is mid-green. It is good for baskets and mixed containers. Half hardy; Zones 9–10. Willems, Belgium, 2008.

'Boogie Woogie'

This is a strong growing upright and bushy cultivar that grows to a large plant quite quickly with mid-green foliage. The medium-sized single flower has a rose-bengal tube, rose-bengal sepals held half up with reflexed tips and a quarter flared mauve corolla with red veins on the slightly furled petals. Half hardy; Zones 9–10. Waving, UK, 2016.

'Brey'

One of the many recent European releases, this Flemish cultivar is rather unusual. The flower is a medium to large double with a long pale coral-rose tube, pale coral-rose

'Alan Swaby'

'Anne Reid'

sepals held horizontally with green tips and a full flared corolla whose petals are orange-red at the base and pale cyclamen-purple at the ends, veined with red. The plant is very free-flowering and its growth habit is a trailer with mid-green foliage. It should be very good in a basket on its own or in mixed baskets and containers. Half hardy; Zones 9–10. Michiels, Belgium, 2008.

'Chris Bright'

With an upright self-branching habit, this fuchsia has small single flowers with a pink tube, pink sepals held horizontally with recurving tips and a light powder-pink corolla with red anthers and a pink style. The small foliage has a mid- to dark green top surface. It is very suitable for growing in small pots and as a miniature or quarter standard. Half hardy; Zones 9–10. Fleming, UK, 2008.

'Debron's Black Cherry'

As soon as this cultivar starts to come into flower you will see the origins of the name. The buds, prior to opening are very round and dark, resembling a cherry. The growth is upright and bushy with bright mid-green foliage which is a perfect foil for the dark flowers and buds. The single flower has a dark reddish-purple tube and sepals, held slightly down with reflexed tips. The corolla is quarter flared and dark purple. This cultivar is listed in the Pacific Northwest hardy list and has a very hardy parent. Hardy; Zones 7–9. Monnier, USA, 2012.

'Debron's Black Cherry'

'Debron's White Linen'

This is a very full double-flowered cultivar, and the white blooms stay white even in the sun. It has upright and bushy growth, which becomes slightly lax with the weight of the flowers. The very full double flowers have white tube tinged green, white sepals and a very full white corolla. Half hardy; Zones 9–10. Monnier, USA, 2012.

'De Groot's Floriant'

Resulting from a species, *F. andrei*, crossed with the cultivar 'Fugi-san', this is an unusual upright shrub with medium to large mid- to dark green foliage. The medium-sized single flowers have a long red tube, short horizontal red sepals and a short orange corolla. The hardiness is unknown but treat as tender. Tender; Zone 11. de Groot, Netherlands, 2007.

'Jaspers Lightning'

This is one of the several new triphylla type introductions from the Netherlands produced by crossing triphylla cultivars with other fuchsia cultivars. Strong growing and upright with mid- to dark green serrated leaves, it does not self-branch easily and needs pinching to make it bushier. The single flowers are held in terminal clusters and have a long white tube, short white sepals tipped green and a pale pink corolla. Quite spectacular when in full flower. Tender; Zone 11. van Aspert, The Netherlands, 2014.

'Lind'

This new German cultivar has a lax bush or stiff trailing manner of growth with medium-sized mid-green foliage. The large double flowers have a cream tube with pink blush, cream to pink horizontal sepals, darker pink underneath, and a full red corolla, flushed orange at the base. This fuchsia will do well in baskets or mixed containers, and might be worth trying as a weeping standard. Half hardy; Zones 9–10. Strümper, Germany, 2007.

'Lynne Patricia'

This has attractive medium-sized double flowers with a dark rose tube, sepals that are rose at the base, changing to white with green tips, and a white-flushed violet corolla with rose streaks. It has upright self-branching growth with medium-sized mid-green foliage, and is very suitable as a pot plant or for use in mixed containers. Half hardy; Zones 9–10. Swaby, UK, 2007.

'Chris Bright'

'Maggie Rose'

'Scarlet Jester'

'Maggie Rose'

This is a strong-growing bushy cultivar with medium-sized single flowers with a deep rose tube, long semi-reflexed deep rose sepals and a deep blue to violet corolla with the petals striped pink. The medium-sized foliage is an attractive shade of lime green. It is excellent as a pot plant, and should make a good standard. Half hardy; Zones 9–10. Waving, UK, 2006.

'My Little Gem'

This very pretty little cultivar from Gordon Reynolds, excellent in small pots, has small single flowers with a pale aubergine tube and sepals, and a corolla that opens dark purple and fades to aubergine. The flowers are held semi-erect off the small mid- to dark green foliage and the growth is small, self-branching and compact. This fuchsia is suitable for exhibition, and probably worth trying as a miniature standard. Half hardy; Zones 9–10. Reynolds, UK, 2008.

'Nicki Fenwick-Raven'

This new hybrid has tiny single flowers, although they are quite large for an Encliandra. The tube is long and greenish-white, and the sepals are white and recurved, but on ageing they mature to pink, then red. The corolla opens white but when mature becomes pink, edged with red. It is possible to see flowers of differing colours on the plant at the same time. The upright growth reaches 1–1.2m (3–4ft) high, with tiny fern-like, dark green foliage. Being an Encliandra, the plant may prove to be slightly more hardy than the present half hardy classification. Half hardy; Zones 9–10. Morrison, UK, 2008.

'Pat Bastiman'

This beautiful new cultivar has quite long upright and arching growth. The plentiful small to medium single flowers have a pale pink tube, pale pink sepals held horizontally with reflexed tips and vivid deep cerise corolla. These contrast beautifully with mid- to deep green leaves. Half hardy; Zones 9–10. Wilkins, UK, 2022.

'Pavilion Princess'

A lovely trailing fuchsia, excellent for basket or hanging pot use. The long cascading growth are teeming with single flowers with a long white tinged with lavender tube, long white tinged with lavender sepals, darker underneath and held half down with reflexed yellowish green tips. The corolla petals are reddish-purple shaded lavender at the base. Half hardy; Zones 9–10. de Cooker, The Netherlands, 2015.

'Scarlett Jester'

This triphylla type resulting from the hybridization of triphylla cultivars with a very hardy fuchsia magellanica variant has resulted in a much tougher variant. It has long arching growths with terminal clusters of long tubed red flowers with a slightly lighter corolla. An excellent garden subject superb in a large pot. Half hardy; Zones 9–10. de Cooker, The Netherlands, 2015.

'My Little Gem'

'Suffolk Splendour'

This fuchsia was released in 2009 and was named in honour of the Stowmarket and District Flower Club's 50th anniversary in Suffolk, England. The large double flowers have a magenta tube, reflexed magenta sepals and a very full fluffy white corolla. It is an upright bushy plant, suitable for pots and large containers. Half hardy; Zones 9–10. Welch, UK, 2009.

'Toby Foreman'

This new upright self-branching floriferous cultivar makes a superb pot plant or standard. The flowers are medium-sized singles with a deep rose tube and sepals, and an attractive cream-white corolla. The flowers stand out well against the neat mid-green foliage, making it a very striking plant. Half hardy; Zones 9–10. Waving, UK, 2007.

'Victorian Speed'

This is a new Flemish cultivar with a lax bushy or stiff trailing growth habit, with many large double flowers. The flowers have a rose tube with rose sepals hanging down that partially encircle the red and purple petals of the full corolla. The foliage is slightly matt mid-green and its habit of growth makes it excellent to

'Vorarlberg'

use in hanging baskets and containers, especially because it is so floriferous. Half hardy; Zones 9–10. Michiels, Belgium, 2008.

'Vorarlberg'

This trailing cultivar has medium-sized semi-double flowers with a pale pink tube, shell-pink sepals with yellow-green tips that are deeper pink underneath and a soft pink flared corolla. The growth is lax and

trailing with mid- to dark green foliage, making it an interesting cultivar to grow in hanging containers or possibly as a weeping standard. Half hardy; Zones 9–10. Klemm, Austria, 2007.

'Widnes Wonder'

This distinctive new cultivar has profuse small single flowers with a white tube flushed pink, slightly recurving white sepals flushed pink and darker pink underneath, and a tight corolla that opens dark violet, maturing to purple-pink. It has small self-branching compact growth with neat mid-green foliage. It is excellent for small pots, and should be easy to grow as a small standard, the miniature type probably being the most suitable. Half hardy; Zones 9–10. Bright, UK, 2009.

'Windsor Castle'

This is an attractive floriferous single flowered fuchsia which displays its flowers well against the pale green foliage. The small to medium single flowers have a pale rose tube, pale rose sepals, held horizontally with reflexed tips, and a quarter flared lavender blue corolla. The hybridizer who had previously served with the Blues and Royals gained permission to use the name. Half hardy; Zones 9–10. Birt, UK, 2020.

'Toby Foreman'

'Widnes Wonder'

'Windsor Castle'

CALENDAR OF CARE

Fuchsias are undemanding plants, and many of the hardy varieties, once planted in the garden, will give pleasure for years with little or no attention. However, if you want to grow the more showy, non-hardy fuchsias, or to try training shapes or propagating your own plants, you will need to know what to do when, to ensure the best results.

This calendar of care describes the best time to carry out important tasks, such as encouraging dormant plants back into life, re-potting shooting plants to give them a good boost, caring for standards to make sure they will flower well from year to year, taking cuttings and planting up hanging baskets and containers, all shown season-by-season. It has tips for maintaining a hardy fuchsia bed and ways to keep fuchsias at their best through the summer with correct watering, feeding and protection of the roots from the sun, and gives details of how to prepare fuchsias for the dormant or slow-growing winter storage period.

Left: In midsummer, the stunning large double flowers of the fuchsia 'Marcus Graham' look fantastic. They have a waxy white tube, broad white sepals with a pink flush, and a full salmon-pink corolla with lighter splashes.

Top left: The striking white and deep blue single flowers of the recently released cultivar 'Geoff Oke', named in honour of the secretary of the British Fuchsia Society, make it a superb small patio pot plant.

Top middle: With a long deep pink tube, green sepals and an orangey corolla, the flowers of 'Jungle' are borne on spreading growth.

Top right: 'Ruth King' has double flowers with a pink tube and sepals and a lilac and white compact corolla, excellent for the centre of a mixed basket.

Spring care

Spring is often the most exciting time for the fuchsia grower, with many things to do and the fuchsias developing rapidly. You may be taking cuttings, re-potting plants, visiting nurseries to buy new and replacement plants, shaping and growing on fuchsias and planting up baskets and containers. Fuchsias will be growing very quickly and you can end up rushing from one project to the other, having to look after far more cultivars than you ever intended to grow. Once you are successful at taking cuttings, you may have too many healthy new plants, and it is very difficult to throw any of them away. Take heed of the advice of an experienced fuchsia grower, and stick to the plan you made in the winter.

IN THE GREENHOUSE

Throughout the early spring months, temperatures in the greenhouse can vary widely. On sunny days it can get very hot, while during the night temperatures can still drop below freezing. Some shading will be required on the inclined glass that faces the sun to prevent scorching of young plants.

Fuchsias will be growing very strongly and need pinching, potting on and turning, but don't forget that any plants needed for early flowers in the garden will take 10–12 weeks from the last pinch to begin flowering. If there are any overwintered plants that were not re-potted in the late winter, these should be done in early spring, potting down if necessary.

POTTING ON

1 Use a smaller pot inside the next-sized pot as a mould and fill the gap with potting compost (soil mix). Gently lift out the inner pot.

2 Knock the plant out of its pot and drop it into the prepared mould. Tap on the ground to settle the contents, and gently water in.

Continue to take cuttings of plants you want to propagate, especially those that you bought recently. Move plants outside on suitable days to start the hardening-off process. Start to plant up containers ready for putting out permanently when all danger of frost has passed. Grow on any plants that you are training as standards or other shapes, remembering to re-pot

Top left: The small red-and-purple-flowered hardy cultivar 'David' is easy to bring into flower in the spring using a greenhouse. Many other hardy single-flowered fuchsias treated in this way can be encouraged to flower early.

Left: The trailing fuchsia 'Irene Sinton' needs removal of yellowing leaves and careful watering in the spring to avoid botrytis. The large double flowers have pink sepals and a pale lilac corolla splashed with pink.

them, loosen their ties and remove the side shoots or pinch them out when required to maintain the shape.

Watch the plants closely for signs of pests and diseases, since at this time of year infestations can start. Aphids, in particular, can very rapidly infest plants, and it is better to catch them early. If you are worried about vine weevils then late spring is a good time to apply a biological nematode to protect against them. The nematodes can be used when the soil temperature is above 5ºC (see also page 245). Toward the end of the spring, as the day length gets close to the maximum, apply additional shading to reduce the temperatures in the greenhouse.

THE HARDY BORDER

If you have plants in the hardy border that you have not cut back in late winter, prune them in the early spring when conditions are good and green shoots are appearing from the base of the plant. Clean out any germinating weeds from the border, give it a dressing of a general fertilizer, and hoe a mulch of garden compost into the soil surface. If there are any inter-planted bulbs, delay the hoeing until you are sure where they are to avoid damaging the shoots. If you have any spring-flowering shrubs among the fuchsias, wait until they have finished flowering, then prune them back to the desired shape and size, remembering how much growth they will make in the summer. Watering is not normally necessary except in exceptionally dry periods. Toward the end of the spring, when all danger of frosts has passed, plant new hardy fuchsias to fill any gaps, or replace those that have not survived the winter, remembering the design.

THE GARDEN

Plant out summer bedding fuchsias that have been properly hardened off at the end of the spring when the danger of frost has passed, and bring containers outside. Be ready to protect them with fleece if there is an unseasonable cold snap.

WARMER CLIMATES

By this time in the season, the plants are growing very strongly, and may already be in flower. Staking and tying, watering, feeding

and mulching permanently planted specimens are now the main tasks. Shading will also be required in the greenhouse and for other specimens planted out in exposed positions by the use of shade netting or similar protection against the strengthening sun.

THE SHADEHOUSE

This resource, which is essential in warmer climates, comes into its own at the end of the spring and allows pot plants to be grown when the temperatures regularly climb into the mid-30s Celsius (mid-90s

Above: Standing plants outside on mild spring days is important to harden up the growth. This miniature standard of the hardy cultivar 'Tom Thumb' has been put out in the open air on a bright day to kick-start this process.

Fahrenheit). It provides some shade from the sun, and a more humid atmosphere, which the fuchsias love. The care needed includes the regular watering, feeding and turning of the pot plants, watering the gravel base to increase humidity and moderate the temperature, and cleaning up any dropped leaves to avoid disease.

Summer care

Throughout the summer, fuchsias are at their peak. This is the time to take the opportunity to relax and enjoy them as much as possible. Visits to other gardens, displays and nurseries to see fuchsias in flower may give you some exciting ideas for the next season. However, you will need to carry on with some ongoing maintenance to keep your own plants at their best. The most important task is to continue with all necessary watering and feeding. The bulk of the watering and feeding applies to containers and baskets, but do not forget that the hardy border and summer bedding will need watering in long dry periods and will benefit from occasional additional foliar feeding to boost the growth.

GENERAL SUMMER TASKS

In the early summer, carry out any necessary further planting of the hardy bed, but complete this before midsummer to give the new plants the maximum time to establish before the winter. Hoe through the hardy border, or use a surface mulch to control the weeds until the fuchsias have made enough growth to suppress most of the weeds. If the border is under-planted with bulbs or inter-planted with shrubs, remove the old bulb leaves as soon as they have died down and prune any shrubs as required.

If you still have plants in the greenhouse, use maximum shading and ventilation and

Top: The lovely double flowers of 'Lillian Annetts' are a spectacular sight throughout the summer months.

keep the floors and any gravel on the benches wet to increase the humidity, but if the temperatures are regularly above 27°C (80°F) fuchsias will grow better outside or in a shadehouse.

WATERING AND FEEDING

All the plants in containers should be watered and fed regularly, and all old flowers and seedpods or berries should be removed to ensure the plants put all their energy into further flowering. Take special care with baskets, as these are most likely to dry out, especially in warm windy conditions, and are often difficult to rewet. When they are properly rewetted, there should be a steady slow dripping of water as the excess drains away. If the water

gushes through and stops draining quickly, check that the compost (soil mix) is properly wet, and if necessary take the basket down and immerse it in water until it is really soaked through.

Watering is best carried out in the early morning, and if necessary a little more in the evening, but try to avoid watering in the middle of the day, although wetting the ground around groups of containers to increase the humidity helps on the hottest days in the summer. If you have any plants in pots plunged into the borders, do not forget to water and feed these. Depending on how hot the temperatures are, fuchsias can sometimes go through a period in the hottest part of the late summer when the flowering is not very prolific, but as the days

DEADHEADING, REMOVING DEAD LEAVES AND WATERING

1 Use a pair of small nail scissors or a sharp knife to remove any dead or dying flowers to tidy up the plant. Removing these before the formation of seedpods promotes flowering.

2 Remove any seedpods (the ovaries left when the flowers fall) to ensure the plant continues to flower. If left on the plant, the seedpods will ripen to form edible (but not very tasty) berries or fruit.

3 Remove dead and dying leaves. If they fall into soft stem branches, they could cause botrytis and rot. They will often just snap off, using your fingers, or can be cut with scissors.

4 For fuchsias in pots up to 20cm (8in), a small watering can is easier to use than a large one. The flow of water is more controlled and easier to direct to the right place.

CHECKING TIES

TAKING CUTTINGS

1 Check that ties are not tight on trained shapes such as standards. If wire ties are used, this is very important, as they will cut into the growing stem and cause scarring.

2 Ties made using PVC tape are best as they hold the subject quite firmly with a wide area to spread the pressure. They also stretch slightly as the stem grows.

1 Take cuttings from the parent or stock plant, ideally cutting just below a node. If the growth is too short, take a cutting just above a node. These root nearly as well.

2 A gravel tray propagator, full of strips of cuttings in individual cells. While the top is open, check if any watering is required or any dead leaves need removing.

get shorter and the humidity returns in the mornings, there will be a second flush of heavy flowering.

TRAINED SHAPES

Any plants that you are growing into standards and other trained shapes will need continuing attention, with further stopping, tying, turning and potting on as needed. Remove any flower-buds produced.

Keep an eye out for any sign of pests and diseases and take prompt action, if necessary. The most likely pests are aphids, red spider mite, whitefly and moth caterpillars throughout the summer, and the main disease is fuchsia rust in late summer and early autumn.

SUMMER CUTTINGS

You can take cuttings in the summer, but it is often difficult to find good cutting material without buds, and the temperatures can be too high for good rooting. Reserve your efforts for new cultivars, where you will perhaps only have one plant and need to propagate some more as an insurance against losing it. Try to find a cooler area to place the cuttings in the propagator – they should be out of direct sunlight but it should not be too dark.

Right: This large fuchsia, flowering in an old ornamental pot, will need plenty of watering and feeding during the hot summer months.

Autumn care

The autumn season is a busy one with many tasks to carry out, but the timing is very dependent on the nature of the weather. This is the time to preserve your fuchsia collection by preparing your plants for the rigours of winter. There are different methods and techniques that can be used depending on the facilities you have at your disposal and the local winter climate in your area. These guidelines are written for those readers who live in areas of the world that have frost in the winter, but for those who live in frost-free areas, the autumn season means simply pruning your plants to induce a dormant period and ensure that you have a bushy plant with fresh growth for the next year.

GENERAL AUTUMN TASKS

Any pot plants that you plan to overwinter in their current pots should be treated with a proprietary vine weevil killer, unless you have used a biological control earlier in the year. Otherwise, the eggs and larvae might eat the roots over the winter. An alternative is to pot back plants before putting away for the winter, removing any vine weevil. Potting back gives the plants fresh compost and encourages new, healthy root systems. You can also do this in the winter or early spring when conditions are suitable.

Take cuttings from any plants cut back at the end of the summer when they have made new shoots, and from any other plants you want to keep if you can find suitable non-flowering shoots.

Clean the greenhouse and staging, then sterilize it, clean the glass and remove the shading. Put back the insulation, if necessary, and check that the heating system (if any) is in good working order.

PREPARING PLANTS FOR DORMANCY

In mid-autumn, dry out any fuchsias you wish to store in a dormant state over the winter. When they are quite dry, cut them back by about two-thirds, and remove any remaining leaves. Leave the cut stems to heal over for a few days before watering

Top: Triphylla fuchsias will flower right through the autumn until the first frosts. Continue feeding the plants in order to maintain vigorous flowering.

Right: With proper care, hardy cultivars such as 'Richard John Carrington' will continue flowering well into autumn. This cultivar has single flowers of bright cerise and blue-violet.

POTTING BACK

1 Stop watering until the plant is quite dry. Knock it out of its pot, in this case a 15cm (6in) one, then remove the old potting compost (soil mix).

2 A dry, gritty compost comes away easily from the plant. It now has only a small amount of compost left on it and is ready to re-pot into a smaller pot.

3 Choose the smallest pot the plant roots will comfortably fit into, in this case an 11cm (4¼in) pot. As plants become older, some root pruning may also be required.

4 Fill the new pot with fresh potting compost. Push it down well, ensuring that you fill all the gaps, tapping the pot to help it to settle, then water in sparingly.

again. If any stems continue to bleed sap, lay the pots on their sides until the bleeding has stopped so that the sap does not run back down the stems, causing rot. Spray the remaining wood and soil surface with a combined insecticide and fungicide to kill any overwintering pests or spores.

Store the plants for the winter in the greenhouse, either on the benches if the greenhouse is cold, or on the floor under the staging if it is heated to a minimum of 5°C (41°F). If you do not have a greenhouse, store them in a frost-free shed, cellar or garage, wrapping them in paper if necessary to keep the frost away.

Trained shapes that are to be stored in a dormant state in the greenhouse can be treated in a similar way, though the pruning needs to be appropriate to the shape. Clean off all the leaves and spray the wood with a suitable treatment against red spider mite, which tends to overwinter in the bark of old specimens. Trained shapes that are to be kept in green leaf should be sprayed to kill any insects, moved into the heated greenhouse in good time before the frosts and kept ticking over. These shapes are best stored standing upright.

LATE AUTUMN TASKS

When the first frosts are threatening, break up the hanging baskets, checking for any signs of vine weevil, and cut back and pot up any plants you want to keep for the next year. These plants are also good for encouraging into growth for early cuttings in a heated greenhouse. Treat any plantings in mixed pots, troughs and containers in the same way, while specimen plants can be simply cut back and overwintered in the same pot.

When the first frosts have blackened the leaves of any non-hardy fuchsias growing in the borders that you want to keep for the following year, lift the plants, cut back the stems by one-half to two-thirds, remove the dead leaves, then pot them up and store with good ventilation for a few days, and finally place them in storage. Lastly, clear away the dead leaves and compost them unless the plants have suffered from significant fuchsia rust, in which case the leaves should be disposed of.

CUTTING BACK A HANGING POT

1 Leave the hanging pot outside, allowing exposure to a few light frosts. Bring the pot into the greenhouse to dry out before pruning.

2 Using a sharp pair of secateurs, cut off all the long growths, plus any that are crossing each other or are weak or damaged.

3 When the pruning is completed, the plants have been cut back to the edge of the pot and form a dome shape over the top of the pot.

TREATING AGAINST VINE WEEVIL

There are now biological controls on the market that will control vine weevils in a natural way. Nematodes can be applied in late spring, however early Autumn is also a good time to do this as the small grubs are particularly active now.

1 Carefully read the instructions before use. Pour the diluted solution of the nematode treatment into a small clean watering can.

2 Apply the treatment as a soil drench to the pots. Stand the pot in a plant saucer to catch any drainage and allow it to re-absorb. You may wish to do two applications to be absolutely sure.

Left: This weathered terracotta (clay) pot planted with a hardy fuchsia will continue to flower well into the autumn, provided there are no early frosts. Keep feeding and removing seedpods and old flowers from the growth to help it to continue flowering vigorously.

Winter care

At this time of year, most fuchsias are stored away in their dormant state, or settled in the greenhouse, just ticking over in green leaf. It is a good time to sit back and browse through the next year's fuchsia catalogues. During the previous season, you will probably have seen and made note of fuchsia varieties you would like to try. Many nurseries now make their catalogues available on the internet, and are happy to take orders this way, or by email. Order as early as possible to ensure you get your selection in good time during the next season. You may also want to tackle the more energetic task of preparing the ground for new hardy fuchsia beds or hedges when the weather is suitable.

THE HARDY BED

When frost has killed and removed the leaves from the stems in the hardy fuchsia beds, cut back any of the growth that is not woody. This is usually about the last third of the last season's growth. In very cold areas or for fuchsias you planted in the previous season, draw some soil up over the stems and add some extra winter protection in the form of dry leaves, straw or similar insulating materials.

In milder areas, the end of the winter is the time to prune fuchsias back hard as they start to make growth, before the stems are growing so strongly that they will bleed when pruned. In colder areas, this is a job for the early spring.

IN THE GREENHOUSE

For a frost-free greenhouse, maintain a minimum temperature of 1°C (34°F). For a heated greenhouse, which will keep most fuchsias ticking over in green leaf and protect more tender varieties like Triphyllas in their dormant state, keep a minimum of 5°C (41°F). It is possible to use higher temperatures, but this increases the heating cost considerably. Open the ventilation in the greenhouse on days when the weather conditions allow.

Top: 'Alf Thornley' is a lovely pink and white double-flowered bush which grows well in the greenhouse.

Right: Placing plants under the staging in a heated greenhouse in winter will keep them in green leaf. This method works well, as long as the glass extends close to ground level.

Right: Fuchsias grown from cuttings in late spring and not allowed to flower over the summer. These plants grow on in green leaf over the winter to make flourishing specimen plants the next year.

Keep watering to a minimum, and if possible water in the mornings. The plants, even the defoliated dormant ones, should be kept with the root ball just moist, although they will normally stand being dry for a few days in the winter. For the plants in green leaf, quickly remove any dead or dying leaves to minimize the chances of botrytis. Turn the plants regularly and keep an eye out for any pests and diseases, treating if necessary.

In the later part of the winter season, encourage dormant plants to start into growth by spraying the hard wood with water, which will encourage buds to break. Plants in green leaf will start to grow as the day length increases, and you can take early cuttings from these plants. These cuttings are excellent for growing standards, or for any other forms of training needing a long growth period.

Standards and other trained shapes are best kept standing upright, either as dormant plants in the frost-free greenhouse, or ticking over in green leaf in the heated greenhouse. Being upright ensures that the sap rises to the head of a standard, and will initiate the new growths needed. For a pillar, cone or pyramid, it

helps to suspend the plant horizontally, and rotate it in the horizontal axis, to ensure that all the lateral growths get some period of being vertical to boost the sap flow.

DORMANT PLANTS IN STORAGE

Check any plants in dormant storage periodically. Often books will tell you to keep the plants in an area just above freezing, with a temperature of 0–4°C (32–39°F). Realistically, this is often difficult to achieve in a cold climate unless you have a cold cellar, or a garage kept frost-free. The essential point is to keep them above freezing and ensure they do not dry out.

If the temperature gets warmer for a period, dormant plants may start into growth, and when stored in the dark, produce long white straggly growths. Simply remove these. When it is warm enough to bring the plants out into the light they will start to make normal growth.

WARMER CLIMATES

If you live in an area that is free from winter frosts, induce the dormancy period by pruning to reduce the size of the plant and promote new growth from the base, which will make the plant a better shape next year.

PRUNING A FUCHSIA IN LATE WINTER

1 This 'Thalia' plant has been kept dormant through the winter, and is now starting to make new small growths.

2 Trim the wood of the branches back carefully just above the lowest strong buds, using sharp secateurs.

3 The aim is to obtain a fuchsia that is balanced in shape, with good growth from low down on the plant.

Useful addresses

GENERAL

Barbara's Fuchsia website
www.collectingbooksandmagazines.com/
web/fuchsia.htm
Website from the central Blue Mountains,
New South Wales, Australia

Dave Clark's website
www.fuchsiaclark.co.uk
Pictures of his raisings and a lot of useful
information on fuchsia culture and hybridizing.

**Deutsche Dahlien-, Fuchsien - und
Gladiolen-Gesellschaft eV (German Dahlia,
Fuchsia and Gladioli Society)**
www.ddfgg.de
A gallery of fuchsia pictures and a fuchsia
finder, all in the German language. There are
links to search by name, properties or breeder
(hybridizer) of 11,500 fuchsia varieties.

Just Fuchsia by Yo Yo
www.eonet.ne.jp/~yoyo-
ensoleile/index_en.html

Fuchsia Finder
www.fuchsiafinder.com
Website of Eddy de Boever with a database of
fuschia cultivars with plenty of pictures. Also a
useful fuchsia cultivar search tool for UK and
Europe.

Fuchsia Magic
www.fuchsiamagic.com

Chris Martin's wonderful collection
of fuchsia photographs.

Irene's website
www.ideboda.nl
Interesting information and pictures;
in Dutch/English.

Jack Lamb's website
www.jacklamb.free-online.co.uk
UK national collection of species.

The Plant List
www.theplantlist.org
A comprehensive list of all known plant
species, and the definitive list on genus
Fuchsia.

UNITED STATES
American Fuchsia Society
www.americanfuchsiasociety.org
The first national society, founded in 1929. It
contains varied information and access to the AFS
registration database for fuchsia varieties online.

**Crescent City Branch of the
American Fuchsia Society**
www.crescentcityfuchsiasociety.com
Contains interesting material about
gall mite-resistant fuchsias.

The Earthworks Fuchsias Nursery
www.fuchsias.net
18034 SE 248th St, Covington,
WA 98042
Tel: +1 253 226-1210

The Fuchsietum: A Garden in Portland
www.fuchsietum.com
A wonderful garden in Oregon with a real focus
on fuchsias.

Northwest Fuchsia Society
www.nwfuchsiasociety.com
A lot of useful information and links.

**Orange County Branch of the
National Fuchsia Society**
www.ocfuchsiasociety.com
Basic fuchsia care and other links to fuchsia
societies

Dancing Oaks Nursery and Gardens
www.dancingoaks.com
17900 Priem Road
Monmouth
OR97361

San Diego Fuchsia and Shade Plant Society
Secretary: Richard Hubbell,
15420 Olde Highway, 80#175,
El Cajon, CA 92021-2427
Tel: +1 619 443-3706

Oregon Fuchsia CSociety
www.oregonfuchsiasociety.com
Tel: +1 503 246-7920
Plant nursery in Portland, Oregon

Flowers by the Sea
www.fbts.com/fuchsias/
PO Box 89
Elk
California, 95432

Taylor Greenhouses
www.taylorgreenhouses.com/fuchsia.html
6203 Dahlberg Road
Portland
NY 14769

CANADA
**British Columbia Fuchsia and
Begonia Society**
www.bcfuchsiasociety.com

Jolly Farmer Products Inc.
www.jollyfarmer.com
56 Crabbe Road, Northampton,

New Brunswick, E7N 1R6
Tel: +1 800 695-8300

Richbar Nursery Ltd
www.richbargolfandgardens.com
3028 Red Bluff Road, Quesnel,
BC, V2J 6C6
Tel: +1 250 747-2915

UNITED KINGDOM

British Fuchsia Society
www.thebfs.org.uk
History of the society and other information
including links to many useful websites and
individual fuchsia nurseries.

The Duchy of Cornwall Nursery
www.duchyofcornwallnursery.co.uk
Cott Road, Lostwithiel,
Cornwall, PL22 0HW

Tel: +44 (0) 1208 872 668
Email: sales@duchyofcornwallnursery.co.uk

Fuchsia Flower
www.fuchsiaflower.co.uk
Website incorporating the Lancaster,
Morecambe and District Fuchsia Society

Roualeyn Nursery
www.roualeynfuchsias.co.uk/
Trefriw
Conwy
LL27 0SX

Irish Fuchsia and Pelargonium Society
www.ideasforgardens/IrishFuchsiaSociety/
index.html
Secretary: Pat McCrea,
36 Carnmoney Road
Glengormely, Co. Down, BT36 6HP,
Northern Ireland
Tel: +44 (0) 28 9083 6918
Email: mccrea-patricia@hotmail.com

Little Brook Fuchsias
www.littlebrookfuchsias.co.uk
Ash Green Lane West, Ash Green,
Nr Aldershot, Hampshire, GU12 6HL
Tel: +44 (0) 1252 329 731
Email: carol@littlebrookfuchsias.co.uk

Salford & Bolton Fuchsia Society
www.salfordboltonbuchsiasociety.co.uk
Excellent website with society news,
articles, photos, links to other local groups etc.

The Fuchsia Centre
www.fuchsiaplants.co.uk
Thornton Nurseries
Reservoir Road
Leicester, LE67 1AR

AUSTRALIA
Brenlissa Online Nursery
www.brenlissaonlinenursery.com.au
Tel: +61 (0) 438 393 578

Nurseries Online
www.nurseriesonline.com.au
Useful website with links to local fuchsia
nurseries

Fuchsia Fantasy
75 Lillico Road, Lillico, TAS 7310
Tel: +61 (0) 3 6428 2884
One of the major fuchsia nurseries in Australia

Metamorphosis Fuchsias
44 Hastings Ave,
Melbourne, VI 3029
Tel: +61 (0) 3 9748 5562

NEW ZEALAND

Maidstone Nursery
S.H.1. Otaki North
Tel: +64 (0) 6 364 7013
Email: buzz@xtra.co.nz

The National Fuchsia Society of New Zealand
contact via their Facebook page

SOUTH AFRICA
Western Cape Fuchsia Society
www.safuchsias.co.za/index.php/wc-fuchsias
Information and photos.

Index

'Emma Louise'

'Joan Cooper'

'Pink Marshmallow'

'Little Beauty'

Fuchsia colours and terms

The flower colours of fuchsias are widely described based on the Horticultural Colour Chart system developed by R.F. Wilson and published by the British Colour Council in collaboration with the Royal Horticultural Society in 1938, now long out of print. A reproduction of those colours commonly used in the descriptions in this book is set out in the grid below.

COLOURS

carmine	carmine-rose	coral pink	imperial-purple
mallow-purple	mauve	neyron-rose	orchid-purple
rose-bengal	rose-madder	turkey-red	wisteria-blue

TERMS

Epiphytic: Describes plants that grow above the ground surface, using other plants or objects for support, but are not parasitic.

Paniculate: Describes a plant whose flowers are borne in clusters (panicles or racemes), and they often simultaneously include both flowers and fruit.

Pelargonium: Term used for all varieties formally commonly known as geranium, for example zonal geranium. The term 'geranium' now applies to the hardy variants such as the cranesbill.

Petaloids: Smaller petal-like structures within the corolla that can also be fused with other flower parts such as the stamens.

Raceme: An indeterminate (i.e. not terminated by a single flower) flowering stalk with a series of flowers on stalks branched from the main stem, with the oldest flowers at the base.

Self, or self-coloured: In which the tube, sepals and corolla of the flower are all the same or very similar colours.

Sub-raceme: A smaller flowering branch with fewer flowers than the main raceme.

Ternately: Arranged and growing in groups of three (of leaves).

Acknowledgements

The publisher would like to thank the following for kindly allowing photography to take place in their gardens: Abbotsbury Gardens, Duchy of Cornwall Nursery, Elizabeth Coles, John Nicholass, Kath van Hanegem, The Lost Gardens of Heligan, Mike and Julie Daw, Paul and Rosemary Weekes, RHS Rosemoor, RHS Wisley, and Silver Dale Nurseries.

Thanks to Carol Gubler/British Fuchsia Society for permission to take photographs at the BFS London Show.

The publisher would also like to thank the following for allowing their photographs to be reproduced in the book (t=top, b=bottom, l=left, r=right, m=middle).

Alamy: 79tr, 81tr, 83b, 86b, 87b, 149tl, 149tm, 149tr.
Amy Christian: 44t.
Country, Farm and Garden: 229tr.
Lucy Doncaster: 33tl, 243b.
Tim Ellerby: 10m, 13br, 19m, 24tl, 24tr, 33tr, 36m, 38bl, 41b, 50bl, 50br, 58tl, 63m, 65bl,

78bl, 89m, 93tl, 96b, 97tr, 97m, 104b, 108br, 130t, 139t, 140t, 143b, 160tl, 163tr, 163b, 165tr, 190br, 193br, 199tl, 230br, 232b, 233t, 236tr, 237bl, 242t.
Felicity Forster: 71b, 72m, 75bl, 78t, 80t, 87m.
Rog Frost: 11tl.
GAP Photos: 79tl, 108t.
Carol Gubler: 149bl (courtesy of DEFRA).
iStockphoto: 148bm.
Manfried Kleinau: 166tr, 170t, 199b, 222t, 237t.
Rainer Klemm: 233bl.
Chris Martin: 11tr.
John Nicholass: 31t, 31br, 38br, 42t, 51tr, 52t, 53bl, 53br, 54t, 55r, 56bl, 56br, 58br, 65tr, 72b, 75bmr, 76t, 77t, 77bl, 78br, 92t, 104m, 106t, 107b, 119br, 122t, 123bl, 123br, 137t, 138t, 145tm, 145tr, 145ml, 145mr, 158br, 162b, 164tr, 175b, 188tl, 192tr, 195bl, 195br, 215tr, 221tl, 223tl, 224br, 227t, 228b, 231b, 234 all, 235 all, 236tl, 236tm & b, 237m & br.

'Wilson's Pearls'

Photolibrary: 23tl, 43b ('Keizerskroon', 'Monte Carlo', 'Johann Strauss'), 45tl (*Daphne retusa*), 45bl (*Forsythia* x *intermedia*), 46b, 47bml (*Buxus microphylla* 'Faulkner'), 81b, 102m, 109t, 150br, 229b.
Kath van Hanegem: 42b.
Henk Waldenmaier: 165tl.
Steven Wooster: 22t, 27br, 132m, 166b, 168br, 231tl.

Hardiness and zones

Plant entries in the directory of this book have been given hardiness descriptions and zone numbers. Other than plants listed as hardy, the hardiness descriptions are for plants grown in pots, while the zone numbers refer to plants in the ground.

HARDINESS

Tender: May be kept at a minimum temperature of 7°C (45°F).

Frost tender: May be damaged by temperatures below 5°C (41°F).

Half hardy: Can withstand temperatures down to 0°C (32°F).

Frost hardy: Can withstand temperatures down to -5°C (23°F).

Hardy: Can withstand temperatures down to -15°C (5°F).

ZONES

There is widespread use of the zone number system to express the hardiness of many plant species and cultivars. The zonal system used, shown here, was developed by the Agricultural Research Service of the United States Department of Agriculture. According to this system, there are 11 zones in total, based on the average annual minimum temperature in a particular geographical zone.

The zone rating for each plant indicates the coldest zone in which a correctly planted subject can survive the winter. Where a plant's hardiness is borderline, the first number indicates the marginal zone and the second the safer zone.

This is not a hard and fast system, but simply a rough indicator, as many factors other than temperature also play an important part where hardiness is concerned. These factors include altitude, wind exposure, proximity to water, soil type, the presence of snow or shade, night temperature, and the amount of water received by a plant. These kinds of factors can easily alter a plant's hardiness by as much as two zones. The presence of long-term snow cover in the winter especially can allow plants to survive in colder zones.

KEY TO ZONES
These maps show the zones in Europe and the USA. The temperature ranges apply worldwide.

Zone 1	Below -45°C (-50°F)	
Zone 2	-45 to -40°C (-50 to -40°F)	
Zone 3	-40 to -34°C (-40 to -30°F)	
Zone 4	-34 to -29°C (-30 to -20°F)	Zone 8 -12 to -7°C (10 to 20°F)
Zone 5	-29 to -23°C (-20 to -10°F)	Zone 9 -7 to -1°C (20 to 30°F)
Zone 6	-23 to -18°C (-10 to 0°F)	Zone 10 -1 to 4°C (30 to 40°F)
Zone 7	-18 to -12°C (0 to 10°F)	Zone 11 Above 4°C (40°F)